The **Philadelphia** One-Day Trip Book

The Philadelphia One-Day Trip Book

101 Exciting Excursions In and Around the City

By JANE OCKERSHAUSEN SMITH

EPM
PUBLICATIONS, INC.

1003 Turkey Run Road   McLean, Virginia 22101

Library of Congress Cataloging in Publication Data

Smith, Jane Ockershausen.
  The Philadelphia one-day trip book.

  Includes index.
    1. Philadelphia (Pa.)—Description—1981–   —
Tours. 2. Philadelphia Region (Pa.)—Description and travel—
Tours. I. Title.
F158.18.S58   1985   917.48'110443   85-12858
ISBN 0-914440-82-9

EPM Publications, Inc., 1003 Turkey Run Road,
    McLean, Virginia 22101

Printed in the United States of America

Cover photograph by Fred J. Maroon
Cover and book design by Tom Huestis

To Ann with love

Contents

Introduction

Summer

Autumn

Winter

Spring

Introduction

Philadelphia, which had the largest English-speaking population outside of London before the American Revolution, has three centuries of history to explore. Because of its liberalism and intellectuality the city attracted many of the most brilliant minds of its day. Philadelphia still attracts the talented and forward-looking. In and around this exciting, ever-changing city there are a myriad of diverse and off-beat excursions to make, many that are ignored in official city and area guidebooks and that even long-time residents may have overlooked.

These economical one-day vacations are for families, friends, lovers and loners. *The Philadelphia One-Day Trip Book* tells you how to explore on your own without the auspices of a group or organization. With it you can discover the best season in which to visit and by referring to the Annual Calendar of Events you will learn when special events will be taking place that add additional reasons for visiting. In all, you will find here everything you need to know to plan 101 fun-filled forays.

With minimal amounts of planning and expenditures you can go day-tripping in four directions from Philadelphia. Be sure to check the Geographical Cross Reference when you plan your trip; you may want to combine several selections for a full day's outing. Go east into New Jersey to Victorian Cape May whose appeal extends to historians, antique buffs, architectural enthusiasts, nature lovers and sportsmen. Traveling south you can explore Maryland's Eastern Shore and visit quaint towns like Chestertown, or head over to historic Annapolis, the capital of Maryland. Farther south but still within easy driving distance are the numerous attractions of Baltimore and Washington. To the north, the Pocono Mountains offer scenic vistas of natural woods, streams, lakes and waterfalls; you'll also find artist colonies, steam trains, covered bridges, wineries, old canals and specialty museums with everything from dolls to theatrical costumes. The Pennsylvania Dutch country to the west offers a network of sites featuring ethnic food and handicrafts. A visit to the Lancaster area also gives you a chance to gain a better understanding of the Amish and Mennonite peoples who live in this part of Pennsylvania.

The excursions included in *The Philadelphia One-Day Trip Book* can be enjoyed throughout the year. Though you will find them arranged seasonally, this is not meant to restrict you to visiting certain sites only during certain seasons. It is designed to encourage you to plan outings that capitalize on seasonal variations—garden blooming schedules, for example, migratory birds, or historical re-enactments. A visit to the Longwood Gardens conservatory can be a genuine balm to the spirit when the countryside is covered with snow and the skies are gray. Yet each season at Longwood has its special appeal. The often arbitrary seasonal divisions are simply a means to get you to view day-tripping as a year-round option.

There are a few key steps you should take before starting out. First, read the entire description of your destination. You may discover it is not open on the day you plan to visit or has only a half-day schedule. It is always a good idea to call before you venture forth because hours of operation and admission rates can change as rapidly as the weather.

Once you have determined that your choice of site is indeed open, give some thought to your family's special interests. Will this trip appeal to everybody? Most excursions won't, but you may be able to work out some double-feature trips that offer something for everyone. A trip to Hawk Mountain will hold older family members entranced, but fidgety youngsters may have trouble sitting still on the mountain promontory. They can have their innings with a ride on the WK&S Railroad nearby. A visit to Morristown National Historical Park can end with a refreshing swim in Sunrise Lake. Some spots provide their own eclectic mix: at Hagley Museum, for example, you can explore the antique furnishings and restored garden of Eleutherian Mills, then take a jitney ride to the powdermill to learn how gunpowder was made in the early days.

Flexibility is frequently the key to successful family forays. If you've planned to include three sites and you discover your first stop is having a special festival, why not relax and spend the whole day? An advantage of these one-day trips is that most are close enough to return another time—and it's easy to revisit your favorites. Do be sure to read the whole book so that you can expand your list of outings. Your planning should also take the weather into consideration. If everybody is anticipating an outing and it suddenly rains, you don't have to stay at home. There are many exciting indoor destinations—the Merritt Museums, Villa Pace, Please Touch Museum, Fireman's Hall or the London Town Brass Rubbing Centre to name just a few.

Another way to make sure that your trip proceeds smoothly is to pack the car wisely. If you're on a limited budget your only expense will be the gasoline if you choose one of the many government operated free sites and carry a picnic lunch. Even if you don't plan to lunch al fresco it is a good idea to bring a snack and a cooler to take care of inopportune hunger pangs and thirst. A pillow in the back seat may encourage younger family members to rest enroute. And if your destination is an indoor site you may want to pack a ball so that active children can work off extra energy at a nearby park. Sweaters come in handy if the weather changes. An absolute must to include is an up-to-date, detailed regional map. The map and directions included in the book will orient you but it is still a good idea to carry a larger map. Philadelphia, like many cities, has a confusing habit of using colloquial or "old" names for routes that do not appear on the maps. For example, Route 30 is often referred to as the "Lancaster Pike" and as "Lincoln Highway." The signs can be confusing without a map to provide reassurance about route numbers.

Do consult the book's Topical Cross Reference to help you plan trips around special interests. With it you can zero in, for example, on such diverse fields of interest as food and wine, the military, transportation or religion. For history lovers there are living history museum villages such as The Colonial Pennsylvania Plantation, Hopewell Village, Bethlehem, Hagley Museum, Quiet Valley Living Historical Farm, the Peter Wentz Farmstead and Waterloo Village. These sites give visitors a chance to see how their earlier counterparts lived. Change is no more a hallmark of living history than it is of natural history. Consider the migratory flights of birds of prey you can see at Hawk Mountain or the annual passage of waterfowl along Cape May County, at Eastern Neck Wildlife Refuge or at the Tinicum National Environmental Center.

Change is never more apparent than at gardens. Shifting seasons bring to flower a wide spectrum of delights. Garden enthusiasts often appreciate the chance to visit conservatory collections during bleak winter months. Morris Arboretum is one attraction that has something of interest year round.

Gardens, the arts, history, scenic splendors, off-beat museums and spots with particular appeal to children—there is fascinating variety here. One of the charms of short trips is the chance they give you to explore new areas of interest. So don't limit yourself. One-day trips not only expand horizons, they lift every day life out of the humdrum and provide treasured memories for the future.

Summer

Ashland's Pioneer Tunnel Coal Mine and Steam Lokie

Deep into the bowels of the earth the miners were carried on small cars, into the damp, chill depths of the anthracite coal mines in Mahanoy Mountain. On many mornings the miners entered the inky depths before sunup and they spent the day in a dim, carbide-lit tunnel hacking away at the deeply embedded coal. At its peak the Pioneer Tunnel in Ashland, Pennsylvania, produced 400 tons of coal a day.

What was once a tedious, dangerous ordeal can be a fascinating experience today, thanks to a group of public spirited volunteers in Ashland who have reopened Pioneer Tunnel. Their efforts give you the opportunity to get an in-depth look at a real Pennsylvania coal mine. You need have no concern over safety as the mine is inspected daily. They have timbered up the entire mine since it reopened including the first 100 to 200 feet that had caved in when the mine was dynamited shut in 1931. Like the early miners, you will be taken into the mine on old mine cars. The guides are themselves experienced miners. Even though you are told that no miner ever died in Pioneer Tunnel you still feel overwhelmed when you look up and realize you are 500 feet below the surface.

Once inside you'll get a chance to walk down the gangways, or tunnels. The guides explain what was involved in mining coal in this "adit" mine. Adit means that the tunnel was driven into the rock horizontally at right angles to the coal seam. You'll be able to peer down lighted shafts that lead from one level to the next more than 200 feet below. With a little imagination you can picture the miners struggling along the steep inclines each with 250 pounds of necessary gear.

The tour takes about 35 minutes. As you leave the cold depths, the guides turn off the lights for just a minute so that you can experience the inky blackness of the subterranean shafts. The temperature stays at about 50 degrees year-round, so be sure to bring a sweater or jacket.

After your trip down the mine you can board a steam lokie for another kind of ride. The lokie is an old-fashioned narrow-gauge, steam locomotive called the Henry Clay that once hauled coal cars. It takes you on a 30-minute, three-quarter-mile trip along Mahanoy Mountain and the site of an old strip mine. Mammoth Vein was an immensely thick vein of anthracite coal that pushed its way to the earth's surface. The coal was simply scooped up by huge steam shovels. The 250-foot-high wall of solid rock left by the strip mining extends to the west as far as you can see. It gives mute testimony to the harmful effects of strip mining.

There is yet another example of mining you'll see on your train ride. Mahanoy Mountain also has its "bootleg" coal hole. During the Depression, men defied the dangers and the law to obtain coal to heat their homes or to sell for much needed cash. From the highest point on your ride, you can see for 20 miles. Ashland looks like a toy town at the foot of the mountain.

The Ashland Pioneer Tunnel Coal Mine and Steam Lokie is open daily from May 30 to Labor Day weekend from 10:00 A.M. The last Lokie ride leaves at 5:30 P.M., the last mine tour, at 6:00 P.M. During May and from Labor Day through October it is open on weekends only at the same hours. Admission is charged and there is a picnic area and playground equipment adjacent to the tunnel.

Before you head home there is one more stop you should make. Two hundred yards from the tunnel is The Anthracite Museum of Ashland. With photographs, models, graphics and actual equipment, it shows how coal was located and extracted. It also gives more details on the life of a Pennsylvania miner. The museum is open Tuesday through Saturday from 9:00 A.M. to 5:00 P.M. and Sundays from NOON to 5:00 P.M. From Memorial Day to Labor Day the museum is open Monday through Saturday from 10:00 A.M. to 6:00 P.M. and Sunday from NOON to 6:00 P.M.

For serious geology buffs there is still more to see. Just 1½ miles from Pioneer Tunnel is an exposed fault which has proved to be a rich site for fossil hunting. The Pioneer Tunnel Office will arrange for a fossil hunting tour.

Directions: From Philadelphia take I-76, the Pennsylvania Turnpike west. Then take I-176 north to Reading. From Reading take Route 61, north to Ashland. The Pioneer Tunnel will be on your left at the top of the town.

Barns-Brinton House and Chaddsford Winery

Side-by-side in the picturesque Brandywine Valley are two dissimilar but appealing attractions: the Barns-Brinton House and Chaddsford Winery.

They actually have more in common than is immediately apparent because the 18th-century **Barns-Brinton House** was a tavern as well as a home. Although the house no longer offers "ye accommodation of Man and Horse," guides in colonial garb are on hand to welcome guests.

William Barns built his tavern on the Great Road between Philadelphia and Maryland in 1714, using brick instead of the more common native fieldstone. The house was constructed in the Flemish bond pattern, accented by black headers. On the upper wall on the west gable end there is a decorative double diamond design in the brickwork. The restored structure has retained its original floor plan.

You'll first enter the barroom of the tavern which Barns operated from 1722 to 1731. Hinges and other hardware are original and are believed to have been done by Barns himself as he was also a blacksmith. It's the cage bar that intrigues most visitors. The wooden grill could be closed and locked at night to protect the tavernkeeper's stock. It leads to speculation that it gave rise to the use of the word "bar" to mean a counter from which drinks are served.

Visitors can try to guess the purpose of a well-worn hole in the newel post by the narrow winding staircase that leads to the public sleeping quarters. It is called a "distaff hole" because it held the distaff from the spinning wheel so that it could be set up near the window for light.

After William Barns's death in 1731 the house changed owners several times. It was eventually purchased by James Brinton in 1753, remaining in the Brinton family over 100 years. The Chadds Ford Historical Society purchased the building in 1969 and have restored and furnished the tavern as a Living History Museum. It is now open June, July and August on Saturday and Sunday from NOON to 5:00 P.M. There is a nominal admission charge.

You leave the house as you entered it, by the original entranceway now lined with beds of medicinal, culinary, ornamental and aromatic herbs. A short walk across the grassy grounds takes you to the adjacent **Chaddsford Winery**.

The winery opened in the summer of 1983 and already has established a reputation among Pennsylvania wineries. The young couple that own and operate the winery, Eric and Lee Miller, have a background in the industry that far exceeds their years. Eric Miller's parents established New York state's first farm winery, Bernmarl Vineyards. Lee Miller co-authored a book about east coast wineries and helped found the magazine *Wine East*. The couple brings both knowledge and enthusiasm to this Chester County winery.

In the remodeled barn they explain how grapes are crushed

and the juice is fermented, barrel-aged and bottled. After your tour you can taste the wines made at Chaddsford. Tours and Tastings are given on Saturday from 10:00 A.M. until 5:30 P.M. and on Sunday from NOON to 5:00 P.M. You need to call (215)388-6221 to arrange a tour if you plan a trip on a weekday although the winery is open for tastings and sales from 10:00 A.M. to 5:30 P.M.

Directions: From Philadelphia take I-95 south to the Wilmington, Delaware area. Exit on Route 52 and continue north about ten miles to the intersection with Route 1. Make a right on Route 1 towards Chadds Ford. In about 1½ miles you will see both the Chaddsford Winery and Barns-Brinton House on the right.

The Colonial Pennsylvania Plantation and The Tyler Arboretum

Did you know that houses could be dissected? Through painstaking architectural research at **The Colonial Pennsylvania Plantation** it was possible to trace about 90 percent of the changes at this old farmhouse and uncover its past: when it was first constructed, how the original design was altered and when different rooms were added.

Though the farm was started between 1705 and 1724, it is the tumultuous days of the American Revolution—the 1770s—that are recreated here. And you will be actively included in the process of recreation and restoration that makes this a "museum in the making." Since the farm is only 15 miles from Philadelphia you can become quite actively involved if you choose. As a volunteer you can help reconstruct a building, learn old-fashioned fireplace cooking or, perhaps, spinning. Drop-in visitors may also occasionally lend a hand with the farm chores—cutting the curd for cheese, carding wool or dipping candles.

Like the Peter Wentz Farmstead, this plantation appears as it would have looked in the 1770s. The furnishings and equipment are not preserved in a hands-off museum format, but rather are there to be used. In many cases the furniture, utensils and tools are made right at the farm, using the old methods. As at the Peter Wentz Farmstead the colors are bright and unfaded and nothing is mellowed with age.

It is interesting to note that although a farm family at that time would have been sufficiently well-off to be able to set aside a room for formal entertaining, the furniture was still more sturdy than comfortable. It wasn't until the Victorian period that seats were upholstered and provided the comfort of springs.

Although this part of Pennsylvania was primarily Quaker and many of the farmers did not leave to fight in the Revolutionary

War, the farms were nevertheless affected by the fighting. A local farmer, Benjamin Hawley, made these entries in his diary:

28 August 1777   *"Clear morn, then some Clouds; Draw'd in all the hay."*

11 September   *"Very hot; finished harrowing the rye; the English Engaged the Americans; the latter defeated with much loss."*

12 September   *"Cloudy; putting up fences that the American Soldiers [broke] in their retreat."*

13 September   *"Some Clouds; Some of ye English Soldiers had Sundries to ye value of 8 shillings and did not pay."*

The Colonial Pennsylvania Plantation recreates farm life in surprising detail: fields, orchard, kitchen garden, still room, root cellar, springhouse and barns. The farmer may solicit advice from you on what crops to plant. As early as the colonial period Pennsylvania farmers practiced crop rotation. There is likely to be a field of clover or grass interspersed with the major crops of wheat, potatoes, rye and oats. The plantation has instituted a breeding program to develop animals that more closely resemble those of 200 years ago. On a farm this size records indicate that a family would likely have kept two or three horses, three or four cows, five or six sheep, a sow and boar, plus an assortment of fowl. By visiting at least once during the spring, summer and fall you'll get a picture not only of the daily chores but also of the larger seasonal activities such as planting, shearing and harvesting. The plantation is open on weekends from 10:00 A.M. to 4:00 P.M., April through November. There is an admission fee. The Colonial Pennsylvania Plantation is located within the Ridley Creek State Park and picnic facilities are available in the park.

Adjacent to Ridley Creek State Park is **The Tyler Arboretum** which has more than 4,000 plants and trees within its 700 acres. Twenty miles of hiking trails will give you a chance to see roughly 380 species of native southeastern Pennsylvania plants. Some of the most interesting specimens in the collection are not native to this area. The arboretum is noted for its giant sequoia, which was planted here between 1856 and 1860. It now stands over 65 feet tall and boasts a nine-foot circumference. Camera buffs have a real challenge in capturing this striking beauty. Other unusual trees include the multi-trunked ginkgo, a cedar-of-Lebanon, a tulip tree and a bald cypress which is 100 feet tall. Specialty areas at The Tyler Arboretum include the Pinetum and the Fragrant Garden for the visually handicapped.

The Tyler Arboretum is open daily at no charge from 8:00 A.M. until dusk. There is a bookstore and gift shop which you can visit from 9:00 A.M. to 4:00 P.M.

Directions: The shortest route to The Colonial Pennsylvania Plantation from Philadelphia is via Route 3, the West Chester Pike but it does take you through congested areas. The Schuylkill Expressway, Route I-76 west to the Valley Forge Interchange often can be quicker. Take Route 202 south to Route 252. Go south to Route 3 at the Newtown Square Interchange. The main entrance to Ridley Creek State Park is three miles west on Route 3. For the Tyler Arboretum continue south on Route 252 past Route 3 to Route 1 and make a right. The Tyler Arboretum is located at 515 Painter Road in Lima, just two miles north of Route 1 using Route 452 to Barren Road.

Delaware Water Gap Trolley and National Recreation Area

Delaware Water Gap once was the end of the line for resort-going Philadelphians who would come by trolley to this vacation spot in the Pocono Mountains. The ride took about 9½ to 10 hours and required six transfers. Now you can drive it in 2½ to 3 hours and get on the trolley after you arrive. You'll be given a guided tour of the scenic and historic high points throughout the lower portion of the Delaware Water Gap National Recreation Area. As you drive along the steep, stony Delaware River, approaching the town of Delaware Water Gap, it is not hard to understand why during the 1800s this was the third largest resort area in the U.S.

Long before then, the Shawnee Indians inhabited the area. Indian relics and artifacts have been recovered by archeological teams working along the river. Today, however, the name Shawnee is more closely associated with a resort offering year-round sports in a Victorian atmosphere.

Many well known entertainment figures have been frequent guests at Shawnee. You'll hear about them aboard your trolley trip. You board the trolley at the Delaware Water Gap Trolley depot on Route 611 in the center of the town. Fred Waring lived here from 1940 until his death in late 1984. He did his broadcasts from the local playhouse, as did old-time radio favorites Fibber McGee and Molly. You will also pass Waring's workshop where he published music. Jackie Gleason came to Shawnee years before he made Ralph Kramdon a familiar figure in homes across the U.S. "Diamond" Jim Brady built the Castle Inn for the famous dancer of the 1920s, Irene Castle. Children who may be non-plussed by such dated trivia usually perk up when the home of

Captain Kangaroo's sidekick, Mr. Greenjeans, is pointed out to them.

History goes back much farther on this trolley ride through the lower portion of the Delaware Water Gap National Recreation Area. There are still remnants of the original home of Louis Depue, the first white settler in this part of Pennsylvania. Later in the colonial period, Benjamin Franklin commandeered a home at Shawnee to use as a base from which to subdue the local Indians. The stable for this early fort now serves as the gate house of Fred Waring's home.

Nature lovers get a good bit of geological lore. The trolley stops at the Point of the Gap where you can clearly see how the Pocono Mountain range developed from a great upfold in the earth's crust. Over millions of years the water cut a gap through the rocky range leaving visible tilted layers on the rocky surface. This ridge at Point of the Gap was once 20,000 feet high. The tail end of the giant Wisconsin glacier came down through the Delaware Water Gap.

The Delaware Water Gap can also be explored on the miles of hiking trails and by water as there are canoe launching sites within the recreation area. A bit farther north but still within the Delaware Water Gap is Dingmans Falls. You can see two waterfalls on an easy three-quarter-mile-look hiking trail. The Visitors Center has an audio-visual program and exhibits on the natural world of the Pocono Mountains. The center is open from late April through the end of October.

One other area of interest within the park is the century-old Millbrook Village. This is not simply one town that has been restored but a representative look at American life in this mountainous area during the mid-1800s. Old homes, from rustic log cabins to comfortable farmhouses, are complemented by commercial concerns: a general store, grist mill, blacksmith shop and shoemaker's shop. There is also a school, a church and an old cemetery to help draw you into the past.

The roughly one-hour-long Delaware Water Gap Trolley runs on the half-hour beginning at 9:30 A.M. and continuing throughout the day. There are also twilight tours at 6:00 and 7:00 P.M. Even on warm days you may need a sweater or jacket in late afternoon because it gets cool in the tree-shrouded gorge. There is a $2.50 fare for the trolley ride. For additional information call (717)476-0010. Even if you forego the trolley ride be sure to drive through the town of Shawnee.

Directions: From Philadelphia take the Pennsylvania Turnpike Northeast Extension. Continue north to Exit 33, Route 22 east. From Route 22 pick up Route 33 north to Interstate 80 east. Take I-80 to Exit 53. From the exit continue straight into the town of

Delaware Water Gap. At the light you will see the Water Gap Trolley depot. It is about an hour farther to the Dingmans Falls area. Get back on I-80 west and continue to Exit 52. Follow Route 209 north to Dingmans Falls. At the blinking light in Dingmans Ferry turn left and follow the signs.

Edison National Historic Site

A good idea for a different one-day trip is the laboratory and home of Thomas Alva Edison, a man who had more than his share of good ideas. He was, for a long time, the holder of more patents than any other individual although now a few gifted inventors have surpassed him. His total was 1,093, with the first granted in 1869 when he was only 22.

More than half of all of Edison's patents were invented at his West Orange Laboratory in New Jersey. A model for both Bell and Westinghouse laboratories, Edison's "invention factory" was established in 1887. He wanted a lab where he could translate his ideas into "useful things that every man, woman and child wants . . . at a price they could afford to pay." Edison achieved his goal and in fact would boast that his lab could build anything from a "lady's wristwatch to a locomotive."

Continuous daily 1½-hour tours offer a glimpse of how Edison realized his creative ideas. They trace the development of an idea from his "thought bench" at his nearby home to his "work bench" at the lab. Most visitors start their lab tours with an Edison invention that became an integral part of the world's recreation time—the phonograph. Although this was actually invented at Menlo Park in 1877, he put it aside for ten years. When he opened his West Orange laboratory one of his first projects was to work on improving the phonograph, his favorite invention and the one he called "his child." You will see the original 1877 tinfoil phonograph here as well as many of Edison's later models.

The decade long delay on the phonograph was to allow Edison time to work on yet another important invention, his incandescent bulb and lighting system. The light bulb and the Pearl Street Power Station were among his most significant contributions. You will also see some of the earliest movies ever made, including The Great Train Robbery of 1903. Considered the first feature film ever made, it was only ten minutes long. You will appreciate the scope of Edison's operation as you tour the chemistry lab, machine shops, library, business office and a replica of the world's first motion picture studio. Edison liked to joke that his labs were stocked with every imaginable substance he and his staff might need in their work—as he put it, "Everything from an elephant's hide to the eyeballs of a United States Senator."

You'll get to learn more of Edison the man when you tour his nearby home, Glenmont. Be sure to make a reservation for the house tour as soon as you arrive at the Edison National Historic Site. They accommodate visitors at Glenmont on a first-come, first-served basis, and space is limited.

The 23-room Victorian mansion was not built by Edison but by a New York businessman who was convicted of embezzling company funds which he used to furnish the mansion in opulent Victorian style. He wrote Edison from prison to tell him how he should run Glenmont. Though he lived here 45 years until his death in 1932, Edison's house has undergone considerable renovations that have given it a decor of the 1920s and 1930s. Thomas Alva Edison is buried in a simple plot behind the house. His wife, Mina Miller Edison, is buried beside him.

The Edison National Historic Site is open daily from 9:00 A.M. to 5:00 P.M. Guided tours begin at 9:30 A.M. with the last complete tour starting at 3:00 P.M. Families and individual visitors do not need reservations but all non-family groups of ten or more do have to have reservations and need to call well in advance: (201)736-1515. Glenmont is open only Wednesday through Sunday afternoons. A nominal admission fee is charged at this historic site, but those under 16 and over 62 are admitted without charge.

Directions: From Philadelphia take the Schuylkill Expressway, I-76, south and cross the Benjamin Franklin Bridge to New Jersey. Continue on I-76 to the New Jersey Turnpike. Follow the New Jersey Turnpike north to the Garden State Parkway. Continue north on the Garden State Parkway to East Orange, Exit 145. Bear left leaving exit and take I-280 west. Continue on Route 280 west until you reach Exit 10. Make a right turn at the first traffic light and a left at the next traffic light. You are now on Main Street. Continue through three traffic lights. You will be able to park free across from the Edison National Historic Site. Walk down Lakeside Avenue to the entrance gate.

Fireman's Hall and Elfreth's Alley

Descended in a direct line from the very first fire department in America, **Fireman's Hall** in downtown Philadelphia captures the long and colorful history of fire fighting in this country. Benjamin Franklin, who in 1736 founded the first fire company in the colonies, the Union Fire Company, on December 7, 1736, would be delighted with this restoration which is a direct lineal descendant of the Union Fire Company Franklin began.

Leather buckets, from the colonial days of fire fighting, were supplanted by hand pumpers as you'll see in the story of fire fighting that enfolds in the museum exhibits. Probably the oldest piece of rolling stock on display is one of the three fire wagons the Common Council of Philadelphia ordered from England in 1730. It was sold in 1764 to the Middle Ward Fire Department in Germantown, where it was called "Shagrag." Another of the old pieces is a rare 1815 Hand Pump. This old wooden fire wagon looks like it would have been in dire jeopardy if it got anywhere near a fire. It's a wonder that it survived.

The upstairs displays have as their focal point the colorful stained glass window that shows a firefighter saving a young victim from flames. You will be given an overview of the rise of the Paid Department, or salaried firemen. Small models of early equipment are dwarfed by actual pieces of rolling stock. One rather grand piece is the Spider Hose Reel built in 1804. It's as elegant as a gladiator's chariot. The mirrors on each side of the reel look like shining shields, and the brass bells and wrought iron lanterns give it more dazzle.

More prosaic tools of the trade hang on the walls. There are firemen's helmets including a collection from foreign countries, also some oversize equipment like the life net that took 14 firemen to hold, and a modern asbestos fire fighting suit.

A memorial room is dedicated to Philadelphia fire fighters who have died in the line of duty. The helmets hung above the plaques are fire scarred, scorched and blackened. If this room reminds visitors too much of the tragic aspects of fire fighting, their mood should lift when they enter the wheelhouse of a fireboat. This wheelhouse replicates that of a fireboat in one of Philadelphia's three Marine Fire Fighting Units. You can take the helm and steer toward the Philadelphia skyline painted in a mural. In another recreated area you see the living quarters of early professional fire fighters, complete with chief's office and sliding pole. A tape fills the room with the voices of firemen telling about exciting moments on the job. The human side of fire fighting is also brought clearly in focus in a film shown at Fireman's Hall.

Back downstairs in the old fire hall of the station that was active in the 1870s there are more large wheeled pieces. Many of the pieces are the traditional fire truck red. You'll see an 1896 red ladder truck, the 1907 pot-bellied Metropolitan Steamer, a 1903 cannon wagon and a 1870 fire wagon hose carriage.

Fireman's Hall is owned by the city of Philadelphia, and there is no admission charge. The museum is open Tuesday through Saturday from 9:00 A.M. to 5:00 P.M. It is located between Race and Arch Street at 2nd and Quarry Streets.

Just a half a block up the street is another Philadelphia landmark—**Elfreth's Alley**. The 30 houses that line this old town alley were built between 1728 and 1836, making it the oldest residential street in America. The alley was named for Jeremiah

Elfreth and was the home and shop for carpenters, printers and other craftsmen. Even Benjamin Franklin is reputed to have lived here once. The oldest house is number 122 which was built in 1728. At number 126, the Mantua Maker's House Museum, built in 1762, you can see a display of various items made by residents of the alley from 1750 to 1800. Included are pottery and pewter and such utilitarian items as the clay roach trap that caught the varmints with molasses. Once a year on the first Sunday in June the residents of Elfreth's Alley have an open house and you can tour these privately owned homes. The little museum is open from 10:00 A.M. to 4:00 P.M. daily at no charge.

Directions: From city center go down Race Street to 2nd Street and turn right. Fireman's Hall will be on your left as will Elfreth's Alley. There is limited on-street parking. Parking is also available at the Philadelphia Parking Authority Location at 2nd and Walnut Streets, just a short walk down 2nd.

Fort Delaware State Park

Prisoners who were held at Fort Delaware during the Civil War referred to it as a "chamber of horrors." Children may be amused to hear that in the 1860s farm families across the river from the fort would scare their youngsters into behaving by threatening to take them to the fort and turning them over to the guards. Nowadays it is a treat, not a threat, to get to go to Fort Delaware.

Part of the fun of this outing is getting to the fort. Fort Delaware is on Pea Patch Island in the Delaware River, just one mile offshore from Delaware City. On weekends and holidays from April through September the cruiser *Miss Kathy* leaves from the Clinton Street Dock at frequent intervals from 11:00 A.M. to 6:00 P.M. The 15-minute boat ride, for which there is a nominal charge, is incentive enough for many kids; in fact, the rougher the water the more they seem to enjoy the ride.

You may wonder at the island's unusual name. A popular explanation is that in colonial days a boat carrying peas ran aground on this 178-acre mud flat. The cargo spilled out of the beached boat and the peas sprouted in the sandy soil, creating an island. Look around as you explore the island and see if you can spot any peas still growing there.

The brief trip from the island dock to the fort is made by jitney. After entering the Sally Port, or main entrance, you should take time to see the 30-minute film, *The Story of Pea Patch Island.* You'll discover that as far back as 1812 there was a rough earthwork fortification built on this island to protect Philadelphia from the British. The fort you see now was not started until 1848. Covering six acres and within a 30-foot moat, Fort Delaware is larger than Fort Sumter.

It is an excellent example of our early coastal defense system and is considered by many architects to be the finest example of brick masonry work in the country. The granite walls are 30-feet thick in places, rising to a height of 32 feet. Members of the Fort Delaware Society and other interested individuals have been taking classes in brick pointing, learning how to repair the old brickwork.

The fort was operational just two years before the Civil War began and was used during the war to house prisoners of war. Though no shots were ever fired in battle at this fort many lives were lost because the crowded conditions led to an unhealthy environment. By August 1863 there were 12,500 captives at the fort. A story is told about the escape of one of the prisoners during the cold winter of 1863–64. The Delaware River had frozen over and many of the Northern soldiers went skating on the river in their off-duty hours. For many prisoners from the Deep South this was their first exposure to winter sports. One group of Floridians was so interested in the skating that the Northern guards let them use their skates and try their luck. They floundered and fell, of course, and one prisoner making more ludicrous pratfalls than the others got farther and farther from shore. When he was well beyond musket range he straightened up and with real skating style made his escape.

People can appreciate why he wanted to leave when they see the dungeons. On your self-guided tour you can go from these lower depths up to the ramparts. At the top you get an excellent perspective of the entire island. At the northern end there is a bird sanctuary. If you have time take the nature trail to the observation platform overlooking the nesting area for egrets, herons and ibis.

Directions: From Philadelphia take I-95 south. Take Delaware Exit 4, Route 7 east to Route 13. Exit on Route 72 east to Route 9 into Delaware City. Turn left at the traffic light onto Clinton Street, to Delaware State Park dock on the canal.

Harpers Ferry

The summer heat doesn't seem to affect the costumed gentleman who is dressed in a heavy jacket, long-sleeve shirt and wide-brim hat. As he explains to the crowd gathered around him, that although he can get a good job at the armory it worries him to live in this community because of its unhealthy location on the water. The air off the water is so full of impurities that even in the heat it's best to keep your body covered. The town is Harpers Ferry, and the time is the mid-19th century.

A day spent at this recreated site at the confluence of the Potomac and Shenandoah Rivers will give you some surprising insights into the Civil War era. Several tours are offered by the National Park Service. Since guns are the key to understanding Harpers Ferry, "The Guns of Harpers Ferry" makes a good start. You are invited by an overdressed young gunsmith to imagine that you too are a skilled craftsman employed by the federal armory that President Washington urged Congress to establish in Harpers Ferry. The hour-long tour takes you to Artillery Square where volunteers demonstrate the early flintlock musket and flintlock rifles.

Watching the flintlock musket being fired makes it easy to see why it needed improvement. It often takes more than a few trials to get the gun to fire; though this can be embarrassing before an audience it was downright dangerous before the enemy. Nor was that the only danger. The loading of the flintlock gave rise to the expression, "going off half-cocked."

Early guns were made by hand. In 1819, at his rifle works on Virginius Island in Harpers Ferry, John Hall developed a breech loading flintlock rifle that had machine made interchangeable parts. The replaceable parts, which made repairs possible on the field, brought changes to the armory too. Now craftsmen as well as parts could be replaced. Previously workers at the Harpers Ferry armory had taken advantage of the monopoly they held on repair work. The incidence of drinking, gambling and absenteeism was very high among them. In one year the factory superintendent missed 123 days. After the development of interchangeable parts and the advent of the time clock and set work schedules, the problems continued, this time due to the workers' reluctance to accept these new conditions.

This all came to an end in 1841 when the percussion rifle, the new Hall rifle, eliminated the flint. Its ignition system was based on a cap of fulminate of mercury. Soldiers on both sides of the Civil War went into battle carrying this weapon. Except for the fire engine house now known as the John Brown Fort, none of the 20 buildings of the armory still stands. Markers indicate where the guns were once stored. A museum in the Master Armorer's House off Arsenal Square depicts how the guns were made.

It was the federal armory and arsenal at Harpers Ferry that led to the single most historic incident associated with this town— John Brown's Raid on October 16, 1859. Another of the National Park Service's tours deals with this raid. A gentleman dressed like a middle class merchant tells you the tale of John Brown, a man who few could explain. After the tour you should stop at the John Brown Museum and see the six pictures of Brown; each reveals a different man. He was indeed a man of many faces.

His raid was Brown's attempt to force the southern states to renounce slavery. An earlier slave revolt in 1831 led by Nat Turner had resulted in Virginia's legislature coming within one vote of abolishing slavery. John Brown believed another revolt might convince the wavering southerners. He intended to seize the 100,000 guns in the Harpers Ferry arsenal awaiting shipment. He would then establish a provisional government in the mountains with a black president and from this refuge he would invade the south with his black army.

To accomplish his grandiose scheme he needed the guns of Harpers Ferry. He did have 1,000 pikes to arm the blacks while they learned to handle guns, a new skill for many as they had been forbidden to carry arms. What really upset the residents of Harpers Ferry during the raid was the sight of several blacks carrying guns, a signal of profound trouble. John Brown's band of raiders was actually very small, only 22. He had believed that blacks would flock to his banner once his raid was successful. Your tour at Harpers Ferry will take you to the fire engine house where John Brown and his men took refuge with their hostages after seizing control of the armory and arsenal. This is where you will hear the story of the raid. Like so much of history it is full of ironies, humor and missed opportunities. It makes a grand tale and they tell it well!

The day he was hanged John Brown wrote a message that foretold the great conflict that was to come in 17 months. The Civil War in Harpers Ferry is the subject of another hour long tour. On Saturday afternoons at 4:10 P.M. there is a two-hour hiking tour of the town that also takes in the graveyard above Harpers Ferry and Storer College, a radical institution of higher learning that educated both blacks and women. At 8:30 on Friday and Saturday evenings you can see a program on the park green. "Hearts and Minds," often repeated, reveals how Harpers Ferry has changed our lives as well as the course of history. A day spent at the park, however, will cover most of this information.

If you don't care for tours, you can explore on your own. Background information on these free tours plus times for each is available at the Visitors Center in a seven-minute film. There is a 30-minute film on the raid at the John Brown Museum. Several of the town's main streets have been restored and you can wander among historic buildings and quaint shops and restaurants. The Dry Goods Shop on Shenandoah Street is stocked as it would have been in the 1850s. It has a special price on pieces of the rope that was used to hang John Brown. A sign advises men of Harpers Ferry to buy a Colt pistol to protect their women and children. Next door is the Provost Office that brings back the days of martial law at Harpers Ferry. The town changed hands eight times during the war.

Combining the historic with the scenic you can climb above the town to Jefferson Rock. When Thomas Jefferson took in the view from this vantage point he declared it "worth a voyage across the Atlantic." Not to detract in any way from Harpers

Ferry's very real scenic appeal, it is worth mentioning that Jefferson up to that time had never crossed the Atlantic.

Nature lovers may want to extend their day by taking a hike on Virginius Island, site of the John Hall Rifle Works, or crossing the river to explore Maryland Heights. A picnic lunch along the river will make this an inexpensive excursion as there is no admission charge for the buildings. The Harpers Ferry Visitors Center and Exhibits are open daily 8:00 A.M. to 5:00 P.M. The first of the summer-only tours begins at 10:00 A.M., and the last tour of the day is at 4:00 P.M. except on weekends when they end with the 8:30 P.M. performance.

Directions: Harpers Ferry is a four-hour drive from Philadelphia. Take Route 30 west past York to the intersection with Route 15. Go south on Route 15 to Frederick, Maryland. At Frederick take Route 340 to Harpers Ferry. Signs at Harpers Ferry will direct you to the Visitors Center parking area.

Hershey

Does the word Hershey conjure up the marvelous taste of chocolate? After a visit to Hershey, Pennsylvania, it will call up many more pleasant associations.

The first impression you are likely to get in Hershey is the rich scent of chocolate which the slightest breeze wafts through the community. Next you'll be visually stimulated by the town's unique street lights and street signs. Where else in America could you see candy-kiss-shaped lights? Few families can resist a candid shot of these street lights or of the street signs at the junction of Chocolate Avenue and Cocoa Street.

You will grasp the scope of the chocolate business and enjoy a scoop of chocolate at Hershey's familiarization center, Chocolate World. This is a good first stop because the parking lot that serves the center and Hersheypark is accessible by tram and shuttle bus to other attractions in this busy town. Chocolate World is open at no charge from 9:00 A.M. to 4:45 P.M. (6:45 P.M. during the summer months). If the kids are in a hurry to get to the rides in the park you can assure them that at Chocolate World they will also have a ride. This ride guides you through the world of chocolate from its beginnings on the cocoa plantations of South America to the finished product made at Hershey, Pennsylvania. Old-timers may remember the tours of the plant itself, which so overwhelmed visitors with the sweet smell of vats of chocolate that it was hours before anyone would want to sample any chocolate. There is no such sensory overload on this ride, and you may well want to stop at the boutiques, restaurants or shops for a taste of the company product. You can buy anything chocolate from one kiss to a ten-pound Hershey bar.

One of the big advantages of this well-laid-out town is that since one parking lot serves all the points of interest families can split up and follow their individual bents. Older kids can head immediately for Hersheypark. (Keep in mind that the easily located Kissing Tower inside the park is a good place to plan a rendezvous.) And the flower fanciers of the family can take their time drinking in the pleasures of the Hershey Gardens.

If a national committee had won their campaign Milton Hershey would have contributed to yet another garden in Washington, D.C. In 1936 he was asked to donate a million dollars towards the establishment of a National Rosarium. He chose instead to develop a garden more or less in his own backyard. Pennsylvanians can be glad he did because the results are striking. It is worth a trip to Hershey just to see the gardens, particularly in early summer and fall when the roses are at their peak. Although the gardens have many specialty areas, roses are the primary focus. There are roughly 35,000 bushes of more than 850 varieties. Roses are featured in the All-American Rose Avenue, the Old-Fashioned Rose Garden and in Mrs. Hershey's personal rose garden.

Other plants are certainly not neglected at Hershey Gardens. Spring arrives in a burst of color provided by tens of thousands of daffodils and tulips, and brilliant azalea and rhododenron bushes. Mid-summer is brightened by the 400 day lily varieties and fall, by the 4,000 chrysanthemums. Tours of the garden include information on the Japanese, Italian and English Formal Gardens. America's past is captured by the Colonial Garden and the Herb Garden.

If you have come to Hershey solely to enjoy the flowers, then extend your pleasure by strolling through the grounds of the Hotel Hershey on the hilltop above the Hershey Gardens. The hotel's formal gardens are attractive and your day can be capped by lunch in the elegant Hotel Hershey dining room overlooking the gardens.

To balance the program for youngsters you may want to stop at the Hershey Museum of American Life before taking them to the rides at the park. This museum presents exhibits from the earliest inhabitants on the North American continent to the collectibles of this generation. There are crude utensils from prehistoric people, intricately crafted Indian baskets, beaded Eskimo clothes, memorabilia from the wars in which America has been involved, a Conestoga wagon and the household belongings that have furnished our homes through the centuries. The collection of Pennsylvania-German artifacts is one of the largest in existence. Another exhibit describes the accomplishments of founder Milton Hershey. They do charge admission at this museum which is open from 10:00 A.M. to 5:00 P.M. During the summer it stays open until 6:00 P.M.

The most well-known attraction in Hershey aside from chocolate is Hersheypark. A redevelopment campaign was initiated in 1971 and today it ranks among America's top theme parks. For animal fanciers a new feature at the park is ZooAmerica which has plants and animals from the five natural regions of North America.

Obviously you can't cover everything in a day, but with the varied attractions at Hershey you can plan a double-feature outing that will come close to pleasing everybody in the family.

Directions: Hershey is a two-hour drive from Philadelphia. Take I-76 (Pennsylvania Turnpike) west to Route 743. Go north on Route 743 to Hershey where the easy-to-follow signs will direct you to the main parking area and to the other points of interest.

Hillwood Museum

Philadelphians who enjoy visiting nearby Longwood Gardens will also want to plan a day trip to the Hillwood Museum and Gardens in Washington, D.C. This garden estate was originally developed by Isaac Peirce, grandson of George Peirce whose arboretum and park formed the nucleus for Longwood Gardens.

Although advanced planning is a must if you want to see both house and garden, it really is worth the effort. Unlike Washington's prestigious national collections, the marvelous array of art amassed at Hillwood is the achievement of one woman— Marjorie Merriweather Post. It is, therefore, all the more surprising to see the scope of her collection and the felicitous combination of styles in her garden.

The house is furnished in a manner fit for a king. In fact, many of the pieces were made for the royal families of Europe. French furniture was a particular favorite of Mrs. Post's. You'll see it throughout the house. The Gobelins tapestries on two sofas and 12 chairs in the drawing room were said to have been a gift from Louis XVI to Prince Henry of Prussia, the brother of Frederick the Great. A portrait of Empress Eugénie is placed between two wall cases of Sèvres porcelain.

The dining room has 18th-century French carved paneling from a townhouse in Paris, and is adorned with four paintings by the Dutch painter Dirk Langendijk. The table is often set with porcelain commissioned by Catherine the Great. The glorious green and clear glass chandelier in the breakfast room has been tentatively traced to a suite designed for Catherine at Tsarskoe Selo.

As the wife of Joseph E. Davis, American Ambassador to the Soviet Union in 1937–38, Mrs. Post was able to purchase many objects confiscated by the regime at the time of the Revolution from the churches and the aristocracy. These were sold by the Soviets during the 1920s and 1930s to finance industrialization. The silver chalices, for example, were sold for five cents per gram weight without any regard for their artistic worth. Only a small percentage of the collection was acquired in the Soviet Union; Mrs. Post continued to collect Russian pieces after her return to the United States. Her collection is now said to be the most comprehensive outside the Soviet Union. Nowhere else in the West will you see displayed the impressive array of Russian porcelain, glass, silver and jewel-studded objects by Carl Fabergé, many of which were made for the Romanov family.

The Russian influence is also in evidence on the estate grounds where you will discover a one-room Dacha, which contains more Russian art. Another country house, this one built like an Adirondack "camp," (albeit in the style to which the aristocratic Mrs. Post was accustomed) showcases her American Indian art and artifact collection. This collection previously displayed at Topridge, her Adirondack camp, was given to the Smithsonian Institution and is now on long-term loan to Hillwood. There is also the C.W. Post Wing with memorabilia and Victoriana collected by Mrs. Post's father.

The grounds are worth exploring not only for these additional exhibition areas, but also because of the outstanding garden. There are more than 3,500 plants and trees in this garden. Mrs. Post took an active interest in the placement of each. According to her daughter, Dina Merrill, who narrates the 30-minute introductory film on Mrs. Post's life that you'll see before your tour, her mother "would think nothing of having an 80-foot tree moved merely five feet in order to improve the view."

The view from Hillwood is magnificent, so obviously she succeeded. From the portico, looking down across the Lunar Lawn, you can see the Washington Monument in the distance. It's six miles from Hillwood. The garden has sections with a natural blending of laurel, azalea and rhododendron, as well as formal areas with a Moorish water canal. There is also a Japanese garden with waterfalls, bridge and lanterns. The roses at Hillwood are one of the joys of a summer visit, and the greenhouse is interesting even in winter.

To make a tour reservation write to Hillwood Museum, 4155 Linnean Avenue, N.W., Washington, D.C. 20008, or call (202)686-5807. If you write be sure to provide alternative dates for a visit as this is a popular attraction. Tours are given on Monday, Wednesday, Thursday, Friday and Saturday. Times are 9:00 and 10:30 A.M., NOON and 1:30 P.M. Admission is charged. It will take about two hours to see the introductory film and house. You'll want to allow at least an additional hour for the other attractions.

Directions: From Philadelphia take I-95 south to the Washington Beltway, I-495. Go west on I-495 to Connecticut Avenue. Take Connecticut Avenue south towards the city and turn left on Tilden Street. Make another left on Linnean Avenue. Hillwood is located at 4155 Linnean Avenue.

Hopewell Village, St. Peters Village and Daniel Boone Homestead

Hopewell Village does for the travel buff what John Jakes's novel *North and South* did for the historical novel buff; it presents a rarely captured look at a paternalistic iron plantation. Like the Hollywood movie sets of the plantations of the Old South, Hopewell looks a lot cleaner now than it did in the 1770s. From the late 18th century until 1883 the furnace ran day and night, filling the air with smoke and coating the village with ash and cinders.

Now the dust is long settled. You can see an idealized, picture-perfect iron-making community, operating as it did between 1820 and 1840. It's interesting to compare the small houses of the iron workers (still planted with their kitchen gardens) with the comparative luxury of the ironmaster's home, the Big House. Like their counterparts in the South, the ironmasters were community leaders. In fact, James Wilson and George Ross, both ironmasters and brothers-in-law of Hopewell's founder Mark Bird, were members of the Continental Congress and signers of the Declaration of Independence. Another Pennsylvania signer, George Taylor, was the ironmaster at Durham Furnace.

When you arrive at this National Historic Site, managed by the National Park Service, you will begin your exploration at the Visitor Center where an easy-to-follow ten-minute orientation slide program provides an idea of how an iron furnace operated. This will, in turn, give you a greater appreciation of what you will see on your self-guided walking tour.

Many of the 17 stops on your tour route are concerned with the iron-making process. Hundreds of acres of wood had to be cut annually to make charcoal for the furnace. You'll see one of the old charcoal hearths and the nearby sod-roofed hut of the collier. The massive iron furnace was the linchpin of the village. There is also a "cast house" where the molten iron was formed into armaments for the Continental Army and such utilitarian products as stoves, sashweights and cookware. Taped messages will help you understand the process as you follow the step-by-step procedure on your tour route.

The voices of these bygone days will also reveal intriguing details about daily life and concerns. Some villagers have serious problems: one worries about child labor, while a widow laments the hardship of her life.

Although interesting year-round, it is in the summer that Hopewell is most alive. During July and August the living history program presents costumed blacksmiths, carpenters, cooks, molders, seamstresses and other craftspeople who tell about their lives and demonstrate their skills. Hopewell Village is open daily from 9:00 A.M. until 5:00 P.M., except Christmas and New Year's Day. The Village is accessible to the handicapped.

Adjacent to this historical site is a natural one—French Creek State Park where you can enjoy a picnic lunch. This 7,339-acre park, with its three lakes, offers a variety of activities. Hiking, fishing, swimming and camping are all possible; during the winter months you can ski, sled, toboggan, skate or even try ice fishing.

Another nearby attraction is **St. Peters Village**, a picturesque Victorian village where you can enjoy lunch, hike along French Creek, and browse through the unusual boutiques. Philadelphians have been coming here for more than a century. While having lunch on the outdoor patio of the Inn at St. Peters you can watch the French Creek Falls, which drop 155 feet in less than half a mile. Lunch is served Monday through Saturday from 11:30 A.M. until 2:00 P.M., both outside and in the Victorian dining room. Dinner runs from 5:30 to 9:00 P.M., Monday through Thursday; 5:30 to 10:00 P.M. on Friday and Saturday nights. A Sunday brunch is served from 11:00 A.M. until 2:30 P.M., and Sunday dinner from 3:30 to 7:00 P.M. If you want to plan ahead you can make reservations by calling (215)469-6277. A bed and breakfast service is also available. An Oom-pah band entertains during the summer from 1:00 to 5:00 P.M. in the beer garden below the Inn.

One more destination that can be included in your day's outing is a stop at the **Daniel Boone Homestead,** just up the road. It was in this untamed part of Pennsylvania that Daniel Boone was born and lived until he was 16. In the woods around his home he learned to hunt and trap. Only the foundations remain of the log cabin Daniel Boone called home. A two-story stone house built in the late 18th century has been furnished to recreate rural life in this part of Pennsylvania. It is interesting to compare this independent rural life with that of the iron workers' at nearby Hopewell.

In addition to touring the old stone house you can get an overview of Boone's life at the Visitors Center. Youngsters can feed the farm animals and during the summer months a blacksmith shop operates on special occasions. Daniel Boone's father was a blacksmith, and as a young boy Daniel learned how to fix his own rifle and musket. Now the area around his old farm is a game sanctuary where deer, raccoon, rabbits, pheasants and quail can occasionally be spotted.

The Daniel Boone Homestead is open for a small charge from 8:30 A.M. to 5:00 P.M., Tuesday through Saturday, and NOON to 5:00 P.M. on Sunday. It is closed on major holidays.

Directions: These attractions are approximately an hour's drive from Philadelphia. Take I-76, the Schuylkill Expressway, to the Pennsylvania Turnpike west. Take Exit 22 at Morgantown and pick up Route 10. At Route 10 turn left, south, for one-quarter mile into Morgantown. In Morgantown turn left, east, on Route 23, and go five miles to the intersection with Route 345. Then take a left, north, on Route 345. This leads into Hopewell, which is only ten miles from the turnpike. Follow the above directions for St. Peters Village and continue on Route 23, then make a left on Route 8 and go north to the village. For the Daniel Boone Homestead, you will also take Exit 22 at Morgantown, then bear left at the McDonalds. Proceed to the intersection and make a right, then very shortly, bear right again on Route 176, north. Follow this road until you see a sign indicating Pottstown. This will lead you to Route 422, east. Continue approximately four miles to the highway division. Stay in the left lane and proceed through a traffic light. Watch for a blue and gold historic marker. Make a left turn and cross over the divided highway. This is the Daniel Boone Road. It leads to the Homestead.

Island Field Museum

For the native American Indian burial grounds were hallowed land. A visit to the even earlier prehistoric burial site, the Island Field Museum in South Bowers, Delaware, lends a deeply felt poignancy to the plea Chief Seattle made in 1855:

"These shores will swarm with the invisible dead of my tribe, and when your children's children think themselves alone in the field, the store, the shop, or in the silence of the pathless woods, they will not be alone . . . Let him be just and deal kindly with my people."

At Island Field Museum a 1,200-year-old cemetery has been excavated. The 125 exposed skeletons remain as they were found. This represents a significant prehistorical find. After the cemetery was discovered in August of 1967 a museum and research center was built around it.

One of the aspects that so excited archeologists was that this cemetery revealed the existence of a previously unknown group of people. They believed these Middle Woodland People lived in this part of North America approximately 1,000 years ago—maybe even as early as A.D. 500. One burial site was carbon-dated at A.D. 750.

Much has been learned from the more than 500 artifacts uncovered at Island Field. Like the Egyptian tombs, this prehistoric cemetery contains the objects these people once used in their day-to-day existence. You will see harpoons, fish hooks, scrapers, awls, knives, fire-making kits, pestles, stone pipes, shell cups, pendants and even a very rare find—a deer antler headdress.

When you visit Island Field Museum you will find out what conclusions archeologists have reached from their study of the artifacts they have found. The presence of intrusive lithics, or stones that are not of local origin indicated that these early people did have contact with other groups. A slide presentation explains the work being done here. The museum has an archeological study collection and a research library with hard-to-find books on regional prehistory. This really is the American history that few of us have studied. It becomes much more meaningful when you can see the tangible reminders of these early inhabitants.

The Island Field Museum can be visited from March through November. It is open at no charge Tuesday through Saturday from 10:00 A.M. to 4:30 P.M., and on Sunday from 1:30 to 4:00 P.M. Phone: (302)335-5395.

Directions: From Philadelphia take I-95 south past Wilmington, then take Route 301-13 south to the Dover area where it will become Route 113. You can reach Island Field Museum from Route 113 by way of Route 19 or Route 120.

Ladew Topiary Gardens

If computer wizardry is too mechanical for you and Hollywood whimsy too theatrical, you may well enjoy the more old-world flights of fancy at the Ladew Topiary Gardens in Monkton, Maryland.

Topiary is the art of trimming, cutting and training greenery into ornamental shapes. It is something of a lost art. Harvey Ladew, a frequent visitor to England, developed a fondness for this garden conceit which has always been a popular feature in the great English gardens. The extent of Mr. Ladew's success at transporting topiary to the United States is attested to by the award he received from the Garden Clubs of America, citing his garden as "the most outstanding topiary garden in America."

But topiary was only one of Ladew's gardening talents. He designed, laid out and planted 15 unique flowering gardens, or "rooms," as he called them. Each garden was designed around a different theme and is separated by a wall or hedge from the other garden rooms. There are flowers in bloom from spring through fall.

Since this garden is located in rural Maryland hunt country, as you enter the Ladew estate it is singularly appropriate to see hunter, horse and hounds in full cry after the fox. But they are not real; they are yews and are just the first example of the marvelous art of topiary. Within this 22 acre green you will see such diverse creations as a topiary Henry Moore sculpture, a lyre bird and unicorn side by side, an antlered reindeer guarding the door and a topiary aviary which, in addition to the lyre bird, includes a dozen swans swimming on waves of yew, French hens sitting on their nests and birds of paradise.

Harvey Ladew had a lively sense of humor and it is very much in evidence in his unusual garden. Where else would one find an apple orchard with a statue of Eve offering Adam an apple? You'll also see posted above the doghouse this unattributed poem:

> "I love this little house because
> It offers after dark
> A Pause for rest, a rest for paws,
> A place to moor my bark."

From the garden teahouse (once a ticket booth at the Tivoli Theatre in London) there is a delightful view of the garden. To enhance your appreciation of this vista the open window has a frame around it, creating the illusion that you are seeing a landscape painting.

Another poetic effort, this one attributed to Hilaire Belloc, will appeal to any garden fancier who has stood bemused by stately sundials trying to fathom just how they work. Around Ladew's sundial you can read this message: "I am a sundial and I make a botch/Of what is done far better by a watch."

This lighthearted effect is also evident in Pleasant Valley Farm, Ladew's home, which, like the gardens, is included in the Register of Historic Places. The hunt motif introduced at the entrance is seen throughout the house. It's amusing to try to count the number of hunting scenes that decorate the furnishings.

Hunting was only one of Mr. Ladew's passions. He was a striking man with a large fortune and considered quite a catch. But he was better at hunting than being hunted, and he never married. He took advantage of his unencumbered state to travel around the world seeking adventures and new friends. Many of his experiences are brought to mind by the mementos. On the wall you can see a note from T.E. Lawrence, the notorious Lawrence of Arabia, who in 1904 complained, "Everything, everywhere is changing." Like his friend Lawrence, Ladew too had adventures with the Bedouin. He crossed the Arabian desert with them and when chilled by the cold night air had the elan to don his dinner jacket, thereby creating a new version of desert chic.

Another friend whose letter adorns the wall was Edward VIII, who while still the Prince of Wales, had occasion to borrow one of Ladew's favorite horses. His note thanks Harvey for the use of The Ghost.

Another wall attests to Ladew's originality and skill as a painter. On his sister's dressing room wall he painted a chest of drawers with bits of undergarments dangling from the opened drawers. Two chairs painted on each side of the chest are also strewn with clothes. This *trompe l'oeil* makes visitors wonder whether his sister's visits disrupted the running of this essentially masculine establishment.

Imagination and determination seemed to influence most of what Harvey Ladew did. When he returned from one of his English visits with a massive oval desk, he discovered that he had no space large enough to accommodate it. This proved no obstacle; he built a room around it. The oval library, lined with 3,000 books, is one of the 100 most beautiful rooms in America. The room even has a secret escape panel.

After sharing Harvey Ladew's world it is hard not to feel a bit let-down. Here is a world where imagination had free rein and cost was no object. It is nice that his world has been preserved for us to enjoy. Harvey Ladew, who died in 1976, seems like a very special person.

Ladew Topiary Gardens are open from mid-April through October. The gardens can be visited Tuesday through Saturday from 10:00 A.M. to 4:00 P.M., and on Sunday from NOON to 5:00 P.M. The house is open only on Wednesday and Sunday; hours are the same as for the garden. Groups can arrange a tour by appointment throughout the year by calling (301)557-9466. Admission is charged. There is a café where you may have lunch and a Visitor Center and gift shop where you will find unusual crafted items, plants and topiaries.

Directions: Take I-95 south from Philadelphia to the Baltimore Beltway, I-695. Go west on I-695 toward Towson. At Exit 27-N, go north on Route 146 past Jacksonville. Ladew Topiary Gardens are five miles past Jacksonville on Route 146, Jarretsville Pike.

Lexington Market and McCormick Spice Company

Philadelphia has its Reading Terminal Market so why try **Lexington Market** in Baltimore? Well, for one thing, this vast market is the oldest continually operating municipal market in the country. For another, it's a fascinating addition to any of the other Baltimore sites you want to explore—Fort McHenry, the B&O Transportation Museum, Maryland Science Center or Baltimore Museum of Industry. All can easily be combined with a stop at this movable feast—you do the moving and they provide the feast. Lexington Market is a veritable United Nations of gastronomical delights.

More than a block of downtown Baltimore is taken up by the two main buildings that house more than 160 stalls. They are rented to butchers, greengrocers, florists, bakers, dairymen, fish merchants and an assortment of ethnic specialists offering pizza, gyros, burritos and subs to name just some of the popular favorites.

Farmers started meeting here in 1783 when John Eager Howard donated some of his pasture to the community. In 1752 Baltimore had reached a population of 250 with 25 homes, two taverns and one church. By the 1780s the town had grown sufficiently to support a market where "city" folk could buy farm produce. It is interesting to note that early Baltimore was America's only walled city. It is debated whether Baltimoreans were trying to keep out marauding Indians, or foraging pigs and geese from nearby pastures.

By the 1850s this market was serving 50,000 people and 600 farm wagons would haul in produce. Three city blocks were in use by 1925 and there were 1,000 stalls offering a full cornucopia of produce. This thriving market was reduced to ashes in 1949. The East and West Buildings, built after that fire, along with the glass-enclosed arcade added in the early 1980s, make up the market you visit today.

You provide your own entertainment at the market; the only amusement is in buying and enjoying the marvelous food. Although it is less fun to watch others buying and trying the edibles, even this can provide more amusing moments than the average sitcom seen on television.

A market stall was the goal of many European immigrants who first eked out an existence with a produce cart on the busy city streets. Some stall renters even today come from families who succeeded in making the transition from cart to market. The key to success for many of these stalls is specialization.

Along with specialization comes special preparation and custom service. There are few other places where you can buy fresh bulk cottage cheese scooped to order, or butter sliced to order. At Lexington the chocolate is hand-dipped and the taffy hand-pulled. The butcher cuts the meat to order and advises patrons on the amount they'll need for dinner parties. For the convenience of out-of-town shoppers some of the stalls have special styrofoam-lined carrying cartons.

While Lexington Market is certainly not as glitzy as Harborplace and not as well known as their "World Famous Lexington Market" sign would indicate, it is a remarkably egalitarian spot. It is indeed the melting pot in operation—with the added bonus of plenty of fresh produce to put in the pot.

Lexington Market is open Monday through Saturday from 8:30 A.M. to 6:00 P.M. Some stalls are also closed on Mondays.

If the aromatic mixture of spices at Lexington Market has stimulated your palate, a visit to the **McCormick Spice Company**, the world's largest processor of spices and teas, will certainly titillate your nose.

Willoughby McCormick, whose motto "Make the best, someone will buy it" is carved over the large fireplace in Ye Olde McCormick's Tea House, started McCormick's in 1889. His first shop was destroyed in the great Baltimore fire. The spice factory has been located at 414 Light Street since 1921.

As soon as you enter the nine-story, saffron-colored building, you will smell the tantalizing aroma of cinnamon and nutmeg. Your tour begins with a 27-minute movie, *The Wonderful World of Flavor*, which provides background information on how various spices are produced and marketed. You will learn that pepper is the world's most popular spice. It has long been valued, in fact, as early as 408 A.D. the Romans ransomed their city from Alaric the Visigoth for 2,000 pounds of pepper. You will also learn about cinnamon, the second most popular spice, and saffron, which is currently the world's most expensive spice.

C.P. McCormick, the company's second president, greatly admired 16th-century Elizabethan England, and he recreated a bit of olde England at his spice plant. After the movie you'll be escorted to Friendship Court by a hostess costumed in an Elizabethan gown. This court contains replicas of the exterior of Ann Hathaway's thatched roof cottage, as well as Shakespeare's grammar school. Here too is Ye Olde McCormick's Tea House where you can have a "cuppa" while you relax. There are collections of old teapots to admire and a variety of aromatic spices to smell. Selected gift items are for sale and McCormick gives visitors a spice chart, selected recipes and often a spice sample.

The tour concludes with a walk around Friendship Court. You will visit the Tea Museum which houses the world's largest book on tea. McCormick also introduces visitors to their gourmet spice shelf and to other products marketed by the company.

Tours are given at 10:00 A.M. and 1:30 P.M., Monday through Friday. There is no charge but they are by appointment only; occasionally walk-in visitors are accommodated if the tours are not filled to capacity. To make a reservation call (301)547-6166.

If you want to expand your outing, plan to enjoy lunch either before or after your tour at the Hyatt Regency's Skylights roof restaurant. The Hyatt, at 300 Light Street, is directly across Conway Street from the McCormick Spice Company. It also faces Harborplace across Light Street. The view from Skylights is second only to the five-sided vista you get from the observation floor of the World Trade Center. Skylights is very popular; to make reservations you call (301)528-1234.

Directions: From Philadelphia take I-95 south. Just outside Baltimore exit for the downtown area on Route 40, the Pulaski Highway. This merges with Fayette Street which will take you into the city. Turn right on Paca Street. The Lexington Market will be on both the right and left sides of Paca Street at Lexington Street. To reach the McCormick Spice Company from the Lexington Market, go up Paca Street two blocks to Mulberry Street. Turn right, continue one block to Eutaw Street. Turn right and go to Pratt Street where you turn left. Continue down Pratt Street to the Inner Harbor area and make a right on Light Street. McCormick's will be on your right just past Harborplace.

Lititz

Few destinations offer the diversity of Lititz, Pennsylvania, the quintessential American hometown of yesteryear. Where else on a Main Street can you get the sound of music mingling with the scent of chocolate? Or visit a shop where you can learn how to make a pretzel?

The town of Lititz was established in 1756. The land was donated to the Moravian Congregation and named in honor of the barony of Lititz in Bohemia where King Podiebrad offered sanctuary to the persecuted Moravians, or Unitas Fratrum as they were also called. The oldest Protestant denomination, Unitas Fratrum was established 60 years before the Reformation in 1467 when followers of John Hus, Czeck theologian and martyr, broke away from the Catholic Church.

The center of community life in Lititz as in any Moravian town was the church. The church you see when you visit Lititz was built in 1786. It is flanked by the Sisters' and Brethren's Houses. Located next to the Brethren's House is the archives and museum which houses an outstanding collection of old musical instruments.

Music was an integral part of the Moravian service. Thus it is not surprising to discover that the Moravians were an important musical force in colonial America. They were the first musical educators; they built many of the first instruments and wrote a substantial number of the religious compositions of the 18th century. They also composed the first chamber music in this country.

The tradition of the trombone choir is closely associated with Moravian music, and so you will see an excellent selection of brass instruments dating back to 1774. The oldest brass instrument in the Lititz collection is a Hunting horn, made in France circa 1750, likely the prized possession of one of the early settlers. Another room has woodwind and stringed instruments. It is a marvel that so many of these old pieces have survived. They have been located, restored, researched and put on display by a dedicated couple, George and Julia Keehn, who with the able assistance of the late R.M. Shank, are largely responsible for making this museum a reality. They offer tours of the museum and provide background information on many of the pieces. To arrange a visit to this unique museum call Doris Allebach, Head Guide, at (717)626-2467, or the Church office at 626-8515.

Directly across the street from the Moravian Church, the Johannes Mueller House will give you an idea of how the early German settlers in Lititz lived back in the 18th century. The main portion of this seven-room house was built in 1792 by Johannes Mueller, a printer and dyer of linen. He lived here with his wife, their four children and his three apprentices.

This house has been furnished with antique pieces donated by the residents of Lititz, many of which were actually made in Lititz. A number of the furnishings belonged to well-known Lititz resident, General John Augustus Sutter, whose elegant two-story brick home just up the street at 19 E. Main now serves as the offices for Farmers First Bank.

The most unusual pieces in the house are two inlaid wooden clocks made by local craftsman, Rudolph Carpenter. His hobby was making incredibly complex inlaid wooden furniture. During the colonial period furniture made out of solid wood was taxed while that made of multiple kinds of wood was not. Evidently the wood was often stained or painted to make detection difficult. Wood was also used for a great many household items including toys. On the second floor of the Mueller house you can see a wooden "slinky" dog, wooden perpetual motion ducks and a two-sided wooden puzzle.

The Johannes Mueller House is open Memorial Day through Labor Day Monday through Saturday from 10:30 A.M. to 4:00 P.M. At other times you can visit by appointment by writing to the Lititz Historical Foundation, 137 East Main Street, Lititz, PA 17543. An admission is charged.

One of your favorite Lititz sites is bound to be the Sturgis Pretzel House at 219 E. Main Street. It's just a block from the Mueller house but you can't miss it because an oversized pretzel hangs outside the door. Billed as the birthplace of the American pretzel industry, this small bakery dates back to 1784. In 1861 a weary traveler stopped at the bakery, and when he was given food returned the favor by sharing the recipe for German hard pretzels with the baker. When the baker did not try the new idea, his apprentice, Julius Sturgis, decided to experiment and the American craze for pretzels began.

The bakery is still making soft pretzels by hand and baking them in the original 200-year-old ovens, but hard pretzels are made by machines, which turn out 125 a minute. Tours are given where you can try your hand at forming a pretzel. Visitors quickly learn the knack of rolling, crossing and shaping, but no beginner can equal the speed of long time workers who can do 40 pretzels a minute. After the tour, few can resist buying some of these tasty snacks. The new horse and buggy pretzels should make a real hit in a lunch box or at a party. The tours are given Monday through Saturday, 9:00 A.M. to 5:00 P.M. The bakery is closed on Sunday. A nominal admission is charged, and appropriately enough your ticket is a pretzel.

Just a few blocks away is the Wilbur Chocolate Company and Factory Candy Outlet. All phases of the candy industry—manufacturing, processing, packaging and advertising—are displayed. Among the extensive exhibits of old candy making equipment, one of the more decorative is a group of more than 150 china and porcelain chocolate pots. Another is a display of hundreds of wood and metal candy containers. For young visitors who are more interested in content than containers they do sell a wide range of candy. You can watch while they make hand-dipped chocolates, and you can also purchase up-to-date supplies for your own kitchen. Wilbur's Factory Candy Outlet is open at no charge Monday through Saturday from 10:00 A.M. to 5:00 P.M. and is closed on Sunday.

Pretzels and chocolates can augment a picnic lunch in the adjacent Lititz Spring Park. If you would rather try the local restaurants you can consider a sandwich and ice cream treat at the Sundae Best just across Klein Street from Wilbur's. On the square in Lititz you can enjoy lunch at the General Sutter Inn, built and operated by the Moravians as an old stage coach stop. Another option would be to drive out to the end of East Main Street to Rome Mill Restaurant where you can enjoy lunch beside a real waterwheel that is located within the restaurant. Next to the restaurant is an old grist mill that you can tour. Rome Mill offers tours daily from 10:00 A.M. to 4:00 P.M. May through October.

Directions: From Philadelphia take the Pennsylvania Turnpike, I-76, west to Exit 21. Head south to Ephrata (see selection on Ephrata Cloister elsewhere in book) on Route 222 and continue south to the intersection with Route 772. Make a right on Route 772 into Lititz where Route 772 becomes Main Street.

Naval Flagships at Penn's Landing

You can quite literally stand in the footsteps of history on the deck of the *U.S.S. Olympia*. Bronze impressions of Commodore [later Admiral] Dewey's footsteps mark the spot on the bridge where he was standing at 5:40 A.M. on the morning of May 1, 1898, when he issued his famous order, "You may fire when you are ready, Gridley." His order marked the start of the Battle of Manila Bay as well as the beginning of America's status as a world power. The guns that Dewey ordered Captain Gridley to fire were the heaviest battery ever fitted to a ship of this size.

The *U.S.S. Olympia* is the sole surviving example of the "New Navy" of the 1880s and 1890s. Flagship of Dewey's Asiatic fleet, she was a protective cruiser that could maintain speeds of 22 knots, considered swift for a ship at that time. It cost $2.9 million to build the *Olympia*, and she was American-designed and built.

Despite her many contributions to American history the Navy was ready in 1955 to scrap this lone survivor of the Spanish-American War. She was no longer of any use and it looked like the "Grand Old Lady," as she was called, was doomed. Then, thanks to a dedicated group of volunteers, The Cruiser Olympia Association, she was painstakingly restored.

When you enter the *Olympia* you will be in the Senior Officers' Mess, and the wood paneling and fine old wood furniture provide ample testimony to the diligence of the volunteers who spent endless hours restoring the ship to its original appearance. Before they took over, one could get wet on rainy days five decks below the bridge. You will quickly realize what a complete world existed aboard these cruisers as you view in succession the ship's store, post office, dispensary, operating room, print shop and barber shop which also served as dentist office on alternate days. Be sure to note the ingenuous methods employed to berth and feed the crew of 440 men.

On the upper deck of the *Olympia* is the wooden casket used when she sailed from Le Havre on her last mission. In it she carried the body of the unknown soldier of World War I for interment at Arlington National Cemetery. From this deck you look down upon the *U.S.S. Becuna* which is anchored beside the *Olympia*. The *U.S.S. Becuna* is a guppy-class submarine that saw action in World War II. She was commissioned on May 27, 1944, as the submarine flagship of the Southwest Pacific Fleet under General Douglas MacArthur. The *Becuna* on her five war patrols is credited with the destruction of thousands of tons of Japanese naval and merchant ships.

The submarine is the last of her type on exhibit. She is 308 feet long, and you can explore from the forward torpedo room to the manuevering and motor room at the opposite end. It is hard to imagine 66 men living in this cramped and confined space. Even the officers' quarters are confining; only the captain has a bed that resembles a normal size bunk. The names of the 16-cylinder engines, Grunt and Groan and Huff and Puff, amuse the kids; but it is the torpedo with cut-aways that really captures visitors' attention. Torpedos don't look that big when you see them being fired in war movies.

These two symbols of America's nautical past are berthed at Penn's Landing at the foot of Spruce Street on the Delaware River. You can visit from 10:00 A.M. to 6:00 P.M. during the summer months and from 10:00 A.M. to 4:00 P.M. in the fall, winter and spring. A nominal admission is charged.

Penn's Landing is located at the very spot where William Penn first landed in 1682 and it is singularly appropriate that you will also find the Port of History Museum at this Philadelphia threshold. Displays within the museum highlight the life of William Penn and the development of this important American city. The museum contains an innovative circular film and slide theater.

An enjoyable way to end your visit is with a ride along the waterfront on the Penn's Landing Trolley. Turn-of-the-century trolley cars take you on a 20-minute ride past such picturesque neighborhoods as Queen Village, Society Hill and Olde City. The conductors, all part of the Buckingham Valley Trolley Association, give you a bit of history about these cars, originally in use from 1904 to 1958. You can catch a ride at Dock Street or Spruce Street from 11:00 A.M. to dusk weekends from Easter to Memorial Day. From Memorial Day to Labor Day, they run from Thursday through Sunday. From Labor Day through December they run on weekends only. The fare is minimal.

Directions: From center city take Market Street down to Front Street and you will find ample parking in the Penn's Landing area. There are two public parking lots plus on-street, two-hour parking; spaces are not difficult to find on weekdays.

New Hope

Ride on a mule-drawn barge on the historic Delaware canal or on the New Hope Steam Railway and experience New Hope, an art colony established in the early 1900s in a little Pennsylvania village along the Delaware River by a group of internationally-known artists. The charms of New Hope include lovely old stone houses that date back to the colonial era, narrow streets and alleys with charming row houses, intriguing courtyards, arts and crafts displayed in shop windows, wooded trails and towpath walks plus the opportunity to sample the competing transportation alternatives that vied for supremacy in the late 1800s and early 1900s.

The barge trips run daily from May through mid-September on an hourly basis. During April and from mid-September to mid-November barge rides are only offered on Wednesday, Saturday and Sunday. The trips are unavailable from mid-November to April. To find out the exact schedule on the day you plan to visit or to make advance reservations you can call (215)862-2842. If you don't have time to schedule a barge ride you can walk along the canal towpath where you'll see the old locks and perhaps one of the barges as it travels along the still water.

Two ferry companies offer 45-minute pontoon boat rides on the Delaware River. Coryell's Ferry, 22 South Main Street, invites you to relax on *The General George Washington*. During the Revolution, Washington crossed the Delaware here on several occasions. Coryell's Ferry is located on the river directly behind Gerenser's Exotic Ice Cream. Try one of the 45 flavors including the offbeat Ukrainian Rose Petal, Jewish Malaga, Magyar Apricot Brandy, Swedish Ollaliberry and Oriental Green Tea while you wait for the boats that leave every 45 minutes from noon to dusk. You can also ride on *The Miss New Hope* operated by the Wells Ferry Boat Rides at the foot of Ferry Street. These pontoon boats run from 1:00 P.M. to dusk every 45 minutes.

The noisier "iron horse" is an entirely different experience from the slow, tranquil barge ride. You'll buy your ticket for the 8½ mile steam train ride at the quaint New Hope Station where railroad museum evokes the early days of locomotive travel. The New Hope line was built between 1889 and 1890 and gradually supplanted the canal as the major carrier to the region.

On the journey, fans of old movies may recognize the curved trestle bridge the train crosses as the one used on the matinee serial "Perils of Pauline." The train ride through the lovely Pennsylvania countryside gives you an idea why so many artists have chosen to make their home here. You'll travel east to Lahaska and then back to New Hope. At Lahaska there is a collection of shops called Peddler's Village that is worth visiting if you can extend your trip.

The steam train runs on Saturday and Sunday May through October. It leaves New Hope at 1:30 and 3:30 P.M. on Saturday and at 1:45, 2:45 and 4:15 P.M. on Sunday. In November the train runs on Sunday only at 1:30 and 3:15 P.M. The train does not operate December through April. To obtain additional information call (215)750-0872.

Return to New Hope and find a shopper's paradise. The shops along Main Street are filled with unusual antiques and crafts. You can easily spend a whole day exploring the hundreds of shops along the tree lined streets and tucked-away alleys. The shops are open daily year-round from 10:00 A.M. to 5:00 P.M.

If you find yourself wishing that you could tour the inside of one of the lovely old homes, head over to the Parry Mansion on Cannon Square. The Historical Society of New Hope offers tours of this mansion from 2:00 to 5:00 P.M. Friday through Monday. Each of Parry Mansion's ten rooms is decorated in a different style from the late 18th century to the early 20th century.

Be sure to pick up a schedule for the Bucks County Playhouse season which runs from April through November so that you can plan a return visit to coincide with your theatrical favorite. The playhouse is located in an old grist mill and many well-known stars have played at what is now called the State Theatre of Pennsylvania. For up-to-date performance and ticket information you can call (215)862-2041.

Directions: From Philadelphia take I-95 north to the New Hope Exit, Route 32, River Road. Follow Route 32 to New Hope. You can also take either Route 309, Route 611 or Route 263 out of the city and pick up Route 202 which will take you into New Hope. Lahaska's Peddler's Village is located at the junction of Route 202 and Route 263. The train station is located off Bridge Street just before you cross the canal. The barge landing parking lot is located on New Street.

Ocean City Life Saving Station Museum

Many Philadelphians look forward each year to a summer outing or vacation in Ocean City, Maryland. This is a relatively new phenomenon; before the advent of superhighways they would usually go to the Jersey shore. Whether you're a newcomer to the Ocean City scene or an old-timer, you'll enjoy dropping in at the Ocean City Life Saving Station Museum.

This picturesque museum is located at the south end of the boardwalk overlooking the inlet, opposite a new shopping area, Inlet Village. At the museum you will see highlights of this resort town's history through a series of collections designed to captivate all members of the family. It provides a perfect midday break if you're only at the beach for the day, or a great rainy date attraction.

Young boys will love the life saving equipment salvaged from the early days of surf rescue. One of the most unusual pieces is the surfcar, or lifecar. This small metal boat is only 11 feet by 4 feet, a claustrophobic nightmare designed to hold up to four people. The device enabled rescuers to unload more quickly the heavily laden immigrant ships that often ran aground. With the breeches buoy, another popular rescue method, only one person at a time could be saved.

Few visitors know the history of the Life Saving Service; many of us have never even heard about its work. The service was founded in 1848, although the first station didn't open in Ocean

City until December 25, 1878. It was just one of a long series of stations built along the nation's 10,000 mile coast line. The museum covers this service from its beginning to the time it merged with the Revenue Cutter Serivce to form the U.S. Coast Guard. Its collection is the only one of its kind in the country.

The items include early uniforms, oars, old photographs and a full-size surf rescue boat—a 26-foot, double-ended, self-bailing vessel. To give you a clear picture of the service in action, there is a short film on the 1946 rescue of the *Olaf Bergh*, a Norwegian freighter that ran aground at 94th Street in Ocean City. There are also photographs taken at the time; one shows the Norwegian consul watching the removal of passengers by breeches buoy.

The distaff side of the family should enjoy the bathing suit collection from bloomers to bikinis. When families first began visiting the beach at the turn of the century they had to rent suits. When you see these unbelievably unstylish creations you know why bathing suits simply had to get better. One gem from the early 1900s was made out of ten yards of heavy wool.

If your only recently-acquired interest or knowledge of macramé has led you to think this is a new hobby wait until you see the knot board with examples of 50 different knots. You'll learn that for centuries seamen have practiced knotting as a creative outlet during their long hours aboard ship and that, according to the display, the knot predated the wheel.

For decoy whittlers and fanciers there is a not-to-be-missed prize-winning collection of decoys. From 1880 to 1930 when Ocean City was a sleepy fishing village, many local families supplemented their income by hunting. They used both carved birds and live birds (called tollers) to attract waterfowl. One hunter might have as many as a hundred decoys. Fishermen can get an idea of the variety of fish found in nearby waters from the live exhibits in two 250-gallon salt water tanks and from a mounted collection of specimens. Also from the deep is a shell collection, plus an assortment of items retrieved by divers from local shipwrecks.

The most astonishing relic didn't come from the sea, however, but from the raucous hurdy-gurdy of the boardwalk amusement arcade. The laughing mannequin that enticed visitors into Jester's Funhouse in the 1940s and '50s, is still rollicking with merriment. "Laughing Sal," as she is called, by now has become a literary figure. In John Barth's collection of stories called *Lost in the Funhouse* he says, "You couldn't hear it without laughing yourself." Test out his theory when you visit.

Another exhibit, the Building Replica Room, brings back the early days in Ocean City. Eight well-known hotels along the boardwalk have been built on a miniature scale with painstaking attention to detail. You can see a grocery store, a pharmacy, even the Ocean City Life Saving Station Museum itself. Strolling in front of these once-thriving establishments are replicas of tourists like yourselves. Some things never change!

The Ocean City Life Saving Station Museum is open June through September from 11:00 A.M. to 10:00 P.M. daily. During the months of May and October the hours are 10:00 A.M. to 4:00 P.M., Thursday through Sunday. The remainder of the year it is open weekends only from NOON to 4:00 P.M. Admission is charged.

Directions: From Philadelphia take I-95 south to Route 13 south. At Dover continue south on Route 113 until it intersects with Route 50, just to the west of Ocean City proper. The museum is located on the south end of the boardwalk, at the Inlet.

Pennsylvania Farm Museum of Landis Valley

It might be stretching the truth a bit to claim that Henry and George Landis collected one of just about every item found in a house or barn on a typical late 19th-century farm. But the mixture of the many meticulously collected items plus the recreated settings in which they would have been found combines to give you a complete picture of early American rural life.

Begin your look at rural life in southeastern Pennsylvania at the Visitors Center where you will see a short slide presentation. Old photographs introduce you to the Landis brothers who are responsible for this microcosm of life as it once was. A little later in the Yellow Barn you'll see pictures that show what their collection looked like when it was crammed into their modest farm. It was so disorganized it was impossible to appreciate.

Now the museum is organized with special exhibit buildings bringing the past to life through displays and demonstrations. In the spinning and weaving barn a costumed worker will show you how to work the various looms. Curious visitors will see such arcane tools as a flax breaker, walking wheel, heckling comb and scrutching board. In another part of this park-like setting there is a 18th-century Lancaster house that has been moved here and restored as a seamstress' home.

At the pottery shop Pennsylvania redware pottery as well as other styles are on display. Demonstrations let you see work in progress. At the Isaac Landis Gallery, housed in a late 19th-century Landis Valley home, you will see a wide range of folk art. Another shop presents the skills of the printer and the harness maker.

In the transportation building with its wagons, sleds and carriages the Conestoga wagon is the most well-known vehicle. Contrary to popular thinking Conestogas were not used by the pioneers on their westward trek. They used a similar wagon called a prairie schooner. The Conestoga wagon was a freight hauler. Its sloping bed provided no place for passengers, nor was there a place for the driver to sit except the lazy board on the wagon's side. These wagon drivers were hard living men. Many had a habit of smoking potent cigars which have come to be called "stogies." Another expression, "I'll be there with bells on," also originated with the Conestoga wagon. If wagons got mired in the mud, broke an axel or needed help getting back on the road, it was customary to give the wagon driver who came to your aid your wagon bells. Thus, being there with bells on meant arriving without a hitch or problem.

The nearby gun shop with its collection of Pennsylvania and other vintage weapons explains the origin for several other American expressions. "Lock, stock and barrel" once referred to a craftsman who made all parts of a rifle. When the gunsmith demonstrates the tricky procedure used to load a flint lock rifle he'll explain that when powder was put in the flash pan it would occasionally spark and not fire—this was called "a flash in the pan." Also, guns would sometimes go off "half-cocked" before the rifleman was ready.

You can also see the Landis brothers' home which has been restored to its appearance in 1870. You'll start your tour in the old kitchen with its kerosene chandelier and iron stove. In the grooming corner there is a mustache cup and razor strop. The pantry has a pie safe with a lock so that desserts weren't eaten too fast. The ornate stove in the family room has what could be considered the forerunner of the humidifier. Water was put in a tulip-shaped container on top of the stove to add moisture to the air. The wallpaper in the family room is over a hundred years old and the parlor is vintage Victorian from the horsehair furniture to the pump organ.

The Landis brothers might have shopped at the country store with its fully stocked shelves, post office corner with letters in the mail slots and a checkers game on the board in front of the pot-bellied stove. Although you can't buy any of the intriguing items in stock, you can shop at the Weathervane Gift Shop for hand-crafted gifts.

There's so much to see so be sure to allow ample time to explore this farm community. It is open Tuesday through Saturday from 9:00 A.M. to 5:00 P.M. and Sunday from NOON to 5:00 P.M. Admission is charged.

Directions: From Philadelphia take the Pennsylvania Turnpike (I-76) west to Exit 21, Route 222. Proceed south on Route 222 to the Oregon Pike exit. Continue south on Oregon Pike, Route 272. The Pennsylvania Farm Museum of Landis Valley will be on your right.

Quiet Valley Living Historical Farm

Do you regret the demise of the extended family, when several generations customarily lived together? If so, visit Quiet Valley Living Historical Farm and experience this forgotten way of life when guides depicting four generations show you what it was like to live on this nearly self-sufficient homestead from 1765 to 1913.

You'll be introduced to the brave settlers who built the Quiet Valley Farm in 1765. Johan Peter Zepper was a Lutheran from the Palatinate who brought his family to the new world at the invitation of William Penn. Their journey was perilous and only one child, their daughter Catherine, survived the lack of food, water and the rampant diseases that scourged the ship. When the Zeppers arrived in William Penn's colony, the family then had to walk more than a hundred miles to claim their land in the foothills of the Pocono Mountains.

The family expanded in 1777. John Ludwig Meyer, an impressed German soldier, was wounded, captured and imprisoned in Philadelphia after the Battle of Trenton. When the Americans learned he was not a willing combatant he was released, and he stayed in Pennsylvania earning his living as a circuit tailor. His route brought him to the Zepper farm where he not only stayed the night, he stayed a lifetime. He married Catherine and raised his own family on this farm.

There are 14 buildings at Quiet Valley but the farmhouse, a typical Pennsylvania Dutch "grossdawdy house," (see the People's Place excursion elsewhere in the book for another example of this type farm) is certainly one of the most interesting. You might encounter the great-grandmother of the family in the upstairs bedroom talking about the problem of keeping warm on the old farm. Gran also imparts a good bit of folk wisdom in her rural Scotch-Irish dialect. When a youngster in the crowd gets fidgety she advises the young mother to put honey on the thumb and forefinger of each hand and then give the young lad a feather. When she demonstrates this method, she absolutely breaks up her audience. Sitting in her old rocking chair with a gourd hearing aid and a corn-cob pipe, she looks like a vanished bit of Americana.

Another room of the main house that intrigues visitors is the upstairs parlor. One of the women who married into the family in the 1890s was dismayed by the lack of privacy of Quiet Valley. In order to "keep her down on the farm," the great-grandmother gave up her bedroom and converted it into an upstairs parlor for the young bride. However, this parlor is located atop a slanted roof and resembles an amusement park fun house.

The dissatisfied bride was also able to get a "modern" kitchen added to the house in the 1890s. She had a new iron range and a dry sink. But the heart of the house was still the cellar kitchen. In it is the wooden yoke used for hauling water or milk by adding buckets to its hooks. There is speculation that this gave rise to the expression "letting you off the hook" when the buckets were removed.

As you wander around the farm from the smokehouse to the ice house to the old barn, you'll see a variety of farm animals under foot. Sheep, ducks and chickens delight youngsters who also enjoy the hay jump in the barn. Older members of the audience enjoy hearing about the tools the old farmer depended on.

Each and every day food is prepared, animals are tended and the farm chores are done in the authentic manner of this earlier time. On Saturday they bake 30 loaves of bread in the old oven, and throughout the season they make baskets, brooms, candles and other articles they need.

This look at life as it was is provided from June 20 to Labor Day from 9:30 A.M. to 5:30 P.M. and on Sunday from 1:00 to 5:30 P.M. Admission is charged.

Directions: From the Philadelphia area take the Northeast Extension of the Pennsylvania Turnpike to the Lehigh Valley exit. Go east on Route 22 to Route 33 north. Take the Syndersville exit off Route 33 then turn right on Manor Road and follow the signs for three miles to Quiet Valley.

Swiss Pines

Japanese gardens are like abstract paintings; they encourage you to use your imagination and to find your own meaning in what you see. This is certainly true of Swiss Pines in Charlestown, Pennsylvania, where there's an oriental trail garden that encourages you to expand your traditional view of garden design. The stone path that meanders through the "Gardens of Japan" is the only trail of this type in the United States that encompasses both flat and hilly terrain. Where else could you be greeted by Hotei, Benten and Jurajin, the Japanese stone gods that represent health, elegance and longevity?

On your self-guided tour you may encounter water cascading down the hill into a series of pools, or a picturesque wooden footbridge over a pond. Some parts of the trail are almost canopied by the giant yellow bamboo. Although flowers play no significant role in Japanese gardens, during May you will see an exception in a hillside of colorful azaleas.

Many of the garden features are associated with the Japanese tea ceremony. The teahouse (Chosho-Tei), a reproduction of one of the oldest in Japan, was designed by one of Japan's finest contemporary landscape architects, Katsuo Saito. From it you will get a view of the second type of Japanese garden: the static garden. You have already explored part of the stroll garden; now from the veranda of the teahouse you view the Karesansui, or stone garden, framed like a painting by its surrounding fence. As you study this garden many images are suggested by the rocks, carefully placed on the raked white sand.

The more than 70 stone lanterns throughout the Gardens of Japan are also connected with the tea ceremony. Early tea masters borrowed lanterns from old temples and shrines to ornament their gardens and gradually lanterns became an integral part of the oriental design.

Some stone lanterns are called "snow-viewing" because their design is enhanced when they are crowned with snow. This Japanese eye for detail in all seasons and at all times of day is particularly evident in the moon mound, an arrangement of stones planned to reflect the light of the moon. Autumn is particularly felicitous at Swiss Pines because the foliage adds color and the ponds attract migratory birds.

Although the Gardens of Japan are the primary attraction at Swiss Pines there is also an herb garden, a pinetum, crabapple grove, wildflower trail and special areas devoted to rhododendron, irises, roses, ground covers and ferns.

Swiss Pines was acquired by Arnold Bartschi in 1957, and he has donated the land and established the Bartschi Foundation for the study of horticulture, ornithology, conservation and wildlife. There is no charge to visit. Monday through Friday hours are 10:00 A.M. to 4:00 P.M., and on Saturday from 9:00 to 11:00 A.M. Swiss Pines is closed from December 15 to March 15, as well as Sundays and holidays.

Directions: From Philadelphia take the Schuylkill Expressway, I-76, west to Exit 24, the Valley Forge-Route 363 exit. Take Route 363 north until you hit Route 23. Then take Route 23 west towards Phoenixville. Turn left, south, on Route 29. Just before Route 29 passes under the Pennsylvania Turnpike turn right onto Charlestown Road. Swiss Pines is just up Charlestown Road on your right.

Valley Forge National Historical Park

A family excursion to Valley Forge National Historical Park provides a splendid opportunity to instill a sense of pride in our country's past. The story of the bitter winter the young army spent here in 1777–78 is a stirring saga of courage, patriotism, honor and dedication. Exploring this recreated encampment brings alive the victory at Valley Forge.

This victory was not the kind ordinarily won in battle. At

Valley Forge the enemies were starvation, disease and the uncompromising elements. The road to Valley Forge began in August 1777 when the British under General Howe had landed at the upper end of the Chesapeake Bay and headed north toward the patriot capital at Philadelphia. Washington's efforts to halt the British advance failed at Brandywine in September, and again at Germantown, in October. Then with winter setting in, the British established themselves in Philadelphia. The American troops were forced to seek the cold comfort of Valley Forge 18 miles to the west.

To understand what happened during the six months the Continental Army stayed at Valley Forge you should begin at the Visitor Center with the 15-minute audio-visual program. There are four ways you can explore the park. From mid-April through October you can join a bus tour that departs from the Visitor Center. A taped narrative makes this a good way to get an in-depth look at the 2,788-acre park. You can spend as much time as you like at the various stops because you can always catch the next bus. A fee is charged for these tours. Another option is to rent an audio tape and drive yourself. Or you may feel you may get enough information from the park map and the roadside markers at the ten park stops.

A final option would be to bring your bicycle and explore the park along the six-mile cycling trail. It also starts at the Visitor Center and passes all the major points of interest. There are shorter footpaths for those who enjoy hiking and many miles of horseback riding trails. You will also find three picnic areas within the park—Varnum's, Wayne's Woods and Betzwood.

The area near General Varnum's Quarters is the Grand Parade grounds where General von Steuben, formerly of the General Staff of Frederick the Great of Prussia, transformed the ragtag Continental Army into an effective fighting force. One of the major problems the American army faced prior to Valley Forge was the lack of a standard training manual. Although soldiers did have minimal training it was from a variety of field manuals. Thus coordinated battle movements were all but impossible to achieve.

Benjamin Franklin, a notorious Mr. Fix-it, had heard that this problem plagued the Continental troops and it was he who sent Baron von Steuben from Paris with his personal recommendation to see if he could bring order out of chaos. It proved to be a brilliant idea, as within six months the Baron had produced a well-trained army. His work is all the more remarkable seen against the formidable obstacles: the men were weary from long marches and unsuccessful campaigns; they were poorly fed, inadequately clothed and housed. At one point there were 4,000 men listed as unfit for duty. General von Steuben also had to contend with his own limitations; he spoke little English. He labored day and night to overcome all, and part of the victory of Valley Forge can be attributed to his perseverance and skill.

During the summer costumed soldiers man the Muhlenberg Brigade where they demonstrate various aspects of military life in the 1770s. Plan to spend some time at the Isaac Potts House which was used by General Washington as his Headquarters. This fieldstone building has been restored to look as it did when Washington was in residence. At the Visitor Center there is a field tent that was used by Washington when he first arrived at Valley Forge before moving into the Potts House.

In addition to the redoubts, reconstructed fortifications, artillery park and other officers' quarters there are two privately-operated sites within this park. The first is the Washington Memorial Chapel which tells the story of the founding of our country in 13 stained glass windows. During the summer, tours are conducted at the Bell Tower. The chapel's carillon was purchased in 1926 with money collected from the original 13 states. The second, next to the chapel, is the Valley Forge Historical Society Museum with a fine collection of Revolutionary memorabilia. A nominal admission fee is charged.

Valley Forge is a marvelous spot to visit at any time of year. You might want to plan your first visit for the summer months when living history re-enactments bring the camp dramatically to life. A winter's visit captures the real spirit of Valley Forge. You will appreciate our army's accomplishments more fully on a cold, brisk day when there is snow on the ground and a stiff wind blowing across the elevated plain. Often during the winter months, there are hundreds of young Boy Scouts camping "under the same circumstances" as the Revolutionary soldiers. Spring is a delight because the park's 1,000 pink and white dogwood trees are in bloom, and in the fall the bright autumn foliage adds color. The park is open year-round from 8:30 A.M. to 5:00 P.M., except on Christmas Day.

Directions: From Philadelphia take the Schuylkill Expressway, I-76, west to Exit 24 for Valley Forge. Follow the signs to the Visitor Center.

Waterloo Village

Want a one-stop overview of early American history? A visit to Waterloo Village, outside Stanhope, New Jersey, is better than most textbooks at awakening the interest of youngsters in the pivotal periods of our country's past. Take it from history teachers: experiencing history is the best way to remember it. At Waterloo a century of change and development is brought to life.

The saga begins with the Munsee Indians who once inhabited

this part of New Jersey. Indications of their presence were discovered during the October 1743 survey. (A survey stake can still be seen marking the original dividing line between East and West Jersey.) The Indians' sacred burial grounds in the Waterloo area were soon lost as homesteaders staked out their claims to the rich meadowland, and miners searched the highland for ore.

Iron ore was discovered here, as you will learn at the Visitor Orientation Center located in the barn of the old homestead which has been reconstructed as a Meeting House. The slide presentation offered here not only directs your attention to the significant aspects of this National Historic Site, but it also puts Waterloo into historical perspective. And a self-guiding walking tour map available when you purchase your tickets aids you in exploring the village.

Your first stop chronologically is the site of the Andover Forge. When ore was discovered in 1760 a four-fire, two-hammer forge was built. This forge produced such "steel-like" iron that the Continental Congress confiscated the forge in 1778 for the duration of the war so that it could be used to produce iron for armaments needed by the Continental Army.

At the time the forge was built, a grist mill and saw mill were also added. The early models were lost, but replacements built in the 1830s still stand.

Although the ironworks were abandoned for a time after the Revolution, in 1812 Brigadier General John Smith purchased the 282-acre forge tract, for the sum of $13.37 per acre. Being a military man he wanted to celebrate Wellington's victory over Napoleon and so in 1815 he named his forge Waterloo Foundry. Gradually the entire village became known as Waterloo. You can still see five Smith family homes; of these three may be toured. Even from the outside these dwellings reflect the gradually increasing prosperity of the Smith family. The houses range from early stone tenant homes to a Second Empire Victorian mansion.

Waterloo did not achieve its prosperity through the ironworks. It was the canal era that brought boom times. In 1831, the Morris Canal, linking Phillipsburg and Jersey City, made Waterloo Village a lock and plane stop. By 1844 it became a thriving inland port. From this period you can see the Canal House, General Store, Towpath Tavern and the Canal Museum.

In 1847 a gravity railroad was built connecting the Andover Mines and the dock at Waterloo. It was superseded in 1854 by a regular railroad. Thus Waterloo is associated with both the canal and the railroad era. The railroad was the rival for transportation supremacy, and it eventually replaced the canals as the primary route for shipping and trading.

There are 28 stops on the walking tour of Waterloo Village, a microcosm of early America all-too-frequently-overlooked. On weekends during the summer months there are musical concerts featuring jazz, folk, bluegrass and classical artists. Craft and antique festivals are also held. The village is open from mid-April until the beginning of January on Tuesday through Sunday, from 10:00 A.M. until 6:00 P.M. When holidays fall on Monday the village remains open and closes on Tuesday. It is closed on Easter, Thanksgiving, Christmas and New Year's Day. Admission is charged, with no tickets sold after 3:00 P.M. There are picnic facilities.

Directions: Take I-95 north from Philadelphia to I-295. Go west on I-295 to Route 206 north. Take Route 206 to Route 80 west. Take Exit 25 off Route 80 onto Route 206 (again!) for just a short distance, then make a left at the second light on Waterloo Road. Proceed 2½ miles to the entrance of Waterloo Village in Stanhope, New Jersey.

Wyck

Old roses and old world charm can be found in abundance at Wyck, Germantown's oldest house; in fact, one of the oldest houses in the state. The history of Wyck dates to 1689 when Hans Millan, a Swiss Quaker, acquired land on which he built a small house in 1690. When his daughter, Margaret, married Dirk Jansen a second house, separate from but aligned with the first, was built. By 1777 when the house was used as a field hospital during the Battle of Germantown, the two dwellings had been connected at the second floor level.

Not only is Wyck a historic old house but it is also a comfortable old home. Eight generations of Millans have enjoyed life at Wyck. The furnishings and decorative pieces are blended in style and period. They reflect the continued family life from the 18th century to the mid-20th century.

In 1824 major revision of Wyck occurred when William Strickland was commissioned to redesign the interior of the house. He created a suite of sunlit rooms by converting the former cartway separating the two houses into a central conservatory which overlooks both the south lawn and the formal gardens. This suite is beautifully decorated in a comfortable and cheerful style.

A visit to Wyck in late May through mid-June will coincide with the peak blooming season of Wyck's historic old roses. Their form, beauty and especially their fragrance set them apart from the modern hybrid tea roses. The collection at Wyck includes species known to man since ancient times and hybrids dating from 1500 to 1910. Many of the roses at Wyck were planted by Jane Bowne Haines, wife of Reuben Haines who was responsible for the 1824 alterations. She added 22 varieties of roses between 1818–1829, of which 18 have survived or have been re-introduced. A total of 37 different roses now flourish in Wyck's formal box-bordered rose garden.

Wyck is located at 6026 Germantown Avenue. It is open April through December on Tuesday, Thursday and Saturday from 1:00 to 4:00 P.M. To make arrangements for a special tour call (215)848-1690. Admission is charged.

Directions: From center city take East River Drive north to Midvale Avenue. Turn left onto Wissahickon Avenue. At Walnut Lane, turn right to Germantown Avenue and Wyck will be on your right.

Zwaanendael Museum, Lewes and Cape Henlopen State Park

The whale, the swan and the unicorn are all part of the legend that is Lewes, or Loo-is as it is pronounced. Lewes was the site of the first European settlement in Delaware. Thirty-three pioneers arrived here in 1631 on the *De Walvis*, (*The Whale*), to establish a Dutch whaling settlement.

The settlers who reached this peaceful-appearing inlet where the Atlantic Ocean met the Delaware Bay called their community Swanendael, or "valley of the swans," inspired perhaps by the wild swans indigenous to this area.

And now we come to the unicorn, a more tragic element of the Lewes legend. The original Dutch settlers were massacred by the Indians and some blame their death on their unicorn talisman. Their large wooden unicorn was part of the coat of arms of Hoorn, Holland, and when they brought it ashore the curious Indians wanted the Dutch to make them a gift of the unicorn. When their wish was not granted, the Indians burned the stockade and killed the doughty Dutch. To help you visualize this dramatic incident visit the **Zwaanendael Museum** where you will see a model of the first settlement surrounded by a stockade fence.

A new settlement was built but that too was burned on Christmas Eve in 1673. This time the Indians weren't the attackers; it was the Calvert-supporters from the Maryland colony who were determined to keep this territory for their own. If this were not enough, Lewes was twice the prey of pirate raids and was bombarded by the British during the War of 1812. At the museum you will learn how Lewes saved itself from the British with cornstalks.

In a lighter vein there is a collection of antique toys—dolls, cradles, carriages, puzzles, dishes and some old-fashioned transportation models. A stage coach, circa 1860, has its own team of miniature horses. Of a later vintage is the small-scale 1922 Toonerville Trolley.

The Dutch influence is revealed within and without. As you enter the museum you see a portrait of Queen Beatrix and Prince Claus. And the museum building itself is an adaptation of the Town Hall at Hoorn, Holland, home town of many of the first settlers. The colorful brick building with white and red shutters has a statue of David Pietersen de Vries at the top of its peaked facade. He led the first expedition that founded the Dutch settlement over 350 years ago.

This museum is just one of the stops on the historic walking tour of **Lewes**. You can obtain a map of 28 points of interest at the Lewes Chamber of Commerce, in the Fisher-Martin House at 102 Kings Highway. During summer you can also join walking tours given by the Lewes Historical Society. These tours begin at the Thompson Country Store, at 119 Third Street, part of a complex of four restored 18th-century buildings. You won't want to miss this old store even if walking tours are not for you. How many stores still sell penny candy, not to mention homemade cookies and Sally Lunn bread? The store was run by the same family from 1917 to 1960, and the old potbellied stove where regulars would meet to gossip is still there.

The second house in the complex is small but singular. It's a one-room "plank house." Built in 1700, this settler's log cabin has a sleeping loft and crude furniture typical of the pioneer days. One look at the straw-filled mattress in the loft will make beach accommodations look luxurious.

Considerably more elegant are the 18th-century furnishings in the Burton-Ingram House which contains some lovely Chippendale and Empire pieces. The cellar walls are made from ballast carried on one of the early ships that docked at Lewes.

The last building, the Rabit's Ferry House, is also furnished with period pieces, and the walls are an example of the bricknogging technique by which bricks were laid between wooden beams and then whitewashed.

One other stop you should try to make is the Marine Museum-Cannonball House at Front and Bank Streets. There is still a cannonball embedded in the wall from the barrage of April 6 and 7, 1813. The walking tour will also include the Ryves Holt House, the Maull House, the Lightship *Overfalls* and the 1850 Doctor's Office.

If you can't pack in all of these stops, you can at least absorb a good bit of the town's flavor by driving up a few streets before heading for **Cape Henlopen State Park**. This 1,200-acre park is one of the last unspoiled stretches of beach and natural pine forest on the Atlantic coast. The *National Geographic* has described the sand dunes here as a "miniature Sahara." Some one-day trippers may want to relax in the sun and enjoy the surf; those who have energy enough for a hike have a choice of two trails. The Seaside Nature Trail takes you to the top of Hamburger Hill where you will have a marvelous view of the Delaware capes. The trail through the Gordon Pond Wildlife Preserve along the pine woods and brackish ponds provides an opportunity to glimpse rarely seen wildlife.

Obviously this is a lot to see in one day but a morning exploring the town and an afternoon on the beach provide a double-feature outing sure to please nearly everybody in the family. The Zwaanendael Museum is open Tuesday through Saturday from 10:00 A.M. to 4:30 P.M., and on Sunday from 1:30 to 4:30 P.M.; it is closed on Mondays and holidays. The Lewes Historical Society complex is open during the summer months from 10:00 A.M. to 4:00 P.M., Tuesday through Saturday. Cape Henlopen is open during daylight hours year-round.

Directions: From Philadelphia take I-95 south to Wilmington. Exit on Route 13 for Dover, Delaware. At Dover you can either take Route 113 or pick up the scenic bypass, Route 9, which will take you through some nice countryside and small villages. If you take Route 113, continue on to Milford where you will pick up Route 1, to seashore points. Then at Five Points Light continue into Lewes on Route 9.

Autumn

Antietam National Battlefield Site

When you plan an outing within a day's drive from Philadelphia to one of the many battlefields of the American Revolution or Civil War, there are two things you should know in order to get the most out of your visit. First, of course, you need to be able to "see" the battle. Otherwise the parkland will look like the surrounding countryside. Second, you need to understand how a specific encounter affected the course of the war.

Both of these goals are easily met when you visit Antietam National Battlefield. It is not difficult to follow the action here, because it occurred on a single day (September 17, 1862) within this 12-square-mile area. Well marked tour routes direct you to all the encounters of this battle which began at 6:00 A.M. and ended at 5:30 P.M. Following the routes, it is easy to visualize the men under Stonewall Jackson's command hunkered down among the rows of corn, or the 400 Georgian riflemen who gallantly held an essential bridge for hour after bloody hour.

In terms of overall significance, the Battle of Antietam altered the course of the Civil War. General Lee hoped that if he could successfully carry the fighting into the North it would prompt the Union to work seriously toward a negotiated settlement. A second Southern hope was that a win in the North would bring English recognition of the Confederate government. But this was not to be. For the North, their long-awaited Federal victory at Antietam provided President Lincoln with the opportunity to issue the Emancipation Proclamation. He informed the South that as of January 1, 1863, all slaves in territory still rebelling against the Union would be free. This meant that the North was now fighting for two objectives: to save the Union and to abolish slavery.

To become better acquainted with the immediate and long-term objectives of the Battle of Antietam make your first stop the Antietam Visitors Center. Plan to watch both the 18-minute slide orientation program shown on the half-hour, beginning at 8:30 A.M., and the 26-minute live action movie, _Antietam Visit_, shown on the hour starting at 9:00 A.M. The center has an exhibit that includes personal effects of soliders who fought here, as well as four large murals of the battle, painted by artist veteran Captain James Hope. For children and the visually handicapped there is a "touch and feel" Union soldier's uniform and equipment.

From the center you can follow the eight-mile-tour road. If you want full details as you explore, rent the taped tour cassette. During the summer months park rangers give scheduled talks and conduct walks. On weekends from May through October a schedule of volunteer activities will include depictions of Civil War camp life and presentations of historical scenarios guaranteed to bring to life those momentous days.

From taped messages you will learn that battle action began in the morning with an attack by the North on Stonewall Jackson's men who were deployed in a cornfield. Midday saw a pitched battle along the Sunken Road, and in the afternoon there was the encounter on Burnside Bridge.

The tour ends at Antietam National Cemetery. The losses in this one battle were staggering. An estimated 23,000 soldiers were killed or wounded, representing 26 percent of the Confederate force and 15 percent of the larger Federal army. The midday encounter along the Sunken Road lasted for three long hours and cost 4,000 soldiers their lives. Since then Sunken Road has been called Bloody Lane. The Hawkins Zouaves Monument at the top of a hill near Harpers Ferry Road marks the climactic conclusion of the battle. It is a good place to reflect on the enormity of the losses suffered on that one September day in this now peaceful valley. The courage of the men who saw their comrades fall in such numbers, yet continued to fight, is worth remembering.

Antietam National Battlefield Site is open daily year-round, except Thanksgiving, Christmas and New Year's Day. From September through May the hours are 8:30 A.M. to 5:00 P.M. In June, July and August the hours are 8:00 A.M. to 6:00 P.M. There is no admission fee.

Directions: From Philadelphia take Route 30 west, through Lancaster and York, to Gettysburg. Then take Route 15 south to Frederick. At Frederick follow Alternate 40 west to Boonsboro. At the first traffic light in Boonsboro turn left onto Route 34 to Sharpsburg, then make a left at the Lutheran Church onto Route 65 for one mile to the Visitors Center.

Bucks County Vineyards and Covered Bridges

Even those family members who would rather spend their weekends in front of the television set watching "the big game" can usually be persuaded to get out of their armchairs for a wine-tasting excursion. There is an increasing fascination with wine, and while many still think of American wine in terms of California vintages, here on the East Coast vineyards are proliferating.

One of the earliest of the Pennsylvania limited wineries is **Buckingham Valley Vineyard and Winery**, just a short drive from New Hope. It is one of the few wineries in America to offer Estate Bottled vintage varietal wines. This designation is regulated by the Federal government. All, or almost all, the wine labeled "estate bottled" must come from grapes owned or controlled by the winery and it must be grown in a designated viticulture area. If the label reads "Produced and bottled by . . ." it means that that particular wine was made with 75 percent of the grapes from the vineyard on the label. On the other hand, if the label says "Made by . . ." it could mean that as little as 10 percent of the grapes came from the producer's own harvest.

Though Buckingham Valley Vineyard has only 14 acres, it produces 14 different wines, including four dry reds, six white wines and four rosés. You can take a self-guided tour and see the reds aging in their oak casks, and the equipment used to bottle, cork, label and cap the wine. After seeing how it is made you can sample the different varieties. Tours and tastings are from NOON to 6:00 P.M. on weekdays, 10:00 A.M. to 6:00 P.M. on Saturday, and NOON to 4:00 P.M. on Sunday. It is closed on Monday.

Wine-tasting is, itself, an art. It is said if you try more than three or four varieties you are no longer tasting but drinking. When you do sample a variety of wines be sure you eat a cracker, or piece of bread, between wines to clear your palate. To get the most out of tasting, experts advise the following steps:

Always hold the wine glass by the stem. If you hold it by the bowl you will warm the wine and distort the taste. The glass must be colorless so that you can distinguish the color, which ranges from dry straw to deep ruby red. Hold the glass up and observe the color. To test for body, tilt the glass, not too much or you will spill it but just enough to let the wine flow down the side. A wine with body, or good "legs" as it is also called, will roll down the glass in clinging sheets rather than in a rain-like drizzle.

Next you test the wine's aroma. Rotate your glass just enough to swirl the wine around (and again not enough to splash it). This movement will aerate the wine and bring out the bouquet. Because wine fanciers like to do this the wine glass should never be filled all the way to the top.

The final and most crucial test is to determine the taste. Take a small sip and roll it around your mouth. Even if you are a novice you can easily tell if it is sweet or dry. Next decide whether it has a short or long finish, or aftertaste. The final judgment is the most important: do you like it?

At Bucks Country Vineyards and Wineries just three miles outside New Hope wine-tasting is not only in fashion; the owners have gone one step farther and combined the two in a unique wine and fashion museum. The merging of these diverse fields is easily explained. The vineyard president, Arthur Gerold, was also formerly the president of Brooks-Van Horn, one of America's largest theatrical costumers.

So while you are learning about wine- and champagne-making in Pennsylvania you can also browse through a collection of original costumes from some of Broadway's and Hollywood's most noted hits. You will see the magnificent costume Richard Burton wore as King Arthur in *Camelot*, Dorothy's original dress from *The Wiz*, Frank Langella's Dracula garb, the suit Marlon Brando wore as the Godfather and Mary Martin's Peter Pan costume. Other costumes from America's theatrical past were worn by such greats as Katharine Hepburn and Gertrude Lawrence.

Either before or after you see the museum be sure to take the short tour of the wine cellars of this winery. At the end you will have a chance to taste some of its 15 varieties. Most of the wines are made from French-American hybrid varieties of 100 percent Pennsylvania grapes. Some, however, are from native varieties like the Concord, Niagara and Catawba. In the tasting room you will also sample some cheese sent over from the Cheese Factory at The Winery in Reading, Pennsylvania. A bakery at Bucks Country bakes French bread and croissants daily, so you can put together an elegant picnic while visiting here. Hours are weekdays 11:00 A.M. to 5:00 P.M., Saturdays and holidays 10:00 A.M. to 6:00 P.M., and Sundays NOON to 6:00 P.M. There is a nominal charge for adults on weekends.

Why not take your picnic and set out to explore six of **Bucks County's** 13 remaining **covered bridges**? All six are in the New Hope area and can easily be combined with your wine-tasting outing. The covered bridges you will see range from two that were built in 1832 to four constructed during the 1870s. The reason for building bridges with a roof is not definitely known. The most plausible explanation is that the support beams on the sides were given protection from the weather. The covers over bridges are also credited with providing shelter for travelers, shielding animals from their fear of crossing water and keeping the snow off the important river crossings.

All the covered bridges in Bucks County were made in a lattice-style developed by Ithiel Town in 1820. Be sure to get out of the car and study at least one bridge close up so that you can see the series of overlapping triangles with wooden pegs. No arches or support beams were used but these lattice-work arrangements could support a bridge up to 200 feet long.

You will pass the first of the covered bridges before you reach

New Hope. The Van Sant Bridge is just off Route 32, River Road. Check your mileage when you reach the Memorial Building for Washington Crossing State Park. Continue north on Route 32 for 4.4 miles to Lurgan Road then turn left and go 1.5 miles to Covered Bridge Road, where you will turn right and go .6 miles to the Van Sant Bridge. It was built over Pidcock Creek in 1875 and is 86 feet long.

Cross over the Van Sant Bridge and drive for one mile to Aquetong Road where you will turn left and go five miles to Upper York Road. Make a right on Upper York Road and then an immediate left, and go 2.8 miles to Carvesville, an entire village that is listed on the National Register of Historic Places. In the center of Carvesville turn left for one block and then go right on Pipersville Road. This road changes names twice, first becoming Wismer Road and then Carvesville Road. Take this double-named road for 4.6 miles and you will reach Loux Bridge, the second shortest covered bridge in the county at 60 feet. This hemlock bridge is perfect for photographs, framed as it is by an adjacent waterfall and old farm.

To reach the next covered bridge continue through Loux Bridge and go five miles until you reach a dead end. At this point make a right onto Dark Hollow Road and continue for one mile to Covered Bridge Road, where you make a right and proceed .6 miles to Cabin Run Bridge. This is an 82-foot bridge built in 1871 over the Cabin Run Creek.

Backtrack to Dark Hollow Road and take that for 3.2 miles to Cafferty Road. Turn left on Cafferty Road and proceed eight miles to the Frankenfield Bridge over Tinicum Creek. This is one of the longest of the covered bridges, 130 feet.

For the fifth covered bridge continue up Cafferty Road for .2 miles to Hollow Horn Road and make a right. Proceed 1.3 miles to Headquarters Road and turn right. Go .9 miles to Geigel Hill Road. Turn left on Geigel Hill Road and go .2 miles and you will see the Erwinna Bridge, which at 56 feet is the shortest covered bridge in Bucks County.

To see the last covered bridge in this area, return to Geigel Hill Road and proceed .4 miles to River Road, Route 32. Turn left on River Road and go 1.7 miles and make another left turn on Uhlerstown Road; take that .3 miles for the Uhlerstown Bridge. This is the only covered bridge that crosses the Delaware Canal and the only one that has windows.

From here you can get back on River Road and head toward Philadelphia. Or, if you saw the bridges before the vineyards, head back to New Hope. Then go west on Bridge Street (Route 179) in the center of town to the intersection with Route 202. Pick up Route 202 for Bucks Country Vineyard. To reach Buckingham Valley Vineyard continue on Route 202 until it intersects with Route 413. Go left on Route 413 south and the vineyard will be on your left in just two miles.

Directions: From Philadelphia take I-95 north and exit at New Hope on Route 32, River Road.

Bushkill Falls

Older generations generally resist innovative suggestions of the young. So it was when fourth-generation Charles E. Peters recommended to his elders that they charge visitors admission to see the waterfalls on the family property in the Pocono Mountains. The elders doubted that anyone "would pay to see a waterfall," but nevertheless gave him a grudging go-ahead.

Charles fixed up the trail, built a shelter and fashioned a bridge over the falls to high ground. When he opened "Niagara of Pennsylvania" to tourists, he charged an admission fee of ten cents. That was 80 years ago. Admission is still being charged and appreciative crowds are still coming.

"Billed originally as "A Delightful One-Day Auto Trip," Bushkill Falls is that and more: 300 acres of mountain scenery, eight waterfalls and several trails. The longest trail is 1½ miles and takes 90 minutes, but it will give you a chance to see each of these distinctly different falls. The series of three Bridal Veil Falls can only be seen on this longer walk.

Most visitors choose the 45- to 60-minute hike which gives you a view of both the top and bottom of the main falls as well as the Lower Gorge Falls, Laurel Glen Falls and the Upper Gorge Falls. Newly added in 1984 is a short detour off this trail that affords a look at Pennell Falls. If you are in a hurry or not up to a long climb, you can take a 15-minute walk to the Main Falls which, at 100 feet, is the most spectacular of the eight. Comfortable shoes are a must.

Either before or after your hike be sure to take the time to explore the Wildlife Exhibit. It features 80 mounted birds and animals native to Pennsylvania and the Pocono Mountains. If you stop here first, the displays will let you know what you may be able to spot on your walk: red squirrels, for example, chipmunks, snowshoe rabbits, muskrats, woodchucks and beaver as well as birds.

Picnic tables are available and there is also a snack shop. You may want to pack a lunch and then indulge in dessert at the old-fashioned Ice Cream Parlor. Craft shops, miniature golf, fishing and paddleboats provide additional diversions if you want to make a day of it.

Bushkill Falls is located 104 miles from Philadelphia. It is open April through November from 9:00 A.M. to dusk.

Directions: From Philadelphia take the Pennsylvania Turnpike Northeast Extension north to Exit 33, Route 22. Take Route 22 east, then pick up Route 33 north to Interstate 80, east. Take I-80 to Exit 52, then proceed north on Route 209 to Bushkill.

Deshler-Morris House

Most Philadelphians know about—and are justly proud of—Independence National Historic Park, which is situated in the heart of their city. But many area residents are unaware of a suburban adjunct of the park: the Deshler-Morris House in Germantown.

David Deshler, according to family stories, arrived in Philadelphia in 1733 with a bag full of gold and a head full of ideas. By the time he was 29 he was able to start his own business. In 1751 he purchased a modest four-room summer house. As his business grew so did his summer house; by 1772 it was a gracious nine-room, three-story house on the main street.

Deshler may well have wished he had waited five more years before expanding because in the autumn of 1777 his home was commandeered by General William Howe. The British had pursued the withdrawing Continental forces as they fled Philadelphia. They had continued to the outskirts of Germantown where they camped around and took shelter in Cliveden, a substantial estate (see selection elsewhere in book). General Washington, in a surprise maneuver, attacked the British at Cliveden in what is called the Battle of Germantown. Although Howe was able to rally his hard-pressed troops, the Americans harassed the British for the next two weeks. During this tense time Howe made his headquarters in the Deshler house. When Howe returned to Philadelphia, Deshler was able to return to his house.

At David Deshler's death in March 1792 the house was purchased by Colonel Isaac Frank, an officer in the Continental Army. He would eventually find himself playing host to his old commanding officer during the Battle of Germantown. George Washington stayed at this house twice—in November 1793 during the yellow fever epidemic and then again to escape the summer heat of Philadelphia in 1794.

The National Park Service has restored the Deshler-Morris House so that it reflects in part the Washington sojourns. Some of the artifacts date from the time of David Deshler and others, from the Morris family, the last owners. Much of the furniture was made by Philadelphia craftsmen because David Deshler signed the Non-Importation Agreement in 1765 that eliminated the imported luxuries of European design.

There is a controversial portrait of a little girl in the dining room. Some experts believe that only the head and arms were done from a model and that the rest of the picture was pre-painted. In the toy room are playtime favorites similar to those that may have amused the Washington grandchildren. While the children stayed in Germantown young George attended classes at School House Lane and Nellie was tutored at home.

To see an early one-room school house you can travel six blocks up Germantown Avenue and visit the Concord School House. This school was built in 1775 by the residents of upper Germantown; it is not the school attended by George Washington Parke Custis. The original schoolmaster's desk and chair are still here and other 18th-century school items.

The Concord School House at 6309 Germantown Avenue is open April through October on Tuesday from 10:00 A.M. until 1:00 P.M. and Thursday from 1:00 until 4:00 P.M. Tours are by appointment only (call (215)438-6328). A nominal admission is charged.

The Deshler-Morris House at 5442 Germantown Avenue is open from April through December on Tuesday through Sunday from 1:00 until 4:00 P.M. A nominal admission is charged.

Directions: From center city take Broad Street, Route 611 north to Route 1, Roosevelt Boulevard. Go left for just a short way on Route 1 to Route 422, Germantown Avenue. Follow Germantown Avenue into Germantown proper and you will see these two sites clearly marked. The Deshler-Morris House is on the left and the Concord School House on the right.

Freedoms Foundation at Valley Forge

Publicists for the Freedoms Foundation say that in the Philadelphia area the Foundation is viewed like one of the Fiji Islands. People know it exists but aren't really sure what goes on there. Robert Miller, Foundation president, acknowledges that the organization is not well known. "Freedoms Foundation," he says, "is dedicated solely to promoting America and the American way of life."

A visit to the Foundation in its park-like setting just 25 miles outside of Philadelphia can be very stirring. The tone is set before you arrive. A good distance away from the entrance you'll see the special American flag made for Freedoms Foundation. Its bold red and white stripes extend for 42 feet. Also larger than life is the nine-foot bronze statue of a kneeling George Washington looking over Valley Forge. It was at Valley Forge, as most school children know, that Washington and his officers turned the ragged Continental soldiers into a formidable fighting force.

The visit begins with a 24-minute film on the Foundation introduced by the honorary chairman, Ronald Reagan. The film tells about its ongoing educational work, about the many seminars, conferences and workshops held here "on Campus," and about its national awards program to recognize patriotism and civic responsibility.

The Visitors Center was altered in 1985 to encompass the exhibits formerly seen at the Hillendale Museum in Mendenhall, Pennsylvania. They depict the exploration and settling of the North American continent from 1490 to 1890, turning dry facts of textbooks into dramatic experiences of explorers and settlers. The Center also displays copies of the Magna Carta, the Declaration of Independence, the Bill of Rights and other documents of freedom.

The Independence Garden is designed around bricks and stones from the homes of all 56 signers of the Declaration of Independence. Although 12 signers had their homes burned to the ground, five were captured and imprisoned and nine gave their lives, not one signer defected to the British cause. It seems highly appropriate that the non-denominational chapel nearby is called Faith of Our Fathers Chapel. It has a stained glass window duplicating the one in the chapel of the Capitol in Washington.

The exhibits in the Henry Knox Building honor the more than 3,400 winners of the nation's highest military decoration, the Medal of Honor. A 52-acre Medal of Honor grove provides a natural setting for thinking and giving thanks.

The Freedoms Foundation is open for a nominal admission charge by appointment only. To make tour reservations call (215)933-8825 or write Freedoms Foundation of Valley Forge, Valley Forge, PA 19481.

Directions: From Philadelphia take the Schuylkill Expressway, I-76, west to Exit 24, the Valley Forge exit. Follow the signs to Valley Forge National Park along Route 363 north. Once past the park, you take Route 23 west through Valley Forge Village, continuing on to the Freedoms Foundation on your right.

Germantown Mennonite Community

On October 25, 1683, lots were drawn for the Germantown settlement in the Pennsylvania colony. The first members of the community were Quakers and Mennonites, and for a time they worshiped together. By 1690, as more Mennonite settlers arrived from Germany, they gradually began meeting on their own. They elected their own preacher and deacon in 1698. The first Mennonite minister was William Rittenhouse, whose old homestead at 207 Lincoln Drive in Fairmount Park is open for tours. Philadelphia is noted for its Rittenhouse Square, Rittenhouse Street and Rittenhouse Plaza and it is worth investigating the history of this significant Pennsylvania family. William Rittenhouse came to Germantown from Westphalia, Germany, in 1688. His home, which is open for tours, is the oldest Mennonite home in the New World. His great-grandson, David Rittenhouse, who was born in this house on April 8, 1732, was a noted scientist and a patriot in the American Revolution. The house is open from April through October. To arrange a visit call (215)843-0943 or write the Germantown Mennonite Information Center at 6117 Germantown Avenue.

The Mennonite community of Germantown, the first Mennonite congregation in North America, erected a log cabin meetinghouse in 1708. They replaced it with a stone building in 1770. Adjacent to this historic old stone meetinghouse is the Germantown Mennonite Information Center. The Center offers a selection of Amish and Mennonite quilts as well as other handcrafted items. A small museum contains exhibits on the congregation's history. The Information Center is open Tuesday through Saturday from 10:00 A.M. until NOON and from 1:00 to 4:00 P.M.

Just 2½ blocks up Germantown Avenue is an old Quaker house that you can explore. It was completed in 1768 as a wedding gift for John Johnson, Jr., a Germantown tanner. The young Johnsons took an active interest in the Concord School House located across the street (see elsewhere in book). Their home is an excellent example of what is called "Germantown Georgian." It is noted for its fine interior woodwork. During the pre-Civil War period it was one of the stops on the Underground Railroad. The Johnson House is located at 6306 Germantown Avenue and Washington Lane. Tours can be arranged by calling the Germantown Mennonite Information Center.

Directions: From center city take East River Drive (which becomes Wissahickon Drive) to Lincoln Drive exit. Be sure to stay in the center lane and follow the Lincoln Drive signs. Continue on Lincoln Drive to Johnson Street. Turn right and go to Germantown Avenue where you turn right. You will see the Germantown Mennonite Information Center on the left.

Gettysburg Miniature Horse Farm

When this Pennsylvania farm celebrates the birth of a healthy seven-pound, thirteen-inch baby it isn't at all what you'd expect. The congratulations are likely to be for the latest horse born at the Gettysburg Miniature Horse Farm. For Tony Garulo, the ex-sea captain who launched this highly successful attraction, life took an unexpected turn when he visited Argentina and learned about Falabella horses.

He began frequenting the breeding farm of Julio Cesar Falabella and learned that the miniaturization program had been carried on by the Falabella family since the 1860s. One of the early

Falabella favorites was a stallion called Napoleon. Short and stocky, this miniature marvel was only 20 inches high and weighed 70 pounds but he sired many foals and is related to quite a number of horses now at the Gettysburg farm. Napoleon lived to the age of 42, quite a respectable record for a horse of any size.

The downbreeding achieved by Señor Falabella kept the horse proportionally correct, just far smaller than the norm. If you take a picture of a Falabella horse with nothing beside it to indicate size it looks the same as a full-size horse. Other miniaturizers have bred horses with oversize heads and short, stubby legs.

When Garulo ended his maritime career in 1971 he brought 51 of the Falabella horses to Gettysburg. He had obtained an exclusive agreement to be the only Falabella representative in North America.

Even this exclusivity did not prepare Garulo and his partners for the degree of interest the miniatures attracted. Ranging in size from poodle to Great Dane, they delight young and old. They come in a variety of breeds and colors: Appaloosas, English trotters, Clydesdales, Arabians, pintos and palominos. Some are part quarterhorse and part thoroughbred.

As interest has grown so has the farm. Garulo added an 800-seat arena, remodeled the stable so that visitors could see and pet all the horses, added a refreshment and gift shop and began doing four shows a day.

The horses appear to be natural performers. One of the characteristics they have been bred for is disposition; they are very tame and gentle, though some of the stallions may nibble a bit. Like their fullsize counterparts, different breeds excel at different activities. There are jumpers and those that dance and respond to commands; and there are the small Clydesdales that pull wagons. They carry riders up to about 80 pounds.

If you think it would be fun to own one you're right. You would have to own 12 miniature horses before you'd require the amount of feed necessary for one standard-size horse. Numerous well-known personalities have owned Falabellas: the late Princess Grace, Lord Mountbatten, the Aga Kahn, Charles de Gaulle, Aristotle Onassis, Frank Sinatra, the Queen of England and the Dutch royal family. There is a sizeable waiting list for these horses because demand is high. So is the price.

You can see the miniature horses at the Gettysburg farm from April through mid-November. Hours are 9:00 A.M. to 5:00 P.M. daily; during the summer months the farm stays open until 6:00 P.M. Shows are at 11:00 A.M.; 1:00, 3:00 and 5:00 P.M. from Memorial Day through Labor Day. In the spring and fall there is no 5:00 P.M. performance. Admission is charged and rides are extra. Tables are available for picnics.

Directions: From Philadelphia take the Schuylkill Expressway, I-76, west to Route 202 south. Proceed on Route 202 to Route 30 west through Gettysburg. About three miles past Gettysburg on Route 30 you will see a large sign directing you to the farm.

The Glencairn Museum and Bryn Athyn Cathedral

On a clear day you can't see forever, but you can see the skyscrapers and spires of downtown Philadelphia from the tower atop the Glencairn Museum in Bryn Athyn, Pennsylvania which is housed in the castle built between 1928 and 1939 by Raymond Pitcairn, son of the founder of the Pittsburgh Plate Glass Company. From the tower you'll also see the majestic cathedral, begun in 1913 and dedicated in 1919, which he also built.

It is fascinating to learn that to build the cathedral and the castle, Raymond Pitcairn reverted to methods that had proved successful in the Middle Ages. The cathedral which was built first, evolved from models, both scale and fullsize, that were prepared by the skilled craftsmen who clustered around the foundation of the emerging church in workshops reminiscent of the medieval guilds.

The cathedral is noted for its "softness" which was achieved by avoiding straight lines and right angles and by using horizontal curves, vertical bends and slightly bowed lines. The exquisite stained glass windows that filter the sunlight also added to the feeling of softness. However, the art of making stained glass windows was virtually nonexistent in America at that time, so Pitcairn had his workers study the work of 13th- and 14th-century European artisans and then create the windows in shops on the cathedral grounds.

When the cathedral was nearly finished, Pitcairn decided to have the workmen stay on in their shops and build a home for his family in a similar style. Glencairn, his beautiful stone castle, now houses Pitcairn's collection of medieval arts. Many of the objects Pitcairn acquired as models during the construction of the cathedral and others he collected from around the world. The Great Hall on the first floor has six stained glass windows reproduced from the Chartres Cathedral and colors from the windows are picked up in the Oriental rugs scattered throughout the hall. Adjoining the hall is a charming Cloister.

Other floors offer treasures from Egypt, the Near East, Greece, Rome, additional Medieval collections and American Indian pieces. The master bedroom has been retained as it was when the Pitcairns occupied the house.

The extraordinary nature of this museum makes it a popular destination for scholars, artists and students. Since the museum can only accommodate a limited number of guests, visitors must have reservations. Glencairn is open Monday through Friday from 9:00 A.M. to 5:00 P.M. except on holidays. An admission is charged. The only way to explore Glencairn Museum is by conducted tour. You must phone to make reservations for these tours at (215)947-9919 or 947-4200. It is advisable to have an alternate date in case the time you request is booked.

There is no charge or reservation required to visit the Bryn Athyn Cathedral. The cathedral is open daily 9:00 A.M. to NOON except on Sunday mornings when services are held. The cathedral is open daily in the afternoon between 2:00 and 5:00 P.M. On Sundays it opens at 2:30 P.M. Guided tours are given in the afternoons on Sunday, Monday, Tuesday, Wednesday and Friday.

Directions: From city center take Broad Street, Route 611 north to Old York Road, also Route 611. Turn right at the intersection with Meetinghouse Road in Elkins Park. Turn left where Meetinghouse Road ends at Huntingdon Pike, Route 232. At Bryn Athyn turn left on Papermill Road. The cathedral is located at 2nd Street Pike and Papermill Road and the Glencairn Museum is just beyond the cathedral, at 1001 Papermill Road.

Hagley Museum

If you want to take a family excursion to a "theme" park that is more interesting than entertaining and more authentic than ersatz, then head down to the Brandywine Valley in Delaware.

Upper Delaware became a virtual du Pont family fiefdom from the time the du Pont powder mills along the Brandywine River began to prosper. There was a vigorous market for gunpowder and iron in the newly emerging country. As the Brandywine operation expanded into chemicals and textiles, the wealth of the du Ponts increased.

At the Hagley Museum just outside Wilmington, Delaware, you can see the recreated life of an industrial worker in the 19th century. There is so much to see and it is such a picturesque spot that you should plan a picnic lunch and make a day of it. It takes about three or four hours to do justice to the museum.

A jitney takes you around the 200-acre grounds, stopping at more than 24 areas of interest included on the walking tour map. Demonstrators show how the waterwheel, water turbine engine and steam engine were used in the powder mills.

Not only has the gun powder equipment been restored, but also the workers' homes. Community life in the mid-19th century is further revealed by the Brandywine Manufacturer's Sunday School where you can sit at the low desks as a worker in period dress explains the lessons of the day.

Overlooking the powder mills is the wisteria-covered Georgian-style du Pont residence, Eleutherian Mills, built in 1803.

Following the French tradition of sharing the dangers with his workers, Eleuthère Irénée du Pont built his home on the site of the highly volatile powder work mill. The confidence he hoped to instill was undermined several times when the house was severely damaged by explosions, the last and most serious in 1890.

Twelve rooms of the house have been restored and are furnished with antiques to reflect the lives of five generations of du Ponts who lived there. As you leave the house you see the two-acre garden now restored to its 1803–1834 appearance. In addition to the seasonally changing flowers in the *parterres*, there are dwarf fruit trees trained en *quenouille*, a practice popular in France during the 19th century. E.I. du Pont planned his garden to be a mixture of French and American plants.

Also close to the house is a reconstructed summerhouse, an arbor and a barn containing a collection of 19th-century farm tools, weathervanes, wagons, a rare Conestoga wagon and a Cooper Shop. Just down from the mansion is the first office of the du Pont Company. It is interesting to see the precautions taken to protect the candlelit office from the highly explosive powder.

This indoor-outdoor historic complex is well worth exploring. The main museum building tells the story of America's early industrial development through a series of audio-visual presentations, automated displays and a "talking" map. It is a thoroughly professional and eminently enjoyable look at a part of our history all too often overlooked.

From April through December The Hagley Museum is open daily from 9:30 A.M. to 4:30 P.M. January through March the hours are the same on weekends, but on weekdays the museum is open only for a 1:30 P.M. tour. Hagley is closed on Thanksgiving, Christmas and New Year's Day. Admission is charged. Picnic tables are available.

Directions: Take I-95 south to Exit 7, Route 52 north. Follow Route 52 to the intersection with Route 100. Turn right on Route 100 and continue to Route 141. Make a right, continue on Route 141 until you reach the Hagley Museum on your left.

Hawk Mountain

Have you ever experienced "raptor rapture"? You will if you head up to Kittatinny Ridge and the 2,000-acre Hawk Mountain Sanctuary. It's a thrilling sight to see birds of prey on the wing, riding the wind.

At least 15 species of raptors, more commonly known as birds of prey, can be spotted over Hawk Mountain from mid-August through November. The species you see on a particular visit will vary. During September you are likely to sight ospreys, bald eagles and broad-wing hawks. The biggest sighting is usually mid-month when thousands of medium-sized soaring hawks ride the warm air currents. October brings the greatest variety of hawks. You may spot a sharp-shinned hawk, red-shouldered hawk, Northern harrier, Cooper's hawk or rough-legged hawk. As October ends you may well catch sight of the striking golden eagle which rides the cold winds. A chance to see this magnificent bird with its seven-foot wing span is worth braving the colder weather.

If you feel that half the thrill would be lost because you wouldn't be able to identify the various species, then stop first at the sanctuary's Visitors Center to see its collection of mounted birds of prey and to browse through the books. When you're ready to tackle the slopes, you have two options—the South Lookout and the North Lookout. The former is the easier climb; the trail is only three-quarters of a mile. Though experienced climbers may deem it an easy climb, armchair birders should keep in mind the mountain does rise to 1,521 feet and even though the trail is gradual, it's still a climb. If you are really out of shape don't try for the North Lookout; it's a 45-minute hike and involves scaling a few rocky areas. Amateur hikers in sneakers can manage with effort.

Once you reach the top, it's worth the climb. From massive sandstone blocks you gaze over a magnificent 70-mile view. Many of the birds of prey actually fly beneath you. Between 15,000 and 20,000 birds are logged a season and on a "hot" day you may see more than 10,000 raptors. Ironically, a "hot" day usually occurs during cold weather when a front rolls down from Canada. A phone call to Hawk Mountain Sanctuary, (215)756-6961, can give you current flight updates plus projections for the immediate future. It is well to keep in mind that even when there is not a cold front coming through, it is cold on the lookouts, so dress warmly.

Bird-watching requires patience. Be prepared to spend some time waiting. As you wait, there are other wonders to observe. Beneath South Lookout you can see the "River of Rocks," a billion years old. These sandstone boulders wind along the valley floor like a river; water flows not over, but under, them. You may also spot deer in the valley below, but most of the time you will be scanning the sky. Be sure to bring binoculars so you can zero in on the birds once you spot them. Novices get help from more experienced birders who usually are quick to identify the various raptors. In fact, on weekends Hawk Mountain can get quite crowded and regulars try to plan their visits for less frequented weekdays.

Visitors to Hawk Mountain are the beneficiaries of the raptors' practice of daytime migration. (Some birds fly at night using a system of celestial navigation.) Raptors follow the mountain ridges and great kettles of broad-wing hawks soar together on the thermals, the warm air currents that allow the birds to glide from ridge to ridge. Hawk Mountain is the southern ridge of this system; from here on the migrants have to expend greater effort on their southward flight.

Hawk Mountain has been a sanctuary for migratory birds of prey since 1934. It is the oldest refuge offering this protection. Prior to 1934 hunters, not bird watchers, lined the top of Kittatinny Ridge. Surprisingly it was not the government that ended the carnage but Hawk Mountain Sanctuary, a privately-maintained association. The sanctuary is supported by the minimal admission and by annual memberships. There is a small bookstore and rest rooms. Picnic lunches are often enjoyed on the mountain lookouts. Bring an apple or snack even if you don't plan to picnic so that you can munch while you wait. The Hawk Mountain Sanctuary is open 8:00 A.M. to 5:00 P.M. daily.

While in the area why not take a steam train ride on the Wanamaker, Kempton and Southern Rail Road? It has trains and a trolley that meander along the scenic Hawk Mountain Line from Kempton to Wanamaker, a 40-minute, 6½-mile roundtrip. There's time enough to alight and have a picnic at Fuhrman's Grove, explore the nature trails or browse through an antique shop. The railroad runs March through June on weekends from 1:00 to 5:00 P.M. From September through November, when most bird watchers are in the area, the hours are weekends only, from 1:00 to 4:30 P.M. The WK&S is closed December through February. For additional information and updated fares, call (215)756-6469 or (215)437-1239.

Directions: From Philadelphia take the Northeast Extension of the Pennsylvania Turnpike; when it intersects with I-78 go west to Route 143. From Route 143 go four miles to the Hawk Mountain Road, well-marked with Hawk Mountain signs. The WK&S, or Hawk Mountain Line is just five miles south of the bird sanctuary on Route 143 in Kempton.

Historic Fallsington

After the American Revolution the new Congress had to choose a site for the nation's capital. One area that was given serious consideration was the "falls" area of the Delaware River. Today, you can see the quaint village of Fallsington almost as it was in days past.

The village of Fallsington grew around a Quaker meetinghouse that was built in 1690. Meetinghouse Square is still the center of town, now with three meetinghouses facing each other. The

Quakers, or Friends as they call themselves, kept detailed minutes of their meetings which provide a fascinating look at their daily life. William Penn attended the Falls meeting and his home, Pennsbury Manor (see selection elsewhere in book), was often used for meetings before the meetinghouse was built.

From the records we also learn that William Moon was scolded for "marrying his cousin Elizabeth Nutt." On a guided tour of Fallsington one of the restored historic homes you will see is the Moon-Williamson House. Samuel Moon, a well-known cabinetmaker and joiner, purchased the log cabin in 1767. A typical colonial log house, it was built in the tradition described as early as 1679 in this traveler's account:

"The house (we stayed in) was made according to the Swedish mode, and as they usually build their houses here, which are blockhouses, being nothing else than entire trees split through the middle or squared out of the rough, and placed in the form of a square, upon each other, as high as they wish to have the house; the ends of these timbers are let into each other, about a foot from the ends, half of one into half of the other. The whole structure is thus made, without a nail or a spike.

"The ceiling and roof do not exhibit much finer work, except among the most careful people, who have the ceiling planked and a glass window. The doors are wide enough, but very low, so that you have to stoop in entering. These houses are quite tight and warm; but the chimney is placed in a corner. My comrade and myself had some deer skins spread upon the floor to lie on. . . ."

You will see the primitive furniture in the restored Moon-Williamson House, one of the oldest in Pennsylvania still on its original site. You can imagine early pioneer life seeing the spartan rope beds with their straw mattresses and the deer skin rugs on the floor. The settle table demonstrates the common practice of having a piece of furniture serve more than one function. It can be converted from a bench to a table.

The Burges-Lippincott House, another private home that has been restored, reflects a later era. In fact, it represents several later periods. This 18th-century stone dwelling was built in four stages beginning in 1700 and continuing through 1829. It is noted for its carved front door topped by a glass fan and the interior woodwork, particularly the corner fireplaces and the elegant wall banisters. The rooms, furnished with period pieces, suggest a life style far superior to that shown in the Moon-Williamson House.

Across the street is yet another colonial restoration included on the guided tour—the Stage-Coach Tavern. It served as a stopping-off place for travelers between Philadelphia and New York from the 1790s until the 1920s when it was closed by Prohibition. In the Common Room you'll see the card table ready for play, the clay pipe holders and the pewterware to serve a tankard of ale or spirits. The private parlor was used for meetings to discuss town business and politics.

On request your guided tour will also include the Schoolmaster's House built in 1758 according to not one but two fieldstone markers. Tours start at the Gillingham Store which is now the headquarters of Historic Fallsington, Inc. Tours are given March 15 through November 15 on Wednesday through Sunday from 11:00 A.M. until 4:00 P.M. with the last tour beginning at 3:00 P.M. An introductory slide program provides background information on this remarkably preserved community. You can also obtain a walking tour map and explore Fallsington on your own. On the second Saturday in October many of the town's private homes are opened for tours as part of the Annual Historic Fallsington Day.

Directions: From Philadelphia take I-95 north to Exit 413 for Bristol. Make a left at the traffic light and go west on Route 413 to New Falls Road. Make a right and follow New Falls Road into Fallsington. You can also take Roosevelt Boulevard, Route 1, north to Tyburn Road. Then make a right on Tyburn and at the second traffic light make a left into the village of Fallsington.

Indian Steps Museum

When the first settlers arrived at Jamestown, Virginia, in April 1607 they did not build homes and plant crops. Under pressure because they feared the London Company would abandon them if they failed to discover riches in the new world, they spent the spring and summer in a fruitless search for gold. Had it not been for Captain John Smith who supervised the construction of crude cabins and wisely began trading with the local Powhatan Indians, the colony very likely would have failed.

After a time the Indians in the area had so reduced their own supply of surplus food they refused to trade and Smith had to find new sources. In 1608 he sailed up the Potomac River searching for new trade opportunities and gold. He went as far as the Susquehanna River where he encountered the Susquehannock Indians, taller and more warlike than the Virginia Powhatans.

The Susquehannocks and other tribes who used the river for their north-south migrations often hunted, fished, traded and fought along the river bank. The last Indians to inhabit this area, the Shawnese, left in 1765.

The Indian Steps Museum derives its name from the footholes, or steps, the Indians carved into the rocky bank. The steps, unfortunately, are now covered by water. Arrows, spearheads, stone axes and other artifacts left by the hundreds of thousands of Indians who traversed this area have been found along the shores of the Susquehanna River.

In the early 1900s John Edward Vandersloot, a local attorney, acquired 9.6 acres along the Susquehanna River. While preparing the ground for his garden he uncovered arrowheads, spears, tomahawks, stone garden tools and pottery shards. The artifacts introduced him to a hobby he would pursue for the remainder of his life.

Like all collectors, Vandersloot had to find a place to display his finds. His solution provides a fascinating destination for a family outing. He had a great portion of his collection, some 10,000 relics embedded in the walls and floors of his house. Both house and hobby continued to grow. In 1908, the first floor of the house was built; it was followed by the second and third floor and, finally, a tower in 1912. The two massive fireplaces, winding stone steps, stained glass windows and designs all make this a far-from-ordinary museum. John Vandersloot embedded his arrowheads and other relics in designs representing birds, animals, snakes and Indian figures native to the area. The museum also contains traditional displays of artifacts and fossils.

On the grounds which yielded this amazing array of artifacts are picnic tables and a riverside hiking trail. The grounds support an abundant bird and animal population, as well as 70 species of trees. If you visit Indian Steps during fishing season you will notice that there are some great fishing spots along the trail. Boats are also available from a nearby boatyard, and if you choose you can reach Indian Steps Museum by boat. The museum has its own dock. Campers can stop at the convenient Otter Creek Recreation Area, located about a mile upstream at its confluence with the Susquehanna River.

The Indian Steps Museum is open at no charge, but donations are solicited to help maintain this unusual site. The museum is only open April 15 through October 15. Hours are Thursday and Friday from 10:00 A.M. to 4:00 P.M., Saturday, Sunday and holidays from 11:00 A.M. to 6:00 P.M. Special entertainment is scheduled for Sunday afternoons during the summer months.

Directions: Take Route 30 west from Philadelphia to York. At York take Route 83 south. Take Route 83 to Queen Street, Route 74. Go south on Route 74 through Dallastown and Red Lion. Continue through the square at Red Lion to Burkholder Road. Take Burkholder Road to New Bridgeville and pick up Route 425. Continue on Route 425 for eight miles to the museum road. Take museum road for 1¼ miles to the Indian Steps Museum. It is near a small town called Airville.

Maryland Science Center and Baltimore Museum of Industry

You might think a science center and an industrial museum would be on the dry side for a double-bill excursion. Educational but not much fun, right? You couldn't be more mistaken, if the two destinations are the Maryland Science Center and the Baltimore Museum of Industry. And your day's outing can be further enlivened by a lunchtime break at Harborplace where there are any number of culinary choices in all price ranges.

One thing to remember if you visit the **Maryland Science Center** is that it takes two to tango, two to seesaw and at least two to see this center. It is a real hands-on museum and you need a partner to carry out many of the experiments. Like Alice in Wonderland, you will be confronted with signs that say "Try This." Then in easy-to-understand instructions you are directed to place your hands on a meter, stand in a room or talk into an echo tube that extends through several rooms. The second half of the message tells you "what's going on."

This science center is not the type of place you can cover in a hurry—nor would you want to with the admission price comparable to that of the movies, plus an extra charge for the planetarium. You won't want to miss anything and you may be able to get a family rate that saves money. Just be sure to allow yourselves enough time, at least half a day.

Permanent exhibits at the science center explore such topics as energy, geology, antique radios, calculators, exotic fish, computers, the Chesapeake Bay, probability, metrics and space exploration.

The Davis Planetarium creates its own special shows with 350 projectors and a four-channel sound system complete with 12 loud speakers. The dome of the planetarium has a 157-foot circumference and you see the action from horizon-to-horizon when you sit in the 144-seat theater of the stars. The multi-media shows both awe and educate. Bringing visitors back down to earth is no letdown, for there is still the Science Arcade to see. In this educational fun house, you can try some optical tricks with the anti-gravity mirrors or test your optical perception in the distorted room, where visitors find themselves changing into midgets and giants. Special lenses, telescopes, lights, sound and optical devices make science seem like a game.

Speaking of arcades, in the computer exhibit youngsters will find such favorite video games as "Donkey Kong," "Zaxxon," "Centipede" and "Jungle King." It is one of only a handful of its kind in the country. Some parents whose kids spend a lot of time working and playing on computers may find themselves having the binary counter, logic gate and memory bank explained to them, rather than vice versa.

Everyone in the family can test his ability to "think metric" at the science center's metric exhibit. A metrical tic-tac-toe game asks you a series of questions. You'll have another chance to test what you know on "The Chesapeake Jackpot," a slot machine game that asks questions about the Bay. This is part of the permanent exhibit that presents a cross section of Bay life. You can try to experience the fight for survival a blue crab endures amid the perils of the Bay.

From crabs to snakes is but a short jump. One of the 16 live demonstrations is on "Snake Power." In a display of reptilian showmanship a six-foot boa constrictor named Cambridge reveals some interesting facts about snakes.

You can also watch the Van De Graaff Generator in action as it produces one million volts of electricity. More magic show than science demonstration is the reaction of many who watch a tablecloth being pulled from beneath a stack of dishes; it is actually a test of Newton's first law of motion. Chemistry, liquid nitrogen and the testa coil have all been subjects of demonstration at the science center. At the Boyd Theatre films are shown on various scientific topics: volcanoes, the dinosaur, space and evolution

The Maryland Science Center has activities that appeal to all age groups, and while younger kids aren't really relegated to the basement, that is where the special K.I.D.S. [Keys Into the Discovery of Science] Room is located. Operating from 12:30 to 4:30 P.M. on Sunday, this room encourages children four to seven to get involved in activities geared for their age.

The Maryland Science Center is open Monday through Thursday from 10:00 A.M. to 5:00 P.M.; Friday and Saturday from 10:00 A.M. to 10:00 P.M.; and on Sunday from NOON to 6:00 P.M. For additional information call (301)685-2370.

The Baltimore Museum of Industry is just down Key Highway from the science center, although it is too far to walk. The best thing to do is to have lunch at Harborplace and then drive down to the museum. You shouldn't have any problem parking adjacent to the museum during the weekend when the nearby warehouses are closed. This museum is in the middle of the still-active South Baltimore-Locust Point Industrial district. A novel way to approach this museum is by water-taxi. From June through October a water-taxi shuttles from the Harborplace to the museum.

The museum itself is in an old 1865 oyster cannery, the Platt Packing Company. Appropriately the museum's motto is "A Working Museum for a Working City." The weekday bustle of the area is echoed within the museum on weekends. There are three work areas where volunteers demonstrate the skills and tools used in Baltimore's machine, print and garment shops.

Pulleys and belts make a busy work area in the turn-of-the-century machine shop. The belts that run from the floor to the ceiling turn flywheels which power machine tools such as lathes, milling machines and planers. Still useful, these machines enable museum workers to make replacement parts for their own antique equipment.

In the oldtime print shop visitors can "pull the devil's tail." Try pulling the lever on the old printing press and you'll discover why printers came to have over-developed left arms. You will see presses that date back to the 1830s and a model of the Linotype typesetter, a machine which revolutionized the print industry. You will also learn of two American expressions that are believed to be derived from early printing practices. "Mind your Ps and Qs" is said to refer to the composite case with drawers that held individual letters for setting type by hand. The printer had to "mind his Ps and Qs" when he picked out the letters. Another expression, "hot off the press," comes alive when you discover that the ink is still wet when the paper comes off the printing press. In the old days candles were used to dry the wet ink, thus making the paper "hot off the press." Adults and kids alike enjoy having their own opportunity to work the 1900 Poco Press and turning out a single copy with the notation, "I printed this."

In the garment shop you can try out the 1887 Wheeler and Wilson treadle sewing machine. Just a few minutes' effort will make you very glad you didn't have to spend your days as so many seamstresses did in the lofts of Baltimore working these heavy machines. It is interesting to see how specialized some of the sewing machines were. The museum has a belt-looper, both large and small basting machines and a hand-operated button sewer. Even the irons seem to require herculean strength; some visitors can't lift them off the table, much less use them.

An exhibit added in 1984, "Turning on the Power," traces the development of industrial power sources in Baltimore. There is a model of America's first gas lamp, or "ring of fire" as it was called, invented by painter Rembrandt Peale. (The Gas Light Company of Baltimore was the first gas company in America.) This exhibit has three recreated work settings. A tinsmith's shop, lit and powered by gas, is the oldest work setting. You'll see an electrical control room which shows the change-over from gas to electric power. The third is an elaborate electric repair shop, full of interesting household appliances like the 1930s Atwater Kent radio.

The museum has the S.S. *Baltimore*, an old steam engine tugboat, anchored in the water just outside the museum, in the process of being restored.

You can visit the Baltimore Museum of Industry on Saturdays from 10:00 A.M. to 5:00 P.M., and on Sunday from NOON to 5:00 P.M. It is located at 1415 Key Highway.

Directions: From Philadelphia take I-95 south. Just outside Baltimore exit for the downtown area on Route 40, the Pulaski Highway. This merges with Fayette Street which will take you into the city. Stay on Fayette to Pratt Street. Use the Inner Harbor parking lot for the Maryland Science Center. For the Baltimore Museum of Industry, from Fayette Street turn left on St. Paul Street which will become Light Street. Follow Light Street to Key Highway and turn left. Continue down Key Highway to 1415 on the left, the Baltimore Museum of Industry.

The Mercer Mile

"See Henry Mercer's Three Concrete Extravaganzas" may sound like a huckster's come-on. Henry Mercer, however, was no sideshow performer. He was a professional and daringly innovative archeologist, anthropologist, historian and ceramist.

His explorations of the detritus of other civilizations enabled him to spot the "archeology of recent times." That is what he called the spinning wheels, rope machine and salt boxes he spotted at a junk dealer's yard in the spring of 1897, a find which led to the amassing of 40,000 objects that tell the story of work, play and other daily life in this country before the age of steam.

Mercer not only felt a mission to salvage these fragments of Americana, he also had the daring to house them in an incredible cement castle far more likely to be seen on some English moor than in Doylestown, Pennsylvania. The castle is called the Mercer Museum. He designed and built it in 1913 without benefit of architectural blueprints. The castle is always rather cold and damp, and at times in winter it has been known to rain *inside* the castle walls. What great sets for a Hollywood movie there are here among the labyrinth of dark passages, twisting staircases [there are modern elevators as well], high-vaulted ceilings and absorbing, all-pervasive clutter. The use for a movie would surely have pleased Mercer who considered himself a writer in the tradition of Poe and Bierce. You see the influence of the macabre as you wander through the assortment of caskets, hearses and gallows.

The mood changes radically in "A Child's World" where school and play equipment bring to life childhood pastimes of a bygone era. The candy-making display here is just a small example of kitchen-related artifacts to be explored in detail in the rooms on the second floor.

Tools used for more than 50 crafts can be found in four galleries that extend around a central court where other items hang from the high ceiling or are lashed to the railings. A Conestoga wagon and a whale boat are just two of the pieces from the transportation field. As one visitor remarked, "If you can't see it here, it isn't worth looking for."

Henry Mercer was also fascinated with early American redware pottery. Colonial settlers originally made dishes, or trenchers as they were called, out of wood. Later they were made from gray and red clay. After studying the technique Mercer himself began making decorative red clay tiles.

Never one to do anything on a minor scale, he began his factory in 1912 with the massive concrete edifice or "extravaganza" that became the still-operating Moravian Pottery and Tile Works. At first the decorated tiles Mercer produced were used to enhance his home, Fonthill, but it was not long before he was selling them around the world. The tiles grace such haunts of the rich as one of the Rockefeller homes and the casino at Monte Carlo. Mercer's varied designs number approximately 2,000 and include scenes copied from old-fashioned cast-iron stove plates, as well as Indian and Medieval motifs. Prices also run the gamut beginning at $5.00 per tile and going up to $400. A slide show and lecture introduce visitors to the works. After that, you can take a self-guided tour through the cavernous factory.

There is yet one more Mercer "extravaganza" to be visited: Fonthill, his home and the first of his three cement structures. It's fun to imagine the comments of the Doylestown citizenry who watched the turreted, balconied and pinnacled Fonthill go up. Working only with his own ideas and no architect's drawings, Mercer hired local unskilled laborers to build it room by room, improvising as he went along. "Ceilings, floors, roofs, everything concrete," he wrote to a friend in 1909, "You stand up a lot of posts—throw rails across them—then grass—then heaps of sand—shaped with groined vaults then lay on a lot of tiles upside down & throw on concrete. When that hardens pull away the props & you think you're in the Borgia room at the Vatican."

One might believe that the Museum castle would be museum enough but Mercer's five-storied home has endless nooks and galleries filled with memorabilia, as well as walls of tiles. This collection ranges farther afield than that of the Museum including as it does artifacts gathered on Mercer's travels throughout the world. He seems to have kept everything he ever picked up!

You should plan to spend all day exploring the Mercer Mile. Do wear comfortable shoes. All three Mercer sites are open March through December. They are closed Thanksgivng, Christmas, January and February. Only the Mercer Museum is open on Mondays. Hours are 10:00 A.M. to 4:30 P.M. Tuesday through Saturday, and 1:00 to 4:30 P.M. on Sunday. Admission is charged.

Directions: Take Route 611 out of Philadelphia to Doylestown. For the Mercer Museum turn right off Route 611 on Ashland Street and continue to the intersection with Green Street. For

Fonthill continue up Ashland and turn left on Pine Street. Take Pine to East Court Street and turn right. Fonthill is on East Court Street on your right. To reach the Moravian Pottery and Tile Works continue up East Court Street to Route 313 and turn left, proceed about one-tenth mile to the parking lot on the left.

National Association of Watch and Clock Collectors Museum and Wright's Ferry Mansion

It's about time; you'll have the time of your life; time out—it's hard not to think in cliches when you visit the **National Association of Watch and Clock Collectors (NAWCC) Museum** and see the amazing diversity of time pieces housed here. The majority of visitors to the museum are not collectors, although some actually join the organization before they leave.

Appropriately, as you enter the museum you punch in on an old time clock. Along the wall to your right you will see a display of American clocks from 1700 to 1900. The clocks trace the development from brass to wood to spring movements and show that old case clocks were often masterpieces of the cabinet-maker's art. You can also see the component parts of a typical eight-day tall clock.

Some of these early clocks were called "wag-on-the-wall" clocks. This was a clock without a case. Although it was a more economical time piece, few children could resist tampering with the hanging weights. The habit of calling these tall time pieces "grandfather" clocks was inspired by the lyrics of an old song.

An interesting clock is the Sidney Advertising Clock made in 1890. Every five minutes it presents three different ads from a total of twelve held on three drums. A story goes that this concept was put to good use by an enterprising father, Alonzo Stubbs, who had seven marriageable daughters. He bought an advertising clock for his parlor where his daughters entertained their beaus. The father's first message said: "Let those love now who never love before, and those who always loved now love the more." His next placard was more practical: "Gas bills are getting higher." The third restored a romantic mood but the fourth was definitely a warning: "Long courtships cost money and are a great waste of time." The fifth left little doubt of the clock's purpose:

"Let us then be up and doing
With a heart for any fate;
Let's have done with endless wooing
And propose or emigrate."

By the end of two weeks all seven daughters were engaged.

Another direct action clock can be found in the collection of alarm clocks. You can't ignore the wake up message of the "Tugaslugabed." A large coiled spring is attached to a string which when tied to your toe will literally pull you awake. The clock does give an eight second warning, but if the slumberer does not awake the clock spring delivers "a savage yank to the toe."

Also on display are musical clocks and novelty clocks. One is a copy of Grant Wood's *American Gothic* painting called the "wandering eye clock." It creates an eerie sensation, definitely not to everyone's taste. The Anderson bottle clock has been put together piece-by-piece inside a bottle.

Displays also include some of the earliest time pieces to some of the most current. From a Roman ship at the bottom of the Aegean Sea, the world's oldest known time mechanism was recovered—the antikythera believed to have been made about 87 B.C. It shows the position of sun, moon, stars and major constellations. Other early time pieces include the clepsydra or water clock, candle clocks and sundials. In The Old Time Shop you can see cases filled with watches that you might have purchased at a jewelers between 1890 and 1910. Another window on the past overlooks a watchmaker's bench. Don't miss seeing the highly sophisticated "atomic clock."

There is so very much to see that you are likely to spend far more time than you anticipate. You may find yourself agreeing with the mosaic motto you saw when you entered—*Tempus Vitam Regit*—Time Rules Life.

The museum with its well-stocked library on horology is open Monday through Friday from 9:00 A.M. to 4:00 P.M. and Saturday 9:00 A.M. to 5:00 P.M. It is closed on Sundays and holidays. Admission is charged.

Just a few blocks away is the beautifully restored **Wright's Ferry Mansion**. Massachusetts had Abigail Adams and Maryland, Margaret Brent, but Pennsylvania had its own woman who was ahead of her time, Susanna Wright. When she was 29 Susanna purchased 100 acres of land along the Susquehanna River and became known as "the bluestocking of the Susquehanna."

One of her hopes in coming to this virtually uninhabited area was to be instrumental in Christianizing the local Indians and she learned the Shawnah dialect in order to achieve her goal. She operated a ferry crossing on the Susquehanna and the settlement formerly called Shawnahtown became known as Wright's Ferry. She served as the prothonatary, drawing up documents and writing letters for the other settlers in the area. She also practiced medicine and one of the upstairs rooms of the mansion contains drying herbs and plants she would have used. She wrote poetry and kept up a spirited correspondence with many of the country's leading thinkers. She was a particular favorite of Benjamin Franklin and they exchanged ideas and advice.

The mansion was built for Susanna Wright in 1738 and reflects her Quaker heritage as well as her links with England and Philadelphia. The house has been singled out as "the best effort to achieve an exact recreation of 18th-century reality." It has one of the finest collections in the country of Pennsylvania furnishings and accessories made before 1750. The pieces have been chosen because of their historical significance and their architectural purity.

Susanna Wright's austerity can be seen in the curtainless windows and the bare scrubbed floors, but she also had an exquisite artistic sense and a love of beauty. An example is the silk quilt and bedcurtains in her room on the only known example of a Philadelphia Queen Anne high post bed. In fact, Susanna Wright was interested in establishing a silk industry in Pennsylvania, and she had more than 1,500 silk worms herself. The quality of the silk she produced was so good that Queen Charlotte of England wore a dress made from Susquehanna silk, presented to her by Benjamin Franklin, at George III's birthday celebration.

Wright's Ferry Mansion is a special place that reflects a very special lady. When you visit you come away with a new appreciation for a woman who few remember today but who was a generation ahead of her time. Wright's Ferry Mansion is open May through October on Tuesday, Wednesday, Friday and Saturday from 10:00 A.M. to 3:00 P.M. Admission is charged.

Directions: From Philadelphia take the Pennsylvania Turnpike, I-76, west to Exit 21. Go south on Route 222 to Lancaster. Then proceed west on Route 30 to Columbia. Take Route 441, N. Third Street, into Columbia. Turn left at Poplar Street for the NAWCC Museum which is located on the right at 514 Poplar Street. For Wright's Ferry Mansion take Poplar Street down to Second Street and proceed to 38 South Second Street. You will see the restored old home on your right.

Pennsbury Manor

Somehow when you read the history books you get the idea that William Penn, proprietor of the Pennsylvania colony, seeking to oversee his great social experiment personally, settled permanently in Pennsylvania. This is far from accurate, although it may have been close to Penn's original intentions.

Instead, Penn returned to England after only two years in his colony, intending to return promptly and bring his family with him. He went back in response to a threat to his land claims, which were based on a charter he had received from King Charles

II in 1681. From England, William Penn sent regular letters detailing his instructions for his house, gardens and grounds to James Harrison, his steward.

William Penn returned to Pennsylvania in 1699 and in the following spring moved to his completed plantation, Pennsbury, with his second wife. Their son, John, had just been born in Philadelphia. Their stay was to be brief, for after only two years financial problems forced them back to England, this time for good. The country mansion had fallen into disrepair and ruin by the time of the American Revolution.

A major restoration program has brought it back to look as it might have when William Penn was in residence. You may notice that the furniture is not like that seen in the restored homes of Independence National Historic Park. Here the furniture is of an earlier vintage. Some of the pieces were made a hundred years before the American Revolution. This is, in fact, the largest collection of 17th-century furnishings exhibited in Pennsylvania, and it reflects the breeding and wealth of the Penn family. Although he was a Quaker, Penn had a taste for gracious living.

William Penn's letters to his steward also detailed his plans for the gardens. Skilled gardeners were sent to Pennsbury from England and Scotland. During his first visit to Pennsylvania (1682 to 1684) Penn had written home to request "a few fruit trees of the Lord Sunderland's gardener's raising out of his rare collection." Tradition holds that when Penn returned he brought with him 18 rose plants from London. Penn also instructed his gardener to obtain native flowers.

Penn's concerns extended to the outbuildings, or dependencies. Today you will see 21 buildings including the ice house, stone stable, smoke house, plantation office, wood house and bake and brew house. Costumed guides who conduct the tour explain the functions of the buildings. Don't miss the boat house which contains a replica of the barge Penn used for traveling back and forth to Philadelphia.

Pennsbury Manor is open year-round. The hours are 9:00 A.M. to 5:00 P.M. on weekdays and Saturdays, and NOON to 5:00 P.M. on Sundays. It is closed Mondays throughout the year. Admission is charged.

Directions: From Philadelphia take the Pennsylvania Turnpike, I-276, east. Exit at Route 13, Levittown (Exit 29) and signs will direct you to Pennsbury Manor. Turn right at the first light on Route 13; this is Green Lane. Continue on it to Farragut Avenue and turn left. Turn left again on Radcliffe Road. After you pass through Tullytown there will be a Pennsbury Manor sign and you'll turn right for the plantation. Alternatively, take I-95 north to Route 413 south to Route 13 north, and then follow the signs.

Pottsgrove Mansion

When John Potts, a wealthy Pennsylvania ironmaster, completed his Georgian mansion in the 1750s, it was so spacious and attractive that it drew visitors from as far away as Philadelphia. Today a visit from Philadelphia is easier and quicker, so you'll be appreciative that this 18th-century gem has been preserved.

Potts built a dream house that even in its day was considered enormous, but then his family did eventually include 13 children. The sandstone walls are 24-inches thick, which account for its surviving more than 200 years.

As was the custom during colonial times, there was always a welcome for family and friends at Pottsgrove. Children often slept on floor pallets or piled into a big feather bed together to make room for unexpected guests. Tradition says that George and Martha Washington enjoyed the hospitality of Pottsgrove on several occasions.

The ten rooms you'll see on your guided tour are furnished with simple yet elegant furnishings in keeping with Pott's Quaker background. Many of the pieces are Philadelphia Chippendale; although they are of the period they are not original to the house. The expansive front hall where guests were once received is considered one of the architectural highlights of the house.

When you complete your tour of the house you'll want to see the 18th-century flower and herb garden that has been planted by a local garden club. The grounds above the Schuylkill River were once the location of busy dependencies including a grist mill, forge, brewery and other work areas.

Pottsgrove Mansion is open Wednesday through Saturday from 9:00 A.M. to 5:00 P.M. and on Sunday from NOON to 5:00 P.M. Admission is charged.

Directions: From Philadelphia take Route 422 west to Pottstown. Signs direct you to The Pottsgrove Mansion which is off Business 422, not the bypass, just west of Pottstown.

Pusey Plantation

Caleb Pusey's 120-acre Landingford Plantation lay along the only road from Philadelphia to the southern colonies. But living on the main road in 1683 wasn't like it is today. A visit today to the modest Pusey home reveals not only that eight family members and three bound servants lived here once but also frequent overnight guests. Travelers on the Post Road would break their trip at the Pusey home.

Caleb Pusey was a mill manager for the first saw and grist mill set up by William Penn and his partners. Pusey's house is the last remaining house in Pennsylvania where William Penn is known to have visited. One of the artifacts on display in the museum (formerly the schoolhouse) is a reproduction of the weathervane made for Penn's Chester mills. It bears the year 1699 and the initials of Pusey, Penn and Samuel Carpenter, a partner in the mill. You can also see shards of old dishes and other household items that were recovered at Landingford Plantation by the Archaeological Society of Delaware.

The house is constructed of both bricks and stones, rather an unusual mixture. A large piece of millstone has been used to patch the east wall. The 17th-century herb garden is planted within the foundation of the 1682 underground room used by the Puseys during their first winter in Pennsylvania. Pusey's records tell of shelters that settlers "digged in the ground."

You begin exploring the Pusey House by entering the west door and seeing the great stand-kettle. It is similar to those often found in taverns and houses that accommodated larger groups of travelers. In the Pusey House, the kettle was probably used to dye clothes or brew beer rather than for daily preparation of food. You'll also see the back of the bee-hive oven and well. Both indicate that this room was an afterthought, added on after the well and oven were in place. Families who had lived in this house until the early 1960s and had fetched their water in buckets from Chester Creek were chagrined to learn that a well had been hidden beneath their feet all the time. The original well had been filled in many years before and was only rediscovered during the recent archeological dig.

The house holds all kinds of old furniture and household tools. One piece, a walnut cabinet built in 1717, actually belonged to Caleb Pusey. A tool you don't want to miss is the weasel, a clock reel attached to the spinning wheel that measured wool or flax thread. The snapper was set for a certain number of yards and when that yardage was reached the ratchet would go "pop." Thus we learn where the popular children's song, "Pop Goes the Weasel," comes from. The word spinster derives from the fact that most of the spinners in colonial homes were unmarried women.

In the East or Fire Room of the house large kettles hung from a lug pole that was fastened high up in the chimney. It was very hard to move the pots along this wooden pole and accidents occurred frequently. Over the fireplace you'll see a wooden crane that was used to warm the bedlinen and dry clothes. Look for the candlestick with a sharp lower edge that was used during slaughtering time to remove pig bristles.

After touring the house you can have a look at the vegetable and flower garden and the 1790 log cabin that belonged to Caleb Pusey's great-great-granddaughter. It is now the home of the Pusey House custodian.

The Pusey Plantation is open Tuesday through Friday from 10:00 A.M. to 4:00 P.M. Saturday and Sunday hours are 1:00 to 4:00 P.M. A small admission is charged.

Directions: From Philadelphia take I-95 south to Chester. Take the Widener College exit. Follow the signs to Crozer-Chester Medical Center on Upland Avenue. Go left on Upland Avenue to 6th Street. Make a right on 6th Street and go up to Main Street where you turn left. Go to the end of Main Street following the bend of the street to the entrance to Pusey Plantation.

Rock Ford Plantation and Hans Herr House

Rock Ford Plantation in Lancaster, Pennsylvania is a quiet 18th-century oasis that has remained virtually unchanged from the time Edward Hand, a close friend of George Washington, lived there.

The house still has the original floors, stairwells, railings, shutters, doors, cupboards, paneling and window glass. In some rooms the paint on the original walls is more than 200-years old. One reason for its remarkable condition is that Rock Ford has remained in the Hand family through the years. Inventories kept by the Hand family made it possible to reclaim some of the family furniture and to find matching pieces so that if Edward Hand were able to visit Rock Ford, he would recognize it immediately.

Hand rose to the rank of Adjutant General during the American Revolution, and you can see his field desk in the Blue Parlor on your tour of the house. In the dining room you'll see the famous Gilbert Stuart portrait of George Washington. This is one of 11 copies painted on glass made from a stolen copy of this famous portrait taken to China by a sea captain.

Eventually all of the plantation's dependencies will be restored. Currently there are two areas that you won't want to miss. During the spring and summer the garden is especially beautiful. Since Edward Hand was Irish, his garden eschews the formality of the elaborate British boxwood garden. This Irish country garden is full of delphiniums, columbines, lilies, coral bells, daisies, zinnias, snapdragons, marigolds and even random tobacco plants.

On the site of the original barn is an 18th-century stone barn which houses the Rock Ford-Kauffman Museum's collection of folk art. Furniture, decorative household articles in pewter and copper as well as Kentucky rifles made between 1750 and 1850 are just some of the items that fill in the details of life in this part of Pennsyvlania from 1750 to the present.

Rock Ford is open April through November Tuesday through Saturday from 10:00 A.M. to 4:00 P.M. and on Sunday from NOON to 4:00 P.M. Admission is charged.

Another nearby house captures the roots of an even earlier settler. The **Hans Herr House** is the earliest surviving dwelling in Lancaster County and the oldest Mennonite meeting house in America. At the invitation of William Penn, Hans Herr and a small group of Mennonites came to Pennsylvania in 1710. Herr was 72 years old at that time, yet he undertook the ardors of the journey to escape religious persecution in the Palatinate.

The medieval looking sandstone house you will see was built by Hans Herr's son, Christian. The date of construction can be clearly seen on the door lintel as you enter. The year 1719 and the initials CHHR, for Christian Herr. This two-story house has a cellar that extends beneath half the house. The windows of this underground room are 30 inches wide on the inside and less than half that on the outside, providing a refuge in case of Indian attack.

The Herr house is laid out according to a standard Germanic floor plan. The furniture is sparse and plain and represents pieces they would have been likely to use. It is interesting to see the way in which the huge "kas," or wardrobe, can be taken apart almost like a tinker toy. The house has a hidden oven and a cellar door that closes by itself thus preventing younger children from crawling too near the open door.

Before you explore the house stop at the Visitors Center where exhibits will provide background information on the Mennonites and the Herr family. There is also a shed with a display of farm tools and implements, a blacksmith's shop and an old-fashioned garden.

The Hans Herr House is open April through October Monday through Saturday from 9:00 A.M. to 4:00 P.M. From November through March the hours are 10:00 A.M. to 3:00 P.M. It is closed on Sundays, and during January and February it is open only on Saturdays. On the second Saturday in August they hold the Hans Herr House Heritage Day with demonstrations of 18th- and 19th-century crafts.

Directions: From Philadelphia take Route 30 west to the Hempstead Road exit in Lancaster. The Visitors Bureau is in the cloverleaf off Route 30. This is an excellent place to get detailed directions and information on other nearby attractions.

Steppingstone Museum and Susquehanna State Park

A trip to **Susquehanna State Park** near Havre de Grace in Maryland is, historically speaking, meeting Captain John Smith more than halfway. Back in 1608 when Smith began branching out from the waters around the Jamestown colony he sailed to the upper reaches of the Chesapeake Bay in hopes of finding gold among the tribes in the north—or even, some say, the fabled route to the Far East.

From the Chesapeake Bay, Smith sailed up a mighty river about which he said, "Heaven and earth seemed never to have agreed better to frame a place for man's commodious and delightful habitation." Why don't you head down to Susquehanna State Park and discover its delights?

The park's 2,250 acres offer a variety of inducements—historic, scenic and sporting. Within the park are four sites of historic interest. The Rock Run Grist Mill is again operational and visitors can watch cornmeal being ground by water power as it was in 1794. This four-story mill with its complicated gears and pulleys runs on weekends and holidays from Memorial Day through Labor Day from 2:00 until 4:00 P.M. The Miller's House has also been restored, but it is not open to the public.

The restored Jersey Toll House, an important way stop for early settlers in the Susquehanna River Valley, on the other hand, is open for visitors.

One of the prosperous settlers in the area was John Carter who, in 1804, built the Manor House. His home is the third historic attraction in the park. There are 13 rooms, a wine cellar and an indoor smokehouse in this L-shaped building. You may tour from 10:00 A.M. to 6:00 P.M., Memorial Day to Labor Day.

The fourth historic attraction, the **Steppingstone Museum**, was moved to the park in 1978. Rural arts of the late 19th and early 20th century are demonstrated at the museum on weekends from May through September, 1:00 to 5:00 P.M. The collection of hand tools used by local craftsmen gives an in-depth perspective that enables visitors to have a better appreciation for the finished products on display and for sale at the gift shop.

Wool is carded, spun and woven. Colorful examples of the weaving decorate the stone house. Food is prepared over a wood-burning stove in a kitchen filled with intriguing utensils. The formal sitting room and bedrooms are decorated with period furnishings. In the dependencies that supported the farm family, you see a blacksmith, woodworker, tinsmith, broom maker, leather worker, slater and mason at work.

Steppingstone Museum hosts a number of special events. The annual Arts and Crafts Fair with living history, old-fashioned crafts and musical performances is held on the third weekend in June. Hayrides and games your grandparents might have played make the third Sunday in August, Child Games Day, a popular favorite. Finally, the last Sunday in September marks the closing of the farm with an annual Fall Harvest Festival.

Susquehanna State Park is open at no charge daily during daylight hours. There are 70 campsites within the park. If you have time for more than a one-day visit you can enjoy the scenic pleasure of the meandering Susquehanna from your campsite. Many visitors come to the park solely to fish. In April the shad make their way up the river and fishermen vie for a spot along the bank. Pike, perch and bass are also found here. This, in fact, is considered by many sportsmen to be one of the best fishing areas on the East Coast. For information on camping and fishing call (301)939-0643, or the museum at (301)939-2299.

Directions: Take I-95 south from Philadelphia to Exit 6 at Havre de Grace. Follow Route 155 towards Bel Air. After one-quarter mile make a right turn on to Earlton Road and proceed for one-half mile. Then at Qualer Bottom Road turn left for the Steppingstone Museum. For park headquarters continue to Rock Run Road and make a right. You will see the park sign on the right after only a short distance.

Stenton and LaSalle College Art Museum

The stately brick country seat begun in 1723 by James Logan, William Penn's secretary, hardly looks like an economy move to modern visitors. But that is indeed what it was. Logan had suffered a series of business failures in the early 1720s, and he decided to retire to the country while he still had enough capital to establish a workable plantation for his family.

He had begun acquiring land in old Germantown in 1714 while managing the affairs of the colony in Penn's absence. He eventually acquired 511 acres and planned on building an inexpensive stone house. In keeping with his run of bad luck, the quarries failed. In the next two years he was unable to find any other reasonable source of native stones. He finally resumed the work in 1727 using bricks. **Stenton** was completed in 1730. Its name was taken from his father's Scottish village.

Although James Logan's economic fortunes suffered, his political fortunes did not. His jobs included secretary of the province, commissioner of property and receiver general, clerk and later president of the Pennsylvania Provincial Council, chief justice of Pennsylvania and William Penn's Indian agent.

The brick floor you will see in the entrance hall at Stenton was a practical accommodation to the large number of visitors who called on James Logan. Frequently the Lenni-Lanape Indians would camp at Stenton while on their way to Philadelphia.

The constraints of Logan's Quaker beliefs can be seen in the simplicity of both Stenton's design and furnishings. The room interpreted as Logan's study cannot display the one extravagance that Logan enjoyed, his 3,000-book library. It became the nucleus for the Library Company of Philadelphia. Logan was a genuine scholar; in addition to being fluent in seven languages, he conducted both astronomy and agronomy experiments.

James Logan's son, William, followed in his father's footsteps. He acted as attorney for the Penn family and served on the Provincial Council from 1747 to 1776. He, too, made his mark on Stenton. It was William who added the "old" kitchen and piazza. His family also contributed some of the finer pieces of furniture. Each room reflects and interprets one of the three generations to live at Stenton from 1730 to 1780, ending with George Logan.

The stone bank barn was added by George Logan who was intensely interested in agriculture. He turned Stenton into a model farm. His wife, Deborah Norris Logan, transcribed the correspondence of James Logan and William Penn and gained the distinction of being the first woman member of the Historical Society of Pennsylvania.

Stenton is open for tours Tueday through Saturday from 1:00 to 5:00 P.M. There is a nominal admission charge.

While in the area you may want to drop in at the **La Salle College Art Museum** which is open Tuesday through Friday from 11:30 A.M. until 3:00 P.M. and on Sunday from 2:00 to 4:00 P.M. It is closed during the month of August. This gallery, which opened as recently as 1976, presents painting and sculpture from the Middle Ages to modern times. It has already begun one specialized collection of illustrated and printed Bibles. The art is on display in a series of period rooms in Olney Hall at 20th Street and Olney Avenue. No admission is charged.

Directions: From center city take Schuylkill Expressway, north, I-76, to Roosevelt Boulevard, Route 1 north, and proceed to second exit on right. Follow exit bearing left to first traffic light which will be Wayne Avenue. Turn right on Wayne Avenue for one block. You will pass under the railroad. Make a left on Windrim at the first traffic light. Continue alongside the railroad to 18th Street which will be the second light. Make a right on 18th Street and Stenton will be on your left. Continue up 18th Street to Olney Avenue. For La Salle College Art Gallery make a left on Olney Avenue and continue to 20th Street.

Strasburg Rail Road

How about a trip to Paradise? That's not an impossible destination if you head for the Strasburg Rail Road. The ride is so much fun you won't even mind that it's round trip. For kids whose only train rides have been at theme parks this provides an authentic look at old-time railroading.

The Strasburg Rail Road is the oldest short line railroad in the United States. Chartered in 1852, it has been operating for more than 150 years, a record surpassed by only one other railroad in America.

The rolling stock at Strasburg, combined with the old station and water tower, looks for all the world like a miniature train layout—only on a big-as-life scale. It may also remind film buffs of a movie set. If some of the trains look familiar, it's because they have been featured in the movies. Several cars, including the open observation coach, were used in *Hello Dolly*. One engine used in that movie also appeared in *Broadway Limited*. The Willow Brook, which is the oldest standard-gauge coach in the world, appeared in *Raintree County*. Strasburg has a colorful assortment of passenger coaches, freight cars, cabooses and work cars. If Hollywood hasn't employed them all, they at least can star in your home movies.

There are cars to climb on and stroll through, and some puffer-belly-powered engines are in operation for the trip to Paradise. As you start off, the conductor will punch the passengers' tickets and regale you with stories from the early days of rail travel. The 25-minute ride through the Amish countryside may be interrupted at Groff's Picnic Grove. If you have time to make a day of it, pack a picnic and enjoy this special grove accessible only by the Strasburg line. When you are back on the train notice the interior details. All trains in operation have been carefully restored to look as they did in the late 1800s. Coaches have plush seats, inlaid wood paneling, kerosene lamps and potbellied stoves.

For real elegance in rail travel after your train ride climb aboard the special presidential car. Built in 1916, it was used not only by railroad presidents but also by a number of United States Presidents. Harry Truman's 1948 whistle-stop campaign was made in this classy car.

The Strasburg Rail Road is open daily from May through October, with trains running on an hourly basis. It is also open on weekends between April and November, plus the first two weekends in December. There is a charge for train rides.

To put the presidential car at Strasburg in perspective visit the state-owned Railroad Museum of Pennsylvania directly across the street. Here you will see an even bigger assortment of steam and electric trains. This is open at the same hours and does charge admission.

If this railroad stock starts you thinking about the toy trains of your childhood, or about getting a set for your kids, there are two more spots you won't want to miss. The first is the Toy Train Museum just a half-mile east of the Strasburg Rail Road. This is the headquarters of the Train Collector's Association, a group devoted to tinplate trains. Tinplate toy trains are those that are mass-produced rather than hand-built or made from models.

At this unusual museum you'll find a treasury of trains from the early-day models of the 1850–1860s, all the way to current models. Three train layouts provide a background for some of the more than 100 toy trains in the collection. Train movies add to the fun and if you choose to succumb to temptation there is a gift shop.

The Toy Train Museum is open daily from 10:00 A.M. to 5:00 P.M., from May through October, and on weekends when Strasburg is open. It is also open during Christmas week unless there has been a heavy snowfall. Admission is charged.

If you have not lost your enthusiasm for rail-related attractions one more spot can be visited. A lively Lilliputian world awaits you at the Choo Choo Barn, a 1,700-square-foot completely operating train layout. Trains whistle and toot past parades, a baseball game, a complete circus, firefighters battling a blazing house, ski slopes populated with skiers and many more action scenes. The animated scenes are further enhanced when a nighttime ambience is created and the lights come on. Children "oh" and "ah," and grownups are reminded of why they always wanted to have a train set.

The Choo Choo Barn is open daily 10:00 A.M. to 5:00 P.M., from May through October. During the summer months it stays open until 6:00 P.M. In April, November and December it is open on weekends from 11:00 A.M. to 5:00 P.M. Admission is charged.

Directions: From Philadelphia take Route 30 west to Route 896 south, just before the Lancaster area. Follow Route 896 for three miles to Route 741 east. These railroad attractions are on Route 741 in Strasburg, with the exception of the Toy Train Museum which is right off Route 741 on Paradise Lane.

Tinicum National Environmental Center

Country pleasures await you within city environs at the Tinicum National Environmental Center. There is only one other such urban environmental study area in the nation and that is in San Francisco. Tinicum offers an amazing diversity of nature: 4 distinct habitats, 288 species of birds of which 85 nest within the center's 1,200 acres and more than 25 varieties of butterflies.

At the small, utilitarian Visitors Center you can pick up a map and a bird checklist that includes all the birds that have been sighted at Tinicum. It tells you in what season they are likely to be in residence and whether the bird is abundant, common, seen only occasionally or rarely sighted.

The area encompassed by the Tinicum National Environmental Center was once part of the wild-rice marshes that lined the tidal rivers of the Atlantic coast. As early as the 17th century the Dutch settlers began diking these rivers, forming impoundments. Remnants of the old dikes remain, but the main dikes that now form the impoundments were built in the 1930s. One of the objectives of the environmental center, which is run by the Department of the Interior, is to preserve this freshwater tidal marsh, the only one remaining in Pennsylvania.

A 3½-mile trail surrounds the impoundment. If you want to shorten your walk, use the boardwalk across the impoundment. There are five main areas to be taken in. The first can be seen from the observation tower about three-quarters of a mile from the parking lot at the Visitors Center. The tower provides an excellent vantage point from which to spot waterfowl. Be sure to bring binoculars so you can get a close look.

At the eastern edge of the impoundment is the heron rookery. Varieties often sighted here include the great blue heron, black-crowned night herons, great egrets and snowy egrets. You may also spot the green heron though it prefers to nest in the tall grasses and among the reeds. During fall and winter thousands of ducks can be seen in this section. The impoundment also supports a thriving turtle population. You're apt to see red-bellied, snapping and painted turtles and migratory warblers that frequent the shrubs and woods.

Another habitat are the old fields on the eastern edge of the impoundment. The fields are maintained to increase the diversity of the bird population. Among the wildflowers and flowering meadow plants you are likely to spot some of the many varieties of butterflies: the monarch, red admiral, viceroy, painted lady, aphrodite fritillary and red-spotted purple predominate.

At the end of the boardwalk lies a section that is becoming a lowland forest. A little farther on you'll see a stand of young maple, ash and gum trees. The trees provide a habitat for additional varieties of birds: sparrows, warblers, flycatchers, orioles viros and even cuckoos.

To give you an idea of what to look for at different times of the year the managers at Tinicum provide a list of "Phenological Events." Throughout the winter from mid-November to March you are likely to see red-tailed hawks, marsh hawks, kestrels and a variety of song birds. Also commonly sighted are Canadian geese, pintails, black ducks, green-winged teals, ruddy ducks and great blue herons.

From mid-March to May the waterfowl migrate north. The mating season begins for frogs and toads and you're likely to hear their croaking choruses. The mourning cloak butterflies emerge from their chrysalises. April continues the northbound passage of such varieties as the hawks, herons, egrets and sparrows. The tree swallow can be seen again and the carp begin to spawn.

During early May the warblers can be sighted on their annual migration. Sandpipers also pass through Tinicum. Some visitors are surprised to learn that butterflies also migrate; during May you can see the monarchs winging north. In May and June the goslings, ducklings and pheasant chicks leave their nests, in July and August, the young herons and egrets.

By late August and into September the birds begin to fly in the other direction. Sandpipers usually pass first. Then in September and early October the gulls, terns and warblers come south; from mid-October to mid-November, the waterfowl, hawks and sparrows. Nature's continuing cycle always provides something to see at Tinicum.

The Tinicum National Environmental Center is open daily at no charge from 8:00 A.M. to sunset. You may fish at the center, but you will need a license. The waters contain carp, sunfish, perch, catfish, crappie and gizzard shad. Bring your camera, particularly if you have a telephoto lens, and consider bringing your bike. The trail is open to both bikers and hikers.

Directions: From center city take Broad Street south to the stadium complex. From the stadium take I-95 south to the airport. At the end of I-95, follow the signs for I-95 south until you reach Island Avenue. Turn right on Island Avenue and proceed to Lindbergh Boulevard. At Lindbergh Boulevard make a left turn and continue to 86th Street. At 86th Street you will see the entrance sign and a gravel road. The gravel road leads to the parking lot and Visitors Center.

Wheatland

The scene had all the elements of a Hollywood historical drama: the elderly politician in short-sleeves, the folksy porch in the June heat, then the unexpected news—at long last, the party nomination to run for the Presidency! It all happened just that way in June of 1856 when after three unsuccessful bids James Buchanan finally got the Democratic nomination. He would become Pennsylvania's only President. His home is much the same as it was back on that eventful day when he delivered his acceptance speech from his front porch.

Buchanan once said that he "never intended to enter politics . . . but as a distraction from a great grief which happened at Lancaster when I was a young man. . . . I accepted a nomination." He was talking about his broken engagement to Anne C. Coleman, who died shortly after they became estranged. This unhappy experience resulted in Buchanan's remaining a bachelor—the only one ever to become President. His niece, Harriet Lane, served as his official hostess both at Wheatland and while he was in the White House.

Although Buchanan may have entered politics reluctantly, he went on to devote 42 years to public service in various capacities. In fact, his list of titles is formidable. He served in Congress as both a representative and a senator from Pennsylvania. Before achieving his own administration he was Jackson's Minister to Russia, Polk's Secretary of State and Pierce's Minister to Great Britain.

The lavish Victorian ambience of Wheatland reflects his years of travel and diplomacy: Persian rugs, Japanese wallpaper, French lace curtains, Bristol stemware. Some items were gifts from heads of state. The 200-pound fishbowl was a gift from the Japanese Mikado when trade was inaugurated between the United States and the Far East. To commemorate the completion of the Trans-Atlantic Cable there is a message from Queen Victoria. Signed portraits of the Queen and Prince Albert recall Buchanan's years as Minister to Great Britain.

Many of the furnishings represent the White House years. On the large formal dining table, built specifically for Wheatland and never removed, you will see the French porcelain used by Buchanan while he was President. Be sure to note the unusual wine rinsers which enabled guests to rinse their glasses when changing varieties.

After exploring the house you, too, can step out on the famous porch and imagine Buchanan's emotions on that long-ago day. The estate has a garden and several outbuildings. Don't miss the carriage house which contains Buchanan's old Germantown wagon.

Wheatland is open daily from April through November from 10:00 A.M. to 4:15 P.M. Admission is charged.

Directions: From Philadelphia take Route 30 west to Lancaster. In Lancaster take Orange Street, Route 340 west until it branches out onto Marietta Avenue. Wheatland is located at 1120 Marietta Avenue.

York Historic District

To many people's surprise, especially Philadelphians, York was the nation's first capital. When the British captured Philadelphia in 1777, Congress was forced to flee the city. They traveled 88 miles west to York, prudently putting the Susquehanna River between themselves and the British. Congress reconvened in the York court house and drafted the Articles of Confederation, which when adopted served as the nation's first constitution.

History comes alive at the York County Colonial Court House when a three-dimensional dramatic narrative brings you the voices of John Adams, John Hancock, Thomas Paine, Samuel Adams, Philip Livingston, Francis Lightfoot Lee, Charles Carroll, Gouverneur Morris and many others. The court house has been restored to look as it did when the Continental Congress met here from September 30, 1777 to June 27, 1778. Time appears to stand still when you look at the rare tall case clock that marked the course of time for these patriots who proclaimed the formation of the United States of America. Copies of the documents associated with American liberties—the Articles of Confederation, Declaration of Independence and the Constitution—are also on display. The court house is located at 205 W. Market Street.

It was also in York that George Washington came perilously close to losing the command of the Continental Army. General Horatio Gates, hero of the Battle of Saratoga, was headquartered in York during 1778 while Washington stayed with the army at Valley Forge. Congress, either because of proximity or the spell of Saratoga, appointed Gates to the position of President of the War Board. General Thomas Conway then attempted to secure the command of the Continental Army for Gates. The Conway Cabal was thwarted by the Marquis de Lafayette who while attending a dinner party at the Gates house realized that a plot was afoot. His timely toast to Washington as Commander-in-Chief is credited with scotching the plot.

The Gates House is across Pershing Street from the court house at 157 W. Market Street. It contains period pieces representing the furnishings popular in this southcentral Pennsylvania region in the 18th century. Attached to this historic old home is the Golden Plough Tavern. This half-timbered tavern with a pitched roof is worth visiting as it is one of the few buildings in the country constructed in a medieval style. Behind the tavern you'll see the Barnett Bog Log House typical of the homes of German settlers who frequented the tavern after it was built in 1741.

The Historical Society of York County Museum at 250 E. Market Street has recreated a life-size village square. You can stroll down the "Street of Shops" and look into store windows replete with toys, apothecary jars and other necessities of a bygone era. Costumed mannequins also add to the sense of history come alive. In addition the museum has a Revolutionary War collection plus weapons and uniforms from the country's Second War for Independence in 1812.

The attractions of historic York are open Monday through Saturday from 10:00 A.M. to 5:00 P.M. and on Sunday from 1:00 to 5:00 P.M.

There is much more to see in the York area so you may want to stop at the York County Visitors Center just outside the city on Route 30 to obtain additional information. One possible stop is the Bob Hoffman Weightlifting and Softball Hall of Fame off I-83 at Exit 11 as you travel into York. You will enjoy the account of how softball originated, and get an interesting look at weight-lifters, powerlifters, body builders and strongmen. You can visit at no charge Monday through Saturday from 10:00 A.M. to 4:00 P.M. except on holidays.

Directions: From Philadelphia take the Pennsylvania Turn-pike, I-76, west to I-83. Travel south on I-83 to York for about 20-25 minutes. Take the Market Street exit for these historic attractions.

Winter

Alexandria

Most of us are predictable. We follow certain regular habits from which we rarely deviate. Philadelphians who visit Washington, D.C. tend to think in terms of the big national treasures. Neglected are the delights of smaller less well-known, in-town attractions and nearby points of interest. An ideal change of pace is a one-day foray to Alexandria, Virginia, an easy town to reach and an easy town to explore. Most of the city's charming spots can be included on a leisurely walking tour.

Your first stop should be the city's oldest house, Ramsay House Visitors Center, at 221 King Street. One way to get a feel for the city and decide what you want to see is to view the center's 13-minute color movie, *Alexandria*. Informative guides will help you choose from more than 40 brochures on in-town and nearby attractions. A walking tour map and the brochures will help you select attractions certain to suit your interests. You can also pick up descriptive lists of art galleries, museums, antiquarian book and antique shops and restaurants—plus free parking passes for the city's two-hour metered zones. Stop in at the Visitors Center from 9:00 A.M. to 5:00 P.M. daily, except Thanksgiving, Christmas and New Year's Day.

As you stroll along the quaint cobblestone streets you'll notice a variety of architectural styles. Alexandria is noted for its many restored historical homes, also for Captain's Row, the 100 block of Prince Street where the sea captains lived, and Gentry Row, the 200 block of Prince Street where the wealthy lived in large and elaborate houses. Don't miss the alley houses; examples can be seen at 205 King Street and 523 Queen Street. It is said that these were also known as "spite houses" because it was thought they were built to gain control of the narrow passageways or alleys. Another interesting building style is the flounder house. A good example of this design, with its windowless flat-faced side giving it a half-finished look, is at 316 South Royal Street, behind the late 18th-century Presbyterian Meeting House. All of the foregoing houses are private homes and are not open to the public except at times of special tours such as the Christmas Walk.

In addition to the Presbyterian Meeting House, another historical "must" is Christ Church at 118 North Washington Street. George Washington was one of the original vestrymen and you can see Pew 15 which he purchased in 1774, for the colonial equivalent of $20.00. The Lee family also had a pew at this church, where Robert E. Lee was confirmed on July 17, 1853. Christ Church is open 9:00 A.M. to 5:00 P.M. daily, except Sunday when the hours are 2:00 to 5:00 P.M. The gift shop is open April through Labor Day from 9:00 A.M. to 4:30 P.M., and from 9:30 A.M. to 4:30 P.M. during winter.

George Washington was seen not only at religious services in Alexandria. He was a steady customer at the Stabler-Leadbeater Apothecary Shop, at 107 South Fairfax Street, where he picked up his mail. Now a museum, the shop has the largest collection of apothecary jars in their original setting in the country. It also displays early medical implements and patent medicines. You can stop in Monday through Saturday from 10:00 A.M. to 4:30 P.M.

Washington, like many Virginia gentlemen, frequently stopped at Gadsby's Tavern for a meal and the latest news. Now it is both a museum and an operating inn, both run by the city but independently. You can partake of colonial cuisine in the restaurant, and tour the museum's bedrooms, ballroom and ice house. John Gadsby dug the ice cellar in 1805 and sold blocks of ice from the Potomac River for eight cents a pound. Whether you eat at the tavern or take a tour of the museum or do both, it is worth including on your day's itinerary. The tavern is open Tuesday through Saturday from 10:00 A.M. to 5:00 P.M., and Sunday from NOON to 5:00 P.M. A small admission fee is charged.

When George Washington passed through Alexandria on his way to his inauguration in New York, "Light-Horse Harry" Lee who was dining at the Lee-Fendall House at 614 Oronoco Street, quickly wrote the moving farewell address to Washington from the citizens of Alexandria. This house, which has been home to 37 Lees, is decorated with family heirlooms. It is open to the public for a small charge from 10:00 A.M. to 4:00 P.M. Tuesday through Saturday, and NOON to 4:00 P.M. on Sunday.

Across the street at 607 Oronoco Street is the Boyhood Home of Robert E. Lee. One of the bedrooms has been furnished to evoke the presence of young Robert. A parlor is associated with Lafayette, who was entertained here in 1824 when he returned to America to help celebrate the Revolutionary victories. The house is open for touring Monday through Saturday from 10:00 A.M. to 4:00 P.M., and Sunday from NOON to 4:00 P.M. It is closed from mid-December through February 1. An admission is charged.

If you have a second day to give to Alexandria, you should try to see Carlyle House and the Bicentennial Center within Old Town. Beyond this small area there is also Ford Ward Museum and the George Washington Masonic National Memorial.

Alexandria is one of the few cities in the United States to look beneath visible historic structures and explore its archeological sites. You may wish to look at the Alexandria Archaeology program on the second floor of the Torpedo Factory Art Center, 105 North Union Street.

The Torpedo Factory Art Center itself is certainly worth a stop because, in addition to the museum with its artifacts from Alexandria's past, there are studios and workshops of nearly 200 juried professional artists. In the galleries and studios you can see work by painters, potters, fiber artists, batik specialists, printers, jewelers, stained glass workers and musical instrument makers. The Torpedo Factory Art Center is open daily from 10:00 A.M. to 5:00 P.M.

There are many excellent restaurants in Alexandria, each described in a list available at the Visitors Center. If you prefer to picnic you can stop at Founder's Park immediately north of the Torpedo Factory Art Center. Although there are no tables, there are benches facing the Potomac River, as well as a grassy area.

Directions: From Philadelphia take I-95 south. When you reach the Washington area continue on I-95 (which becomes the Washington Beltway) south toward Richmond. Take Exit 1, U.S. 1, to the center of Alexandria, and go right on King Street for the Ramsay House Visitors Center.

Atwater Kent Museum and New Market

Philadelphia brings to life so much of our nation's history that the story of the city itself often gets neglected. If you want to give young children, or visitors to Philadelphia a real survey of how the city got started and how it has grown, the place to see is the **Atwater Kent Museum**.

The original home of the Franklin Institute, the Atwater Kent Museum was built between 1825 and 1826 during the Federal period. Copies of Penn's original plans for the city are in the William Penn room, and maps that show the city's changing profile are in the room called Philadelphia in Two Dimensions. You'll get a brief look at a diverse selection of the city's fire equipment; if you want more, then be sure to visit Fireman's Hall (described elsewhere in this book). The exhibit on city police includes old mug books. Annie Cameron, who was wanted in the 1890s for highway robbery, stares out at her viewers like a mighty tough desperado. The exhibit even includes such rarely covered services as the gas and water departments.

When Philadelphians celebrated their city's 100th anniversary on September 28, 1876, a quarter of a million people turned out for the "Pennsylvania State Day." Souvenirs of this popular event abound in the museum: flags, fans, medals, games and needlework.

Philadelphia's transportation network linked the port with both the old and new world. Ship models represent the city's shipbuilding works, and there are photographs from Hog Island, the largest shipyard in the world prior to World War I. Philadelphia was also one of the earliest cities in America to adopt rail transportation. You'll see a model of the 1829 Stephenson's Rocket and Baldwin's eight-wheeled locomotive.

At the Atwater Kent Museum you can get a well-marked map that will guide you on a short, informative walk around the **New Market** area. You start with the "Archeology at New Market" exhibit, an adjunct to the museum, in the old Bake House located off Lombard Street. Here you'll see all manner of artifacts dug up at the New Market excavations. The self-guided tour continues from Lombard up Front Street to Pine Street and then back down Second Street. This "walk around the block" covers three architectural periods. The first is the pre-Revolutionary Georgian period, of which the Bake House is a good example. The next is the Federal dating from the Revolution until about 1830. Finally there is the Victorian period dating from 1830 to 1900.

The Atwater Kent Museum is open Tuesday through Sunday from 9:00 A.M. until 5:00 P.M., and is closed on major holidays. There is no admission charge. A public parking lot is conveniently located next to the museum.

Directions: The Atwater Kent Musuem is at 15 South 7th Street between Market and Chestnut Streets.

Babe Ruth Birthplace and Maryland Baseball Hall of Fame Museum

Do you know who was born on February 6, 1895? Babe Ruth, and the row home where he was born is now the Babe Ruth Birthplace and Maryland Baseball Hall of Fame Museum in Baltimore. This is an exciting new attraction only seven blocks away from Inner Harbor that presents a multidimensional look at one of the nation's favorite pastimes. If you find you miss baseball during the winter months you can plan a visit to coincide with the Babe's birthday. The museum always plans a gala celebration. Or you can wait until spring and visit at the start of the season. You'll be able to see rare footage of some of baseball's great moments.

The house at 216 Emory Street was scheduled for demolition in 1967, but concerned civic leaders and sports enthusiasts managed to save it as well as the three adjacent houses. The Babe's birthplace was only 12 feet wide and 60 feet long, hardly big enough to house the Sultan of Swat's memorabilia, not to mention the ever expanding collection of baseball items associated with the Baltimore Orioles.

When George Herman Ruth was born here it was his grandparent's home. Young George spent only a short time in the tiny rowhouse. It is, however, the only surviving link with his childhood. His parents operated a tavern on Camden Street and their involvement with the family business meant that young George was left on his own a great deal of the time. Because of his truancy, he was enrolled at the St. Mary's Industrial School. One of the museum's most poignant reminders of the young Babe Ruth is a hymnal he is reported to have used while attending St. Mary's. A note on the flyleaf reads, "World's worse (sic) singer-world's best pitcher." It is signed George H. Ruth.

A "robotic" Babe is on hand to greet visitors and introduce the museum. Sports enthusiasts know they've come to the right spot as soon as they see the big sign announcing "Baseball Spoken Here." Spoken is the right word as many of the displays have taped tributes to the fans, players and sportswriters who enliven the game. There is the Howard Cosell tribute to Earl Weaver and the Baltimore fans that was recorded during the dramatic conclusion of the October 3, 1982 Milwaukee/Baltimore game when the Orioles won the World Series. You can sit in bleachers and watch a 20-minute film on Babe Ruth narrated by Mike Wallace. Sun papers photograph LeRoy Merriken talks about taking the famous photograph of Babe Ruth in action in another audio presentation. Although it is presumed to be a home run shot, the Babe actually was captured hitting a pop up in an exhibition game. There are also recorded interviews with Babe Ruth's family, his team mates and his fans.

The museum planners wisely included some hands-on exhibits for young visitors. There are "touchables" such as bats and gloves of famous players. Babe Ruth's old Louisville Slugger is just one of the bats on display. Older fans will like seeing the 1870 single stitched baseball and the 1910 finger glove.

The museum's focus extends from the Babe to other great Maryland baseball players in the Maryland Hall of Fame Room. It has information on six noted local ball players who are enshrined in the Hall of Fame at Cooperstown. Those interested in baseball "stats" will appreciate the 714 Home Run Club Exhibit that has a plaque for each of the Babe's home runs. The accomplishments of the only 12 players ever to hit more than 500 home runs are also highlighted.

This museum has been designated as the official Baltimore Orioles museum. In the Orioles Room fans can re-live the high spots of 30 years of Orioles' play in a 10-minute video show. And a video and photographic presentation brings back great moments in the careers of each member of the Baltimore Orioles Hall of Fame.

The museum is open April through October, from 10:00 A.M. until 6:00 P.M. on Thursday through Tuesday. From November through March, the museum is open from 10:00 A.M. until 4:00 P.M., Friday through Monday. It is closed during Christmas week, Thanksgiving weekend and on Easter Sunday. Admission is charged.

Directions: From Philadelphia take I-95 south. Just outside Baltimore exit for the downtown area on Route 40, the Pulaski Highway. This merges with Fayette Street which will take you into the city. Continue on Fayette to Greene Street. Turn left and go to Lombard. Turn right on Lombard and go one block to Penn Street. Turn left and continue to Pratt Street where you turn left again. Signs will indicate the Babe Ruth Birthplace on Emory Street just off Pratt Street.

Baltimore & Ohio Railroad Museum and Mount Clare Mansion

On August 26, 1830, the *Philadelphia National Gazette* ran a story on the first road test of Peter Cooper's experimental steam locomotive, the "Tom Thumb." This was the first American-built locomotive to operate on a working railroad line. Previously the fledgling railroads had used horses to pull their cars, after some trial runs with treadmill machines and cars with sails. Riders on the pioneering "Tom Thumb" runs jotted notes to prove that the human mind could still function at the dizzying speed of 15 mph.

In 1927 the Baltimore & Ohio Railroad custom-built a steam-powered replica of the original "Tom Thumb" for the B&O's centennial celebration, the Fair of the Iron Horse. Today this engine is the prize exhibit at the **Baltimore & Ohio Railroad Museum**, in downtown Baltimore. It is fitting that this ironclad should be ensconced here, as the original was built on the site of the museum.

Although the "Tom Thumb" is the star attraction, there are more than 50 other locomotives and full size models in the museum's collection, a collection considered the world's most comprehensive display of railroadiana. Part of the museum is housed in the Mount Clare Station (circa 1830), the nation's first passenger depot. The ornate roundhouse, whose 22 tracks display part of the collection, was built in 1884. You'll see trains from the Civil War, the first time in history that armies arrived at the battlefield by train. The railroad lines were also used during the Civil War for the transportation of supplies. Trains used to transport soldiers in World War I and II are also on display. These trains were called "40 and 8" because they carried 40 men and 8 horses.

Kids enjoy the trains that overflow on the tracks in front and back of the museum. Here youngsters, train buffs and photographers alike may climb into the cab or caboose for a real "hands-on" experience.

The museum also has an elaborate H-O layout to delight model-train buffs. The collection includes tools and memorabilia from the early days of railroading, plus examples of other early modes of transportation, such as the Conestoga wagon, old fire engines and vintage autos. The Baltimore & Ohio Railroad Museum is open Wednesday through Sunday from 10:00 A.M. to 4:00 P.M. Admission is charged.

A visit to nearby **Mount Clare Mansion** will round out your B&O excursion. It was James MacCubbin Carroll who sold the B&O Railroad Company ten acres of land for the bargain price of $1.00 so that they could build America's first railroad depot. Mount Clare is the oldest pre-Revolutionary mansion in Baltimore. This Georgian plantation house was built in 1756 by Charles Carroll the Barrister. Carroll was a colonial leader who helped to write the Declaration of Rights for Maryland, as well as the State Constitution. He was asked to be Chief Justice of Maryland, but declined because of poor health. The house is handsomely furnished with many original pieces and looks as it did in colonial times. Mount Clare is open daily 11:00 A.M. to 4:00 P.M., and Sunday 1:00 to 4:00 P.M. The mansion is closed on Mondays and on major holidays. Admission is charged.

Directions: From Philadelphia take I-95 south. Just outside Baltimore exit for the downtown area on Route 40, the Pulaski Highway. This merges with Fayette Street which will take you into the city. Stay on Fayette to Poppleton Street. Turn left and go eight blocks to 901 W. Pratt Street (corner of Poppleton and Pratt) and the B&O Railroad Museum. For the Mount Clare Mansion take Pratt Street east to Martin Luther King Boulevard, south, and continue to Washington Boulevard. Take Washington Boulevard to Carroll Park on the right. The mansion is at the top of the hill.

Bethlehem

Each year pilgrims from all over the world flock to Bethlehem during the Christmas season. That might seem like an impossible destination for a one-day trip, but not if you head for Bethlehem, Pennsylvania. This is a town that was named on Christmas Eve back in 1741 when the newly arrived Moravian settlers held their religious services in their Gemein Haus. This community log house housed both the settlers and their animals (in an adjoining stable). As they sang "Not Jerusalem-lowly Bethlehem 'twas that gave us Christ" their leader Count Zinzendorf, patron of the Moravian Church, suggested that they christen their new town "Bethlehem."

This Pennsylvania town even has its own Star of Bethlehem, sparkling high above the city from atop South Mountain. The nearly 100-foot-high star can be seen for miles. You will see smaller Moravian stars displayed throughout the entire town during the month of December and candles flickering from the windows of houses and public buildings. Special Lanternlight Walking Tours are conducted and as you near the old Moravian settlement you will encounter one of the largest decorated community trees in the country.

By planning at least three weeks ahead you can make the necessary reservations for the hour-long Night Light Bus Tours. These popular annual tours are led by guides dressed in Moravian attire. They will let you relax and see the sights of this Christmas-bedecked town. You will even ride to the top of South Mountain so you can look down into the valley for a panoramic view of the twinkling Christmas lights. To find out more about these tours, or to make reservations, call (215)868-1513.

In the Christian Education Building of the Central Moravian Church there is a Moravian putz, which is a German term for decoration which has come to be used for teaching Nativity scenes. This putz is composed of hand-carved wooden figures, many originally from Germany. Combining these wooden figures with music and narration, the story of the Nativity is told. They also tell the history of the Bethlehem settlement.

December, with its special Christmas glow, is the best time to visit this historic town. But it is by no means the only time you should visit. If you prefer warm weather excursions you can wait until August when they host Musikfest. At this time a wide range of Moravian crafts, music and food is available.

Bethlehem, spanning three centuries of our country's past, really does not require any special event to warrant a visit. In fact, you might prefer to plan your first trip at an off-time to give yourself a chance to get acquainted with the many attractions of this old town without fighting the additional crowds that predictably accompany the popular annual programs. Whenever you arrive in Bethlehem you should begin your explorations at the Visitors Center, where you can obtain a schedule of daily activities and a self-guided walking tour map. You'll also want to see the half-hour movie, *City in the Wilderness*. Guides costumed in old Moravian dress lead escorted group tours of the

Moravian Community, but these are by appointment only. If you can plan ahead call (215)867-0173 or (215)868-1513.

The walking tour encompasses 26 sites—probably more than you'll have time to include. One stop you won't want to miss, however, is the Gemein Haus, the five-story log cabin built in 1741. Constructed without nails from wood and mud plaster, this is the largest log dwelling still standing in the United States. It not only served as a place of worship but also as a dormitory and craft workshop. Today this community house is a Moravian Museum with examples of early Moravian furniture, needlework, a musical instrument collection, a doll display and religious art— plus a typical kitchen and a schoolroom. There is also a room furnished as it would have been when Count Zinzendorf stayed at the Gemein Haus. It is open Tuesday through Saturday from 1:00 to 4:00 P.M. and, like many of Bethlehem's attractions, it is closed in January. The Gemein Haus is at 66 West Church Street.

Probably the second most significant site to be explored is the 18th-century Industrial Area located along the Monocacy Creek, an easy walk from Main Street. In addition to Bethlehem's Christmas connection, the town is associated with one of the country's largest steel corporations—Bethlehem Steel. The town's industrial heritage goes all the way back to the early settlers who developed an industrial complex of 32 crafts and trades on the banks of Monocacy Creek. Within the 1761 Tannery you can watch costumed workers demonstrate the art of leather crafting. In its heyday roughly 3,000 hides were tanned annually at this massive plant. You can gaze down from wooden walkways at the huge vats where the animal hides were soaked, as you listen to a step-by-step description of the operation. Other early industries are also demonstrated at the Tannery. There is a working model of the 1765 Oil Mill and the 1762 Waterworks. After viewing the small scale model you will visit the reconstructed operating mechanisms of the original waterworks considered to be the first municipal works in the American colonies.

A relatively new addition to the Tannery is the children's Discovery Room. Here youngsters can get in touch with history. Trying on old-fashioned costumes, attempting to communicate via Indian sign language or guessing the use for various unusual tools makes history come alive in a meaningful and memorable manner. This area is open weekends, April through December, and Tuesday through Sunday during the summer months.

These are only the highlights. Other sites to be visited include the Sun Inn circa 1758; the 1810 Federal-style Goundie House; the Annie S. Kemerer Museum, a townhouse filled with the results of a lifetime search for beauty; or the Apothecary Museum, a repository of old medicinal equipment. The latter is open by appointment only. Youngsters might prefer the Lehigh Valley Antique Fire Museum with its old horse-drawn wagons that go back to the early 1800s. Another change-of-pace is offered at the Lost River Caverns just five miles away in Hellertown. Here you can see crystal formations in the caverns, plus a mineral and gem museum.

Directions: Bethlehem is approximately an hour's drive from Philadelphia. Take the Northeast Extension of the Pennsylvania Turnpike to the Allentown exit and go east on Route 22 for Bethlehem. From Route 22 take Route 378 south to Center City Bethlehem (Historic District) Exit 3, and follow the signs to the Visitors Center, located in the 18th-Century Industrial Area at 459 Old York Road.

Conrad Weiser Homestead and Cornwall Furnace and Koziar's Christmas Village

When **Conrad Weiser** was a young boy his family emigrated to New York from Germany. Growing up in the New York colony the youngster became fascinated with the Iroquois Indians who also considered this area their home. His interest and friendship with the Indians was enhanced when he spent the winter of 1712–1713 as the adopted son of the Iroquois Chief Quayhant in northern New York. This experience proved invaluable to him as Pennsylvania's "ambassador" to the Iroquois Indian nation.

In 1729 Conrad Weiser, his wife and children moved west joining a group of Germans who settled at the foot of Eagle Peak in the Tulpehocken Valley of Pennsylvania. He built a one-room Germanic style house for his family with an upstairs sleeping attic. In 1751 he added a second room to accommodate his 14 children. This rustic homestead is now a museum filled with period pieces reflecting the simple life on the frontier during America's earliest years, 1752–1756.

With the help of his large family Weiser operated a farm, which eventually included 800 acres and a tannery. He also served as the colonies' liaison with the Indians. He was highly regarded for his skills in communicating with the Indians and his grasp of Indian affairs. Working with James Logan, the Pennsylvania Provincial Secretary, he helped formulate and carry out a policy that maintained peace with the Iroquois. Near the Conrad Weiser Homestead you'll see a statue of Weiser's Iroquois friend, Shikellamy, an important Indian contact who was responsible for keeping the Delaware Indians under control.

Today on the greatly reduced grounds of this once extensive holding you can visit the graves of Weiser, his wife and several of their children. Legend adds that Indians are also buried here reflecting the harmony of Weiser's long years of peaceful coexistence. A visitors' center provides background information on the contributions of Conrad Weiser to early American history. You can visit Wednesday through Saturday from 9:00 A.M. to 5:00 P.M. and Sunday NOON to 5:00 P.M. Although the homestead is closed on Monday and Tuesday the grounds are open daily from 9:00 A.M. to 8:00 P.M. for picnicking and recreational use.

From the Conrad Weiser Homestead you can extend your outing by heading either north or south. To the south there is yet another site on the Pennsylvania Trail of History—the **Cornwall Furnace**. This remarkably well-preserved iron plantation lets you see a typical iron furnace and the dependent miners' village that is typical of those that once dotted Pennsylvania in the 18th century. It is said that while at Valley Forge, George Washington and the Marquis de Lafayette visited Cornwall to watch the workers cast one of the 42 cannons they made for the Revolutionary army. There is an orientation museum to acquaint you with the work of an iron furnace. This historic site can be visited weekdays from 9:00 A.M. to 5:00 P.M. and Sunday from NOON to 5:00 P.M.

If you head north you will come to a very different kind of attraction, **Koziar's Christmas Village** in Bernville which is open only in the evening. The reason is quite simple. According to Display World Magazine this is the Best Outdoor Christmas Display in the World. Talk about enthusiasm. This family certainly had an abundance when it came to decorating. In 1948, William M. Koziar began stringing lights on his house and farm buildings to the delight of his wife, Grace, and their four children. Each year he added more until the barns, walkways, trees and lake front house sparkled and glittered. There are now more than 500,000 lights, each decoration hand-made by members of the family over the last 40 years.

Visitors start coming in July to see Santa and favorite nursery book characters. Most of the fun is outdoors so remember to dress warmly if you visit in late November or December. You'll view Christmas scenes in 15 glass-enclosed buildings such as the toy shop, Santa's post office, and Christmas in other lands. Two large barns offer a wide variety of ornaments, decorations and gifts. There is also a model train display with 13 running trains and a building filled with decorated trees.

Koziar's Christmas Village opens July 1st and until Labor Day you can visit Wednesday through Sunday from 8:15 to 10:15 P.M. It is closed during the month of September and reopens in October and November on weekends only from 7:30 to 9:30 E.D.T. and 5:30 to 9:30 E.S.T. From Thanksgiving until December 31st it is open week nights from 6:00 until 9:00 P.M. and on Saturday and Sunday nights from 5:30 to 9:00 P.M. It is indeed worth delaying your journey home to see this fairytale display.

Directions: From Philadelphia follow the Pennsylvania Turnpike, I-76, west to the Reading (Morgantown) Exit 22. Take Route I-176 north to Route 422. Go west on Route 422 to the Conrad Weiser Homestead at Womelsdorf. This is roughly 90 minutes from center city. To reach Cornwall Furnace from Womelsdorf take Route 419 south through the picturesque farmland to Schaefferstown, which is an early 18th-century German town with many of the early homes and businesses still standing. Continue through Schaefferstown to Cornwall and follow the signs to the Cornwall Furnace. To reach Koziar's Christmas Village from Womelsdorf take Route 422 west to Route 419 north, then in one mile turn right on Christmas Village Road (this is the second road on your right). The twinkling lights can be seen at a distance looking incongruous amid the rolling Pennsylvania farms.

Discover Dover

Dover, Delaware, is a marvelously preserved reminder of our colonial past. The city was laid out between 1683 and 1717 according to a plan developed by William Penn. The hub of the town both then and now was the Green, where early residents exchanged gossip and goods at market days and fairs. Modern visitors still find the Green the focal point of their walking tour of historic Dover.

Just off the Green at the intersection of Federal and Court Streets is the Visitor Center where you can obtain a walking tour map and information on Dover's numerous attractions. An audio-visual show will familiarize you with nearby attractions. The Visitor Center is open Monday through Saturday from 8:30 A.M. to 4:30 P.M. and Sunday from 1:30 to 4:30 P.M. It is closed on state holidays.

Facing Dover's historic Green is the Old State House, the second oldest state house in the nation still used for state offices. Built between 1787 and 1792, it was occupied by both county and state officials. This restored landmark contains a courtroom, legislative chambers, a Levy Courtroom and county offices. The Governor of Delaware still retains a ceremonial office on the first floor. Delaware holds pride of place, as it was the Delaware convention in 1787 that was the first to ratify the Federal Constitution, thus making Delaware the "First State."

The perimeter of the Green is rich in history. One of the buildings, the oldest clapboard building (circa 1730) in Dover, was the first post office. There are also the multi-named Fisher-Clayton-Comegys-Terry House and the Caesar Rodney House. Your walking tour will take you past numerous other restored houses such as the Ridgely House built in 1728 and the Sykes

House dating from 1812. Both are on the Green. Just two blocks away is the Bradford-Loockerman House. Many of the privately owned homes in Dover are open once a year for Old Dover Days, held the first weekend in May.

One home that is open to the public on Saturday afternoons is Woodburn located on King's Highway. It has been the governor's residence since 1966. Built in 1790 Woodburn is beautifully furnished and has some excellent interior carvings. It is considered one of the best examples of early Georgian architecture in Delaware. Notice the details of the Flemish bond facade, the paneled Dutch door and the 12 pane fanlight window. There is a charming garden and boxwood maze on the grounds. Woodburn is open at no charge from 2:30 to 4:30 P.M. every Saturday, unless it is a holiday.

Your next stop will direct your attention to another branch of government at Legislative Hall, located at the intersection of Duke of York Street and Legislative Avenue. This is where the Delaware General Assembly meets and where you will find the Hall of Records. The Charter Lobby exhibits Delaware's royal charter and other historic documents. Extensive genealogical records are kept in the Research Room, open Tuesday through Friday from 8:30 A.M. to 4:15 P.M. and Saturday from 8:00 A.M. to 3:45 P.M. For information on the Delaware Archives call (302)678-5318.

For those interested in the past another "must" stop is the Delaware State Museum. The nucleus of this three-building complex is the 1790 Presbyterian Church, where John Dickinson wrote Delaware's second constitution. Members of the congregation were the political and military leaders of Delaware. Many of these pivotal figures are buried in the church graveyard, including President Tyler's Secretary of State, John M. Clayton, and Colonel John Haslett. Because of the church's importance to Delaware's past it was deeded to the state in 1950. Today in this old church you will see the original box pews, tin sconces and a spiral staircase. There is also an exhibit on shipbuilding, once one of the major industries in Delaware. Changing exhibits occupy the ground floor on a yearly basis.

The second building was formerly the chapel; today it contains exhibits on early Delaware trades. Here you will see tools from the 18th century used for agriculture, woodworking, weaving and homemaking. Recreated work areas bring to life the work of printers, blacksmiths, cobblers and even druggists.

The Johnson Memorial Building, the third component of the complex, contains the collection of Eldridge R. Johnson, founder of the Victor Talking Machine Company. Early phonographs and records are complimented by photographs of some of the first recording artists.

The Delaware State Museum is on South Governor's Avenue. It is open at no charge Tuesday through Saturday from 10:00 A.M. to 4:30 P.M., and Sunday from 1:30 to 4:30 P.M. Old Christ Church is on the corner of State and Water Streets. Marked by an imposing monument in the church's cemetery is the grave of Caesar Rodney, who rose from a sickbed to ride nonstop to Philadelphia to cast the deciding vote in favor of independence.

Two additional homes in the Dover area are of special interest. Just a short way down Route 113, past the Dover Air Force Base is the boyhood home of John Dickinson. He was known as the "Penman of the Revolution," having written many of the protests against the various oppressive acts levied by England. He was also the author of the 1778 Articles of Confederation. His home, built in 1740, is an excellent example of 18th-century plantation architecture. Unfortunately, in 1804 a fire destroyed much of the interior period paneling and family heirlooms. There are some Dickinson family pieces still on display, however. These include an English bracket clock, an armchair, a teapot presented to John and his bride on their wedding day and other ceramics. The cellar kitchen is unusual, as most plantations had an out-kitchen away from the house. It makes one wonder if perhaps the fire originated there. There is no charge to visit the John Dickinson Mansion which is open Tuesday through Saturday from 10:00 A.M. to 4:30 P.M., and Sunday from 1:30 to 4:30 P.M. It is closed on Mondays and holidays.

Finally, one last stop you should consider is the Allee House at Bombay Hook Wildlife Refuge. Both house and refuge are worth exploring. The Allee House was built in 1753 by a Huguenot family. A good example of a mid-18th-century country house, it makes an interesting comparison with the in-town Dover homes.

Although simple, the Allee House reveals the careful workmanship so typical of colonial architecture. It is built in a Flemish bond pattern. In the parlor take note of the dentil cornice, the recessed arched cupboards flanking the fireplace and the paneled wainscoting on the other three walls. The paneling in the upstairs bedrooms is also considered to be an excellent example of period workmanship. The Allee House is open weekends from 2:00 to 5:00 P.M.

The Allee House's location makes it doubly worth a visit, as this is one of the largest wildlife refuges in Delaware. There are over 12,000 acres of tidal marsh and 1,200 acres of fresh water ponds within this compound. Because of the diversity of terrain, bird watchers have spotted 260 species. Nature enthusiasts have observed 33 species of mammals and 27 different kinds of reptiles and amphibians. There are a number of ways to explore Bombay Hook: you can take an auto tour, hike the refuge trails or, equipped with binoculars, try to spot wildlife from the observation tower. The refuge is open daily until dusk.

Directions: From Philadelphia take I-95 south to Wilmington; take I-495, then exit on Route 13 to Dover. If you want to include Allee House you can detour at Smyrna onto Route 9. The house is located on Dutch Neck Road. Turn left off Route 9 and proceed 2.5 miles to the Allee House.

The Edgar Allan Poe National Historic Site

"Deep into that darkness peering, long I stood there, wondering, fearing, doubting, dreaming dreams no mortal ever dared to dream before." Allow your imagination free rein and you may see him yet, as you stand inside Edgar Allan Poe's bedroom chamber in the modest Philadelphia house he occupied the year before he published that brooding stanza in "The Raven."

Poe moved to Philadelphia from Baltimore in 1838, but he did not live in the little house at 234 North 7th Street until 1843. His six years in Philadelphia proved to be the peak period of his literary life and the happiest time in his personal life. Poe had 31 short stories published. Pay was so minimal, however, that he also worked as a literary critic and magazine editor. On three separate occasions he tried to establish his own magazine, a lifelong aim. He failed each time. Poetry was always his favorite form of expression, but he turned to short stories in order to support his family.

The seven-minute slide presentation at the Poe House acquaints you with the tragedies of the poet's life. He lost both his parents while still a baby. His father deserted his family, and his mother died of TB when he was just two. He was raised as a foster child by John Allan of Richmond, Virginia.

After the death of his foster mother, relations between Poe and John Allan deteriorated. Abandoning hope of reconciliation, the 22-year-old Poe moved to Baltimore to live with his aunt, Maria Poe Clemm. He became attached to Virginia, her young daughter. They married in 1836, when she was just 13.

Maria Poe Clemm managed the household for the newly married couple and moved to Philadelphia with them. As you tour the unfurnished Poe house you can picture the three of them trying to get along on the meager amount Poe was able to earn for his writing. Although they were poor, they did like to entertain the literary and intellectual figures of the day. They usually ate in the wooden shed kitchen that once stood beside the house. In the summer they would invite guests to share an economical dessert of peaches picked from their own tree. A similar tree has been planted to bring back those happy times. This six-room half-house (so called because it was only one room wide) was to be the largest home they would ever share.

No records exist to tell us exactly how the Poe house was furnished, nor indeed how each room was used. National Park Service researchers have an educated guess, however, as to which room was Poe's study and which were the bedrooms of Poe, his wife and his mother-in-law. A trip to the cellar may remind some visitors of Poe's famous *The Black Cat*.

The Edgar Allan Poe National Historic Site is open at no charge 9:00 A.M. to 5:00 P.M. daily except Christmas and New Year's Day.

Directions: From Broad Street go north to Spring Garden Street. Go east on Spring Garden to 7th Street. Edgar Allan Poe's House is well marked with the entrance at 532 North 7th Street.

Ellicott City

The East Coast is rich in towns that time appears to have forgotten. Ellicott City, Maryland, with its narrow streets and winding alleys, is just such a microcosm of an earlier era.

Perched on the banks of the Patapsco River, the town was settled as Ellicott Mills in 1772 by Joseph, John and Andrew Ellicott, Quakers from Bucks County, Pennsylvania. The brothers believed this would be an ideal spot to obtain water power. They also envisioned that the surrounding farmland could be used to grow wheat. Their foresight and skill turned this into one of the most successful milling and manufacturing towns in the East. It also dethroned tobacco as the sole cash crop in Maryland.

The second major impetus to development was the advent of the railroad. Ellicott City, which was just 13 miles from Baltimore, served as the first railroad terminus in the United States. On August 28, 1830, Peter Cooper's engine (later known as the "Tom Thumb") made its first run to Ellicott City. The first passengers jotted notes while traveling to confirm the amazing fact that the human mind could still function at the dizzying speed of 14 miles an hour. The new railroad cars were called the "iron horse" because before this time trains were pulled by real horses. In fact, that is the basis for the legendary race between the Tom Thumb and a horse.

When you visit Ellicott City seek out the old granite stone railroad station which was built in 1830. It now houses the Ellicott City B&O Railroad Station Museum. You can see the Freight Agent's Quarters where he both lived and worked—an economical way to supplement his $400-a-year salary. The Superintendent of Construction's Office upstairs is in the process of being furnished. The Ticket Office and Waiting Room house railroad memorabilia. The larger equipment is on display in the storage and maintenance areas of the old station. In earlier days engines ran on the tracks into the station, where large funnels in the ceiling vented the smoke and steam.

In the second museum building, the 1885 Freight House, you can see an 18-minute *Sight and Sound* show on the founding of the B&O Railroad. Here, too, is the museum's captivating HO Scale Model Railroad depicting the first 13 miles of track. When the house lights dim and the model lights come on the Ellicott City Hotel, Mount Clare, the Baltimore station, as well as the houses, farms, viaducts and other significant sites along this historic route will come alive.

The museum schedule for April through December is 11:00 A.M. to 4:00 P.M. Wednesday through Saturday, and NOON to 5:00 P.M. on Sunday. From January through March the museum is open only on weekends; the hours are the same. Admission is charged.

There is an historic walking tour map to be picked up at the museum to help you explore the rest of Ellicott City. You'll discover, in addition to its historic sites, the town offers a quaint collection of boutiques, emporiums, galleries, antique shops and restaurants. Many of the houses and stores were built in the late 1700s and early 1800s. Although the buildings have interesting pasts, it is the current action which draws most visitors. Whether you are shopping for yourself or doing your holiday buying, the shops display a tantalizing array of unusual items from around the world. The attractions include the popular Stillridge Herb Shop full of dried flowers and aromatic herbs, the West Wind Batik Shop which makes a trip to the Caribbean almost superfluous, a Kitchen Basket for gourmets, Ellicott's Country Store with a potpourri of possibilities, the Owl and Pussycat for pottery and both the Hi Ho Silver and the Mine Shaft for handmade jewelry. Most shops are open Tuesday through Sunday from 10:00 A.M. to 5:00 P.M.

You can plan a lunchtime break at the Continental Chez Fernand, have a front seat on Main Street at the Cacao Lane, grab a sandwich at Baxter's or the Phoenix Emporium or pick up fresh produce at the market for an on-the-spot picnic.

A day trip to Ellicott City will seem like a real vacation. Once you've discovered it you are likely to return to this town where time has indeed stood still.

Directions: Take I-95 south from Philadelphia to the Baltimore Beltway, I-695, then take I-695 west around Baltimore to I-70 west. Continue on that to the Ellicott City exit, Route 29 south. Take this to Old Columbia Pike which will lead to Main Street in Ellicott City.

Ephrata Cloister

Visit Ephrata Cloister and enter another era and another continent. The 11 surviving cloister buildings, medieval in design and European in origin, are administered as an historic site by the Pennsylvania Historical and Museum Commission. The community, 251 years after it was founded, still retains an aura of harmony and otherworldliness. It is at dusk, or on a cold gray day, that the atmosphere of austerity and simplicity is felt most strongly.

Though life in the colonies was hard for all newcomers, the members of Conrad Beissel's Ephrata sect were not content to suffer only the normal hardships of settlement in William Penn's tolerant colony. Beissel's society strove to discipline themselves still more. The sparse nature of their furnishings attest to their philosophy of self-denial. As you tour the Saron, or sisters' house, you will notice the narrow corridors. These were to remind the community of the "straight and narrow path of virtue and humility." The low doors were also designed as constant reminders to members of their vows of humility: wooden benches with wooden "pillows" were reminders of self-denial. Members had to be in bed at 9:00 P.M., but were awakened at midnight for their nightly prayers.

The brothers' quarters, Bethania, was torn down in 1908. A group of married householders also helped to make up the membership of the sect. At its height the community numbered about 300.

Although the members toiled in the fields growing the food necessary for their survival, there was still time for the art of calligraphy, book printing and music—all of which flourished at Ephrata. The calligraphy on display at the Visitors Center is as elaborate as today's laserprints. Illuminated books were a special art form practiced at the cloister. One of the original cloister printing presses, used to turn out books that sold throughout the colonies, is still operational.

Conrad Beissel was one of America's first composers; he composed a number of hymns extolling the tenets of ascetic self-denial. Using the calligraphic art of Frakturschriften, the sisterhood created hand-illuminated song books. Some of their work can still be seen at Ephrata. Eating, like sleeping, was carefully governed by this religious group. Special dietary restrictions were imposed so that the members could purify their voices and perform Beissel's hymns in proper fashion.

Music is still part of the Ephrata experience if you visit on a summer Saturday evening. From late June through Labor Day the Ephrata Cloisters Associates sponsor an hour-long musical drama called the *Vorspiel*. Conrad Beissel's music forms the basis of this presentation. The *Vorspiel* depicts life in this 18th-century religious community.

If you can't attend the musical drama, a slide show at the Visitors Center will also reveal the early life of this otherworldly sect. After your orientation, guides wearing the white garb of Ephrata members will provide an escorted tour of the sisters' house, the austere chapel and the householder's house. From there you are on your own and may explore the alms and bake house, Beissel's log cabin, the print and weaver's shop, a solitary cabin and the old graveyard where many of the original members of the society are buried.

Ephrata Cloister is open Tuesday through Saturday from 10:00 A.M. to 4:30 P.M., and Sunday from NOON to 4:30 P.M. It is closed on Mondays and major holidays. The *Vorspiel* is performed at 7:30 P.M. on Saturdays, and on the last Sunday in July and the Sunday of Labor Day weekend. Admission is charged.

Directions: From Philadelphia take the Pennsylvania Turnpike, I-76, west to Exit 21, the Reading Interchange. Go south on Route 222 to Ephrata. The Ephrata Cloister is located at 632 West Main Street in Ephrata.

George Washington Sampler

In any given February you can take your pick of three separate days on which to celebrate George Washington's birthday. First there is the actual date of his birth, February 11, 1732. Second there is the traditional February 22 date to which his birth date was moved when George was 20 and adopted the Gregorian calendar. The colonies' adoption was late which meant that 11 days were lost. Today, with the Federal holiday bill creating a different date each year on which to commemorate his birthday, you have your choice of weekends on which to plan an appropriate family trip. Unlike the other excursions in this book, you should plan on an overnight stay. A weekend will give you enough time to enjoy more than one of these Washington sampler tours.

The first excursion is to the family home where Washington was born, Pope's Creek Plantation, now the George Washington Birthplace National Monument. The second outing is to Fredericksburg, Virginia and the homes of his mother and sister. The third excursion includes his beloved Mount Vernon and the homes of his two adopted children.

To explore the early years you will head for Virginia's Northern Neck, an area that abounds with natural beauty. This narrow peninsula between the Potomac and Rappahannock Rivers offers many vistas of inlets, creeks and rivers. Life at this Washington family plantation is recreated by the farm's living history program and by the movie, *A Childhood Place*, shown at the Visitors Center.

George lived at **Pope's Creek Plantation** only until the age of 3½, but he did return to spend summers with his older half-brother, Augustine. The modest farmhouse was built by his father for 5,500 pounds of tobacco. The eight room house memorial built in 1930–31 is meant to give you a glimpse of the Washington family's life style. The furniture is representative of the period. There is also an operational kitchen house, weaving room and farm workshop where costumed park personnel demonstrate colonial crafts and chores. You can visit daily, except Christmas and New Year's Day at no charge from 9:00 A.M. to 5:00 P.M.

You can continue over to **Fredericksburg** which is only 38 miles away, or you can plan to explore this second Washington sampler on another day. In Fredericksburg you will see another facet of the Washington family. Here George purchased a home for his mother. As George Washington became increasingly involved in activities leading to the Revolutionary struggle he feared for his mother's safety on the family's country farm outside of Fredericksburg. To protect her he purchased a town house and insisted she move into the city where she would be only a block away from her daughter, Betty. His mother was reluctant to move; she disliked the noise of the city and even objected to the water. Mary Washington was never a self-effacing Southern lady. She had a stubborn streak and for many years she insisted on sending a servant back to her farm each day for fresh well water.

Though she never cared for city living, Mary Washington spent the last 17 years of her life at this house at 1200 Charles Street. It has been carefully decorated to reflect her years there. The house is open daily from 9:00 A.M. to 5:00 P.M. with reduced winter hours. Admission is charged. It is closed on December 24, 25, 31 and January 1.

A back yard path extended from Mary Washington's house to Kenmore where Betty Washington Lewis lived. Fielding Lewis had built this handsome mansion when they married. He died in bankruptcy, however, having lost his personal fortune supplying munitions for the colonial troops. Kenmore is far more luxurious than most rural houses, being particularly noted for its ornamental plasterwork. The Drawing Room, for example, is listed in the book of *100 Most Beautiful Rooms in America*.

After your tour you get a real taste of the past in the cheery out-kitchen. The gingerbread served with your tea is made from Mary Washington's recipe and was once a favorite of George's and Betty's. Kenmore, on Washington Avenue, is open daily from 9:00 A.M. to 5:00 P.M.; from November through March it closes at 4:00 P.M. It is closed on December 24, 25, 31 and January 1. Admission is charged.

George Washington's younger brother, Charles, owned the Rising Sun Tavern at 1306 Caroline Street in Fredericksburg. This was once a "hotbed of sedition" where colonial patriots met to discuss their grievances against England. The tavern has been carefully restored inside and out. Outside is an award-winning 18th-century tavern garden, and inside you will see a collection of English and American pewter in the Tap Room. Hot spiced tea is served in the tavern. It is open daily from 9:00 A.M. to 5:00 P.M. with reduced hours in the winter. Admission is charged.

The third Washington Sampler excursion starts at his beloved **Mount Vernon**, where he died on December 14, 1799. A room-by-room inventory taken at the time of his death has enabled the Mount Vernon Ladies Association to secure 40 percent of the original furnishings. Their task was complicated by Martha Washington's penchant for giving household items as mementos after Washington's death. Admission is charged and hours of operation are 9:00 A.M. to 5:00 P.M. from March through October; other months it closes at 4:00 P.M.

One of the capricious elements of the Washington mythology is that although he is considered the "Father of Our Country" he was, in fact, never a father, despite his lifelong hopes. When he married the widowed Martha Custis in 1759 he unofficially adopted her young children, Jack Parke Custis, age four, and Patsy, age two. When Jack died at the age of 24, after the Battle of Yorktown, Washington (again unofficially) adopted Jack's two youngest children, George Washington Parke Custis and Eleanor (Nellie) Custis. It is visits to the homes of his second family that can be combined with your Mount Vernon visit.

On George Washington's last birthday, February 22, 1799, the youngest of his "children" married. Keeping it in the family, Nellie Custis married George's sister's son, Laurence Lewis. The newlyweds built **Woodlawn** on the 2,000 acres that Washington gave them as a wedding present. It is interesting to visit Woodlawn after seeing Mount Vernon and Kenmore because it was designed to look like the latter and furnished with pieces from the former. A popular feature of Woodlawn is the children's "Touch and Try Room." Youngsters may play with the doll house and try writing with a quill pen. On nice days they may take stilts and hoops out on the mansion lawn. The music room at Woodlawn evokes Nellie Custis's presence in a unique way; tape recordings of her favorite pieces are played so that you can hear them just as she might have if she herself were walking through her house. Woodlawn is open daily from 9:30 A.M. to 4:30 P.M. Admission is charged.

Another part of their wedding gift from George Washington was the grist mill he had owned and maintained a lively interest in for over three decades. He had been visiting this mill when he caught the cold that led to his death. Located across the street from Woodlawn and now reconstructed, The George Washington Grist Mill offers a fascinating glimpse of the ingenuity of our forebearers. A taped message from the miller's wife explains the milling process. An interesting feature of this mill is that visitors are able to view the huge water wheel from four different levels. The mill is not open during February but should be visited if you take this trip any time between Memorial Day and Labor Day when it is open daily from 10:00 A.M. to 6:00 P.M. It is also open on spring and fall weekends but not during the winter months. The phone is (703)780-3383.

The final home on your tour, **Arlington House**, the Robert E. Lee Memorial, was built by George Washington Parke Custis in 1802. He wanted it to serve as a "treasury" of Washington heirlooms. He used the Mount Vernon pictures and china he inherited to recreate the childhood environment he had known at Mount Vernon. This house links two great American families. It was here in 1831 that George Washington Parke Custis's daughter, Mary Anna Randolph Custis, married Robert E. Lee. It is fitting to end your Washington Sampler here because the story of this house begins another epoch of American history, one in which Robert E. Lee played a pivotal role. Arlington House is open daily from 9:30 A.M. to 4:30 P.M. October through March, and 9:30 A.M. to 6:00 P.M. April through September, except Christmas and New' Year's Day.

Directions: For the Northern Neck take I-95 south which becomes the Washington Beltway and continue south on the Beltway to Maryland Exit 7, Route 5. Take Route 5 until it joins with Route 301. Then follow Route 301 to Route 3. Go east on Route 3. The George Washington Birthplace National Monument is 1.7 miles off Route 3 on Route 204.

To reach Fredericksburg from the George Washington Birthplace National Monument take Route 3 west for 38 miles. Fredericksburg Historic attractions are well-marked and the Visitors Center has a walking tour map. If you want to reach Fredericksburg directly from Philadelphia follow I-95 south past the Washington area and take exit marked Fredericksburg Visitors Center, the Route 3 exit.

For Mount Vernon, Woodlawn and Arlington House from Philadelphia take I-95 south which becomes the Washington Beltway and use Exit 1, the Mount Vernon Parkway, south to Mount Vernon. Continue on the Parkway and the grist mill will be on the right just before you reach Route 1 where you will see Woodlawn Plantation. Take Route 1 back towards Washington. Proceed past Alexandria and past the Pentagon to the Arlington Memorial Bridge where signs will indicate the turn off for Arlington House.

Germantown Historical Society Museum Complex

Putting the many historical, religious and architectural Germantown points of interest in their proper time frames is not always easy for visitors. But you can get a sense of the interconnection between all these elements at the Germantown Historical Society Museum Complex.

A span of 300 years of Germantown history is covered at the Visitors Center. The building itself, the historic Federal style Conyngham-Hacker House dates from 1796. Like so many of the town's old homes, it was built by William Forbes as a summer home to allow him to escape the heat of Philadelphia. Here you can see several rooms decorated in various periods and styles. In the Germantown Township room, one of the finest pieces of furniture is the large walnut and tulip wardrobe from 1776. Made of local woods in a German design with English brass fixtures, it nicely illustrates the frequent mix of cultural contributions found in the colonies.

The dining room, with its formal furnishings, reflects a more advanced social and economic status. The peanut design on the top of the Chippendale chest indicates that it was made in Philadelphia. You'll learn how to tell the political affiliation of the original owners of the old grandfather clocks. If a clock retains its lead weights then it is a good bet that the owner was a Tory or a pacifist Quaker; a patriot would have donated any lead to the Continental army for weapons.

Upstairs there is a Federal-Empire room and a Victorian room noteworthy for two decorative pieces: a hanging cloth cartoon about the "The Fatal Effects of the First Steam Coach" and a rare lithopane lamp. Few of these lamps have survived because their overlaid clay panels made them extremely fragile. The scenes on the panels have a remarkable clarity with light shining through.

Next door in the 1798 Howell House is the Germantown Historical Society's Toy and Quilt Museum. The first floor is given over to needlework—samplers and coverlets as well as quilts. A cornucopia of design and fabric, the quilts were sewn of anything from old clothes to stevenographs (colorful ribbons depicting English sporting events). Don't miss the quilt made from old neckties; it indicates a degree of sartorial daring that few men would attempt today.

Upstairs you'll see a part of the Society's 500-piece toy and doll collection. Sharing shelf space are delicate hand-made paper dolls, dressmaker dolls, French fashion dolls and jointed wooden dolls made by Philadelphia toymaker Albert Schoenhut. Cases are jammed with greeting cards, dance cards, vintage toys and school books such as the daunting *Mental Arithmetic* which students had to do in their heads.

Next you'll tour the Von Trott Annex where there is an exhibit on the Great Road, as Germantown Avenue was once called. It was an old Indian trail which bisected the land settled by the first Quaker immigrants. During the Revolutionary War the Battle of Germantown was fought with enemies entrenched on either side of the Great Road.

Across the street in the Clarkson-Watson House (1745), you can see some of the marvelous costumes in the Society's more than 1,000 item collection. The sense of "frozen history" is enhanced by having the mannequins dressed appropriately for the room in which they are displayed. Thus you not only see a selection of wedding dresses worn by various Quaker ladies of Germantown in the formal parlor, you will also see housedresses of the period in the 1880s' kitchen. Work dresses are rarities because they usually ended up as rags. The museum has future plans for a display of underthings and nightclothes in a Victorian bath and children's playclothes in the attic room.

All houses in the Germantown Historical Society Museum Complex are open Tuesday and Thursday from 10:00 A.M. to 4:00 P.M., and Sunday from 1:00 to 5:00 P.M. A single admission includes the four buildings described above plus the Library which is located in the Baynton House.

Directions: From center city Philadelphia take the Schuylkill Expressway north (Interstate 76 west) or East River Drive to Lincoln Drive exit, stay in center lane and follow the Lincoln Drive signs. Take Lincoln Drive to the first traffic light, Rittenhouse Street. Turn right on Rittenhouse Street and follow the signs one block for Wissahickon Avenue. For the Germantown Historical Society Museum Complex take a right on Wissahickon Avenue to School House Lane. Make a left on School House Lane to Germantown Avenue where you turn right. The Visitors Center of the museum complex will be on your right at 5214 Germantown Avenue.

Governor Printz Park and Morton Homestead

Did you know that 38 years before William Penn established his colony, the New Sweden Company already had a settlement in what would become Pennsylvania? The Swedish settlement was to be a base for trading operations with the Indians, not to become a settled colony. Remnants of the brisk trade conducted with the Indians were uncovered by archeologists in the 1930s.

The first Royal Governor of New Sweden was Johan Printz, who arrived in 1643 to expand the fledgling community. He built his home, Printzhoff, up the Delaware River on Tinicum Island.

Archeological remains of his "capital" can be seen at **Governor Printz Park** just south of Philadelphia. The excavations indicated that a fire had burned the settlers' homes in 1645 during the height of a severe winter. Charred remains of logs indicated the location of the first home Printz built. When Printz rebuilt his home, it had imported lumber and furnishings from Sweden and glass windows. Printz and his wife enjoyed this comfortable home for less than ten years. In 1653 he relinquished his command because of increasing disharmony with Peter Stuyvesant, governor of the adjacent New Netherland community, plus lack of support from the New Sweden Company.

Just a mile north of Governor Printz Park is **Morton Homestead**, a reminder of how Pennsylvania's early Swedish settlers lived. It was built by Morton Mortonson, the great-grandfather of John Morton, who was one of Pennsylvania's signers of the Declaration of Independence. The original portion of the simple log and stone house built in the mid-17th century may well be the oldest surviving structure in the state. Simple furnishings are testimony to the austere life led by these often reluctant settlers. Each ship that returned to Europe carried back some who had found the new world not the promised land of economic opportunity. The lack of sufficient settlers contributed to Johan Printz's decision to abandon the New Sweden community.

Of course, some settlers stayed, and at the Morton Homestead a second log house was built in 1698 for Mortonson's son and his family. These two houses were subsequently merged to form one long, narrow structure.

You can visit the Morton Homestead from 9:00 A.M. to 5:00 P.M. Wednesday through Saturday, and Sunday from NOON to 5:00 P.M. The Governor Printz Park is open daily during daylight hours.

Directions: From Philadelphia take I-95 south. To visit the Morton Homestead, just before Chester go north on Route 420 a short distance and you will see the old log house on your right. To see the Governor Printz Park go south on Route 420 to Essington near the International Airport.

Houses of Society Hill

Before the advent of the telephone it was customary to hold "at homes." These were occasions when friends and acquaintances would be sure to find you ready for company. Philadelphia's Society Hill conjures up these bygone days of gracious hospitality. Three old houses with historic significance are "at home" to visitors.

The 18th-century ambience of the Hill-Physick-Keith House makes you feel you should reach for your calling card. This four-story Federal townhouse was built in 1768 by Henry Hill, a

Philadelphia wine merchant. It is the only free-standing town-house that has survived in this old residential district. It is also the only Federal house that is decorated primarily with Federal pieces. Hill's prosperous business enabled him to construct a house and walled garden that covered a third of the block—a marvel of grace, proportion and design.

After Hill's death in 1790 the house was purchased by Abigail Physick who gave it to her brother, Dr. Philip Physick who established a medical office in his new home. The house has been restored and decorated to look as it would have appeared when Dr. Physick lived here. Many of the lovely silver pieces you will see were gifts to Dr. Physick from his grateful patients and others. The city presented a silver bowl to him in appreciation for his courage in remaining in Philadelphia in August of 1793 while the yellow fever epidemic ravaged the population. The silver wine cooler was given to Dr. Physick by Chief Justice Marshall. The doctor removed over 1,000 bladder stones from Marshall without benefit of anesthesia.

Dr. Physick is considered the "Father of American Surgery." His lectures on anatomy and surgery resulted in the University of Pennsylvania giving him the first chair of surgery in the United States. Those interested in medicine will particularly enjoy this house tour because there are display cases filled with Dr. Physick's medical tools, many of which he invented. One of these is the tonsil guillotine. (It's on display at the nearby Pennsylvania Hospital where Dr. Physick was on staff.) Less this sound unduly barbaric, it should be remembered that before this tonsils were removed by tying string to the tonsils with weights on the other end.

The Hill-Physick-Keith House also has a 19th-century city garden with a twisting brick path. Decorating this carefully maintained garden are classical sculpture on loan from the University Museum of the University of Pennsylvania. The house and gardens, at 3231 South 4th Street, can be visited for a nominal charge daily from 10:00 A.M. to 4:00 P.M., and Sunday 1:00 to 4:00 P.M.

One of the hundreds of Philadelphians who did not survive the yellow fever epidemic was Dr. Physick's neighbor, Samuel Powel. His house, at 244 South 3rd Street, was on THE street to live in the fashionable Society Hill district. Samuel Powel was called the "Patriot Mayor" as he was the last mayor of the city under the British and the first under the new republic. His friends included many of the leaders of the young country.

Samuel Powel purchased this townhouse in 1768 just ten days before his marriage to Elizabeth Willing. This elegant home was a perfect showcase for Mrs. Powel who frequently held dances in the ornate ballroom on the second floor. A letter from Benjamin

Franklin's daughter to her father mentions a ball she attended here to celebrate the 20th wedding anniversary of George and Martha Washington. The blue china in the dining room was a present to the Powels from the Washingtons. Another set of dishes with painted hearts and flowers was designed by Mr. Powel as a gift for his wife.

From the dining room you have an excellent view of the garden replanted with 18th-century shrubs and trees. A wooden wall sundial that belonged to Samuel Powel once more marks the time in this lovely retreat. The Powel House is open Tuesday through Saturday from 10:00 A.M. to 4:00 P.M., and Sunday from 1:00 to 4:00 P.M. The last tour begins at 3:30 P.M. During the summer months it remains open an extra hour. It is closed on Mondays. A small admission fee is charged.

One last stop you may want to make before ending your visit to Society Hill is at the Thaddeus Kosciuszko National Memorial at the corner of 3rd and Pine Streets. This Philadelphia townhouse was Kosciuszko's home during the winter of 1797–1798. A seven-minute slide presentation will acquaint you with the contributions made by this Polish engineer to the American Revolution. Displays reveal details of his efforts during the Revolution as well as information on his life. On the second floor, the bedroom he used has been restored to look as it did in the 1790s. The Thaddeus Kosciuszko National Memorial is open daily from 9:00 A.M. to 5:00 P.M.

Directions: From city center go down Market Street and turn right on 4th Street and proceed to Pine Street. You can park along the streets of Society Hill and walk to all three locations.

Merritt Museums

If you hear an exclamation, "What a doll!", it's not a sexist remark, just an accurate one at the lilliputian world created in Mary Merritt's Doll Museum where childhood lasts forever. From a collection of over 5,000 dolls, Mary Merritt has selected 2,500 prize specimens to exhibit.

The "little people" in this collection, which ranks as one of the largest and finest in the country, include every type of doll imaginable. There are rag dolls, china dolls, bonnet dolls, pumpkin heads, wax dolls, French bisque dolls, German jointed dolls, mechanical dolls and even paper dolls. There are also dolls named for their creator such as the Greiner dolls, Joel Ellis dolls and Schoenhut dolls.

Some of the oldest dolls are those made during Queen Anne's reign, 1665–1714. These wooden dolls were often elaborately dressed in silk, brocade and lace. Less ornate are the peddler dolls made during the 1700s and 1800s, often called Notion

Nannies because they were dressed like English peddler women holding their wares in trays and baskets.

Dolls were often used for purposes other than play. In China they used a Doctor's doll to indicate the areas in which a woman felt distress. Some mannequins straddled the line between plaything and fashion model such as the lovely French Fashion dolls. Exact details were adhered to in dress design, wigs, shoes and even hairstyles for the French china and bisque dolls. Women admired them for their fashion forecast and children treasured them because of their beauty. Milliner's models that demonstrated the latest in women's fashions were extremely popular in England and the United States in the early 1800s.

What's a doll without a house to call its own? So more than 50 complete doll houses are on display, the oldest a three-story Queen Anne cabinet filled with period furniture. Also more than 40 miniature period rooms such as a grand French ballroom and a simple Pennsylvania Dutch barn provide an amazingly accurate picture of the times they reflect. They are complete down to the smallest piece of decorative art and household accoutrements that might include selections from the museum's extensive collection of doll dishes.

The museum also has an extensive collection of toys. The world of transportation is represented with shelves filled by trains, wagons, fire engines, boats and carriages. Balance toys, pull toys, whittled hobo arts, playing cards and hobby horses are also on display. If after a visit to the full size reproduction of a mid-19th-century Philadelphia toy shop you feel the urge to acquire an antique toy or doll, you'll be delighted with the wide selection available at the museum gift shop.

Adjacent to the doll museum is the Museum of Early Childhood and the Pennsylvania Dutch. This museum also reaches back into the past and brings alive an earlier era through the household items, toys and arts. An 18th-century frontier kitchen with its dining area and a bedroom are displayed as are period costumes. Indian pottery and baskets also remind visitors of an earlier epoch. The gift shop offers unusual gift suggestions, collectibles such as Indian relics and a selection of more than 100,000 old postcards.

The Merritt Museums are open Monday through Saturday from 10:00 A.M. to 5:00 P.M., and on Sundays and holidays from 1:00 to 5:00 P.M. The museums are closed New Year's Day, Christmas, Easter and Thanksgiving. A single admission price is charged for both museums.

Directions: From Philadelphia take the Pennsylvania Turnpike, I-76, to Exit 23, Route 100. Go north on Route 100 to Pottstown and turn left on Route 422. The Merritt Museums are halfway between Pottstown and Reading on Route 422 near Douglassville.

Morristown

Winters were the real testing ground of the American Revolution, and George Washington's colonial troops spent two bitter cold winters in Morristown, New Jersey. Visitors today fare much better; a cold weather outing gives the best appreciation of the problems that beset the colonial forces. You can add another dimension to your trip by bringing your ice skates so you can enjoy Sunrise Lake if it is open for skating. During the summer there are "living history" vignettes at the park, plus the chance for a refreshing swim at Burnham Pool, operated by Morristown, or Sunrise Lake, a facility run by Morris County Park Commission.

Most Americans finish their schooling with only a sketchy idea of the chronology of the American Revolution, and when they think of the winter encampments they think only of Valley Forge. But in 1776 Washington crossed the Delaware on December 25 and defeated the Hessians. He then went on to beat the British at Princeton prior to leading his tired, cold army to their first winter camp at Morristown, New Jersey in 1777. It was not until the winter of 1777–78 that they camped at Valley Forge. They spent the winter of 1778–79 at Middlebrook, New Jersey, and returned to Morristown in 1779–1780.

The best way to begin exploring Morristown National Historical Park is to stop at the Visitor Center, open from 9:00 A.M. to 5:00 P.M., except on Thanksgiving, Christmas and New Year's Day. Maps of the park and explanatory brochures are available at the center. An eight-minute color film depicts the rigors endured by the Continental soliders during their winters at Morristown. During their second winter camp (at Morristown) 28 blizzards left the army stranded without supplies and reduced the men to a diet of tree bark, shoe leather and—for the lucky ones—company dogs. There is a lifesize diorama of a soldier's hut with a taped message telling about the men who served in the colonial army and the hardships they faced.

You'll find the Wick House near the Visitor Center. This building was used as headquarters for General Arthur St. Clair and the staff of the Pennsylvania Line. Although certainly not so grand as the nearby Ford Mansion, this house was more substantial than most in the area. The simple, homemade furniture is complimented by the pewterware, called "poor man's silver." You'll see indications of the prosperity enjoyed by Henry Wick. His dining room table is a formal Queen Anne piece, although the chairs are in the "Country Queen Anne" style. In the kitchen herb garden adjacent to the house vegetables and herbs are grown and carefully identified.

Your next stop should be Jockey Hollow, where costumed "soldiers" will answer questions about what it was like to camp at Morristown. There are also periodic musket firings and drills at Jockey Hollow. These events occur daily during July and August, and on weekends during the rest of the year as staffing permits. All officers below the rank of General lived with the men at Jockey Hollow. These officers often found it hard to imbue their men with confidence, and only George Washington's compelling leadership held the army together. He successfully quelled two attempted mutinies during their second winter encampment.

Washington's Headquarters is another pivotal section of the park. Here you can visit both the Ford Mansion where the General stayed in 1779–1780, and the adjacent museum. The story behind Washington's use of this home for seven months is a testimonial to his concern and personal regard for his officers. When Colonel Jacob Ford became sick and died during the 1776 New Jersey campaign, Washington ordered a military funeral with full honors for one of his "official" family. Ford's widow remembered Washington's consideration and when he returned to Morristown she invited him to use her home, the finest in all Morristown. Martha joined her husband here and spent most of her time trying to stay warm as she entertained guests and stitched in the upstairs bedroom. Also quartered here was Alexander Hamilton, one of Washington's aides. Perhaps Hamilton did not feel the cold as much as some of the other officers because as the song goes, he had his "love to keep him warm." A romance grew between Hamilton and Elizabeth Schuyler, the niece of Dr. John Cochran, who was the Chief Physician and Surgeon of the Continental Army and a member of Washington's staff. The house where the young lovers met is not part of the park, but it has been restored. It also has an attractive colonial garden. The Schuyler-Hamilton House is at 5 Olyphant Place and serves as the headquarters of the Morristown Chapter of the Daughters of the American Revolution. It is open Tuesday through Sunday from 1:00 to 5:00 P.M., closed on major holidays.

But even Alexander Hamilton, along with Washington's other officers, had little time for romance. Washington kept them busy with scheduled staff meetings and conferences. He utilized the main meal of the day (which was served from 3:00 to 5:00 P.M.) for informal discussions of military matters. The Ford Mansion is open 9:00 A.M. to 5:00 P.M. daily. Costumed interpreters are available to answer qustions as you take your self-guided tour of Washington's Headquarters.

At the museum a 20-minute movie about life at the Ford Mansion during the Revolutionary War is shown on the half-hour. There is also a narrated slide show with more information on the solider's life at Morristown. Displays and dioramas give additional background.

After you have spent several hours exploring Morristown National Historical Park you can include either a change-of-pace stop at the Morris Museum of Arts and Sciences at Normandy Heights and Columbia Roads (where the displays and galleries encourage parent and child "hands-on" interaction), or you can relax at one of Morristown's two beaches.

Just a short drive from the center of Morristown on Mendham Road is the delightful Burnham Pool. This stream-fed pool has a small beach, a sliding board into the shallow water and a raft in the center of the pool. There are changing rooms, rest rooms, a food concession stand, a picnic area and a playground. This is a great place for a summer respite! It is open NOON to 8:00 P.M., from late June to Labor Day. Admission is charged.

Your second option is the Lewis Morris County Park open 7:00 A.M. to dusk with its 300-foot sand beach along Sunrise Lake. This lake also has a raft for sunning, as well as rowboats and paddle boats for rent. There are changing rooms and a place to shower. Although you can't picnic on the beach, there is a lawn area with umbrella-covered tables and piped-in music. You can purchase light food and snacks at the Sunrise Lake boathouse. Summer weekends draw a crowd, so if you arrive much past noon parking is a problem. During the winter there is ice skating on the lake. There is an admission charge for the Sunrise Lake Recreation Area within the park, which is open 11:00 A.M. to 7:00 P.M. on weekends only from Memorial Day to late June. From late June to Labor Day the park is open daily at the same time.

Directions: Take I-95 north to U.S. 1, then go north on I-287. Follow Route 287 to Exit 26B-Bernardsville. Make a right turn at Route 202N (the first stop sign), and then a left at the next stop sign onto Temple Wick Road. This will bring you to the Visitor Center, the Wick Farm and the Jockey Hollow Encampment. For Washington's Headquarters you'll follow the park signs around Sugar Loaf Road and up Western Avenue. Then turn right on Route 24, drive around two sides of the green, and go straight on to Morris Avenue. A map available at the Visitor Center includes the location of the various attractions and will direct you to Lewis Morris County Park which, along with Burnham Pool, is on Mendham Road, Route 24.

Mummers Museum

For a very different excursion why not drive past the colorful outdoor markets of Washington Avenue to the Mummers Museum? Every day is New Year's in this total recall of Philadelphia's annual Mummers Parade. You can't miss this museum because of its bright facade of orange, blue and green tiles. The multi-hued exterior cannot compete, however, with the glittering costumes inside. Called "suits" by the Mummers, some of these get-ups can cost a band as much as $20,000.

Most visitors to this museum don't know the meaning of the word "mummer." The German word "mumme" means disguise and "mummenkleid" means a fancy dress. From Medieval Europe there are stories of costumed Mummers who would silently enter villages to dance and play dice and then leave, all without saying a word. Part of the celebration, as it was carried to America by German immigrants, was the firing of guns to welcome the New Year. In the first parades, called "New Year's Shooter," each marching group fired a salvo. This practice was banned, as was the equally noisy 19th-century "Carnival of Horns."

The parade became a city-sponsored celebration in 1901 and each year it continues to grow. There were 25,000 participants in the 1980 parade.

The Mummers Museum recreates the sights, sounds and ambience. An exhibit designed to suggest a stroll up Broad Street lets you see a selection of "suits" in the three Mummer categories—comic, fancy and string band. There are antique movie viewers, called mutascopes, that enable you to look at highlights from past parades. Rare old photographs capture scenes from the 1880s. And on the museum's telephone listening post you can hear old-timers recall parades of their youth.

If you still have questions, a handy electronic answering board answers the 11 most frequent queries. By now you will, of course, know what is 2.55 miles long, 69 feet wide, 12 feet high and covered with feathers. The answer: Philadelphia's Mummers Parade. If you are wishing that you too were a Mummer and want to see what you'd look like in full regalia, just put your head in the special window and you can Be a Mummer. If that moves you to do the Philadelphia Strut, you can learn the steps from a demonstration display. A distinctive walk that evolved from the Cakewalk, the Strut comes easily with all the music blaring at the museum. Youngsters can push buttons to hear what each instrument in the string bands sounds like, or they can play them simultaneously. The Hall of Fame offers a 45-minute VCR presentation that shows the top ten string bands in the previous year's parade.

It is no surprise that the museum is closed on New Year's Day, as well as Christmas and Thanksgiving. A nominal admission is charged and parking is free in a lot behind the museum. Hours are 9:30 A.M. to 5:00 P.M. Tuesdays through Saturdays; NOON to 5:00 P.M. on Sundays.

Directions: The Mummers Museum is at 2nd Street and Washington Avenue. Go down Washington Avenue towards the Delaware River and turn right on 2nd Street.

The Norman Rockwell Museum

Even better than any family album when it comes to providing a nostalgic look at the past is a visit to the Norman Rockwell Museum in downtown Philadelphia.

What other artist could so perfectly show us "The American Family" as Rockwell did in his series for the Massachusetts Mutual Life Insurance Company? In this amusing exhibit you'll see moments from your own life—the first hair cut, the first prom dress, backyard picnics, a visit to the doctor, the family dog, fishing with Dad, baby's first step as well as the American tourist abroad. Rockwell once said, "I paint life as I would like it to be."

Here at this museum you will be able to see the largest and most complete collection of Norman Rockwell's work. To get a bit of background on his 50 year career you'll want to begin by seeing the short slide and sound presentation on his life and work. Frank Sinatra's moving rendition of "The House I Live In" provides a poignant background to the works of Rockwell.

Rockwell sold the first of his many magazine covers to Curtis Publishing Company in 1916. He was but 22 years old. It is appropriate that the museum is located in the historic Curtis Publishing Building. It was here that Cyrus Curtis founded the *Ladies Home Journal* and rejuvenated the *Saturday Evening Post*. The museum has the entire collection of covers Rockwell did for the *Post*. They date back to 1916 when the popular magazine was five cents a copy. It is interesting to see how many well-known writers contributed to it.

The October 14, 1916 issue, which shows a typical family evening at the theater, features "The Water Cure" by Ring Lardner. On May 5, 1928 you could read the personal memoirs of Benito Mussolini in the issue with a Rockwell cover showing a young girl matching long strides with a hiker. By January 27, 1942, the magazine cost ten cents and the cover shows a young couple reading a brochure entitled "What to do in a Blackout." Rockwell captures a look on their young faces that leaves little doubt that they have their own ideas.

Rockwell not only left us a legacy of our lives he also vividly captured many of the great political, entertainment and sports figures of the day. You'll see portraits of such diverse celebrities as John F. Kennedy and Gary Cooper, and Ronald Reagan and the famous jockey, Eddie Arcaro. There are Rockwell posters and paintings, lithographs and sketches, movie billboards and commercial advertisements. One section of the museum has a replica of Norman Rockwell's studio with a mannequin of the artist hard at work on his front porch. As you view the prodigious output of this artist it will come as no surprise to learn that he worked seven days a week with only a half day off yearly to celebrate Christmas Day.

You can visit The Norman Rockwell Museum from 10:00 A.M. to 4:00 P.M. daily year round. It closes for three holidays— Thanksgiving, Christmas and New Year's Day. There is an admission charge, but children under 12 are free.

Directions: The Norman Rockwell Museum is located at 601 Walnut Street. It is in the heart of Philadelphia directly opposite Independence Hall. When you climb the steps of the Curtis Publishing Building you'll see the entrance to the museum to the left of the main doors.

Odessa

Once the prosperous merchants of Odessa, Delaware, would take one-day jaunts by shallow draft boats up the river to shop and socialize in Philadelphia. Now Philadelphians enjoy discovering the charm of Odessa, a town that represents America in miniature. This quaint port town on the Appoquinimink Creek goes back to colonial times when Dutch and Swedish settlers moved into the area. Quakers followed as part of William Penn's "noble experiment." From the mid-18th until the mid-19th century, Odessa was one of the leading commercial centers of the Delmarva peninsula.

It was the town's significance as a grain port that led in 1855 to its name being changed from Cantwell's Bridge to Odessa. Like its Russian counterpart, the Ukranian city Odessa, this Delaware town was the principal grain market for the region. Six large granaries operated during the village's heyday, with 400,000 bushels shipped annually. The new name change stressed its importance as a grain center in view of the competition from the railroad depot in nearby Middletown.

A walk along the tree-lined streets of this tiny village yields a cross-section of 18th- and 19th-century building styles. On High Street there is the mansion built by Charles T. Polk in 1852. Important to the Odessa community was the old St. Paul's Methodist Church which was begun in 1851. It has been restored with funds raised during the annual Christmas in Odessa house tours. An entire section of the town is on the National Register of Historic Places. Three of the historic structures were donated to the Henry Francis du Pont Winterthur Museum; and these sites may be visited, adding an in-depth view to your stroll through the past.

The oldest historic house museum (and possibly the oldest in Delaware) is the Wilson-Warner House built in 1769 by David Wilson. It stood next to Wilson's store and was built in an L-shape typical of Delaware homes of that period. The furnishings now match the 1829 auction records of the house's contents, when Wilson was forced to sell his land, house and furniture because of business reverses. The home returned to the family when it was purchased by his great-granddaughter, Mary Corbit Wilson, who was also the granddaughter of William Corbit.

Next door is the second house that is part of Winterthur in Odessa, the Corbit-Sharp House. This was built between 1772 and 1774 by William Corbit, the brother-in-law of David Wilson. This dwelling has many special decorative touches like the fretwork railing on the roof and the arched dormer windows. William Corbit had a tannery on the banks of the Appoquinimink Creek and was one of the town's most prosperous citizens.

This lovely Georgian home is filled with family furniture carefully reclaimed with the help of meticulous family inventories. There are samplers stitched by Corbit's young granddaughters in 1823. The upstairs bedroom with its unusual combination of pink and blue, is considered architecturally the most interesting room in the house. But visitors are often more intrigued by the notations made by Daniel Corbit on the inside of his bedroom closet door. He kept a penciled record of the family fortunes there.

It was Daniel Corbit's Quaker wife, Mary Wilson, who in 1860 so objected to the rowdy behavior of the crowds across the street at the Brick Hotel that she waged a successful campaign to have their liquor license revoked. This old hotel is the third building that has been renovated and restored to public use (the Brick Hotel Gallery) as a center of changing exhibitions. The hotel was built in 1822 by William Polk who had purchased the Wilson-Warner House in 1829.

The three Winterthur in Odessa attractions are open Tuesday through Saturday from 10:00 A.M. to 4:30 P.M., and on Sunday from 1:00 to 4:30 P.M. year-round. There are no tours on Mondays, January 1, July 4, Thanksgiving, December 24 or 25. Admission is charged.

Directions: From Philadelphia take I-95 south to Wilmington. Continue south on Route 13 to the junction with Route 299. Odessa, Delaware, is 23 miles south of Wilmington. All three attractions are on Main Street.

The Perelman Antique Toy Museum

Do you have a well-remembered toy from your childhood you'd like to know more about? A visit to The Perelman Antique Toy Museum enables you to trace the history of almost any plaything. Toy trains, dolls, pull toys, marbles and cap pistols are all here in great variety. They represent over a century of childish delight.

One wonders as he looks around a collection as extensive as this, "How did it begin?" Like so many extensive collections, this one began with a single purchase. In 1958 Leon Perelman bought a mechanical bank in an Iowa hobby shop. Had he known it would lead him to amassing the world's largest collection of mechanical and still banks, he might have hesitated. After viewing the display at this museum, visitors are glad he persevered.

Mechanical banks were first introduced in 1867 and remained popular until 1902. This museum has examples of 98 percent of all known types. Quaint vignettes are performed by these banks. A child would eagerly deposit a coin in order to watch the chicken thief tiptoe out of the henhouse for a face-to-face encounter with the police. The thief would dart back into the henhouse and slam the door to the delight of the youngsters. The virtues of saving could be learned by giving Jonah a penny to shoot into the whale's mouth from the safety of a small boat. Savers found amusement in the 1880 bank on which a dentist falls back as he pulls the patient's tooth.

All these high jinks go on in the old Abercrombie House on Society Hill. As any newcomer soon learns, Society Hill in Philadelphia gets its name not from the upper classes but from the Free Society of Traders, a colonial land promotion company. The house was built in 1758 by a sea captain, James Abercrombie. It is fortunately the tallest colonial house in the city; a lot of space is needed to store 4,000 playthings.

On the first floor there are colorful groupings of carousels, ferris wheels and circus riders. Varieties of pull and friction toys are also represented and there is a Noah's Ark made in 1870. Young boys, who have their own toy soldiers, will be pleased by the many military units in the museum's display. There are Medieval knights, Mexican vaqueros, Napoleonic legions, Algerian Zouaves and American Continental troops.

On the second floor there is an amazing array of transportation toys: trains, fire engines and hook-and-ladder vehicles, Model T's, hansom cabs, wagons, donkey carts, trolleys, as well as airplanes and zeppelins.

In the gun display are toy pistols with ornately carved handles. Many of the pistols have the figure of a man or animals mounted on the barrels. When the gun is fired the characters move about kicking, bucking or biting.

The top floor, in addition to dolls and doll houses, features rare play toys. The Zoetrope, or Wheel of Life, which was made in 1880 was called a periphanoscope. It gave the appearance of movement to the revolving picture strips. This was the precursor of cinematography. The German-made magic lanterns and the autoperipatetikon, or automatona figures, were also ahead of their time. One classic is the seated Ulysses S. Grant who smokes his big black cigar turning his head from side to side in satisfaction while puffing out smoke. There are mechanical acrobats, animated musicians and graceful dancers.

The Perelman Antique Toy Museum is open daily year-round from 9:30 A.M. to 5:00 P.M. A nominal admission is charged. You can usually find on-street parking in this relatively uncongested residential area or at the two nearby Penn's Landing parking lots. While in the area you may want to visit the ships at Penn's Landing.

Directions: From center city take Chestnut Street down toward the harbor and turn right on 2nd Street. Continue to 270 S. 2nd Street (corner of Spruce and 2nd).

Please Touch Museum

A visit to most museums can be a frustrating experience for kids. Because children are inquisitive and tactile, they learn best by touching and exploring. Yet all the museum's intriguing objects are roped off, glassed in or protected by signs that say: Please Do Not Touch.

Philadelphia is fortunate to have the Please Touch Museum which offers a wide variety of hands-on exhibits. It is the only museum in the country that is designed specifically for children under eight. It is also ideal for handicapped children under 13.

The enthusiastic volunteers and staff at the Please Touch Museum have set up exhibits that encourage and enhance the imagination. Costumes and masks let children produce their own shows, and uniforms and gear let them pretend they are policemen, firemen, ball players and construction workers. The Tot Spot is a special crawling, climbing and exploring terrain.

Children who love to clown around have the right location—clown alley. It is just part of the Museum's Circus. A performance ring and an animal cage allow kids to become artists or ring masters.

Popular demand has brought back two special exhibits. At the first, the Health Care Center, kids can be nurses, doctors or patients. But most of the patients are dolls. Kids enjoy diagnosing the ills of these docile patients and even performing operations. The second return exhibit area is the Corner Store where fully stocked shelves let children play clerk and customer. They can weigh the produce on the scales and ring up the merchandise on the cash register.

The Please Touch Museum also includes exhibits on science and technology, diverse cultures and the arts. Children can watch and pet small animals in the Nature Center. Working with aides and docents in the Resource Center, youngsters learn how electricity works, what makes an object magnetic or how fossils, shells or stones come to be. The museum staff want their young visitors to gain an appreciation of the folk art of other lands in the Cultural Corner. Although some collectibles are kept behind glass, there are plenty of hands-on exhibits and also costumes to try on. The Virginia Evans Theatre features mime, story telling, puppetry, dance, music and films.

The Please Touch Museum moved into a newly renovated facility in May 1983 in the heart of Philadelphia's cultural community. It is located at 210 North 21st Street, just off the Benjamin Franklin Parkway.

The museum is open Tuesday through Saturday from 10:00 A.M. to 4:30 P.M., and Sunday from 12:30 to 4:30 P.M. Admission is charged. The museum is open to children under eight and their families. Those with handicapped youngsters under 13 should call for information on programs for these children. There must be one adult for every three children. No strollers are permitted on the gallery floor.

Directions: From city center take the Benjamin Franklin Parkway to 21st Street. Turn left onto 21st and proceed one block south to 210 N. 21st Street.

United States Mint

The expression "mint condition" takes on new meaning when you visit the United States Mint at Philadelphia. Watching the shiny coins spill off the assembly line, you find it hard to believe that they are real "money." The large presses stamp out as many as 600 coins per minute. In any group of visitors there's bound to be at least one joker inquiring about free samples.

The U.S. Mint you will tour is the largest of the nation's three operating mints and the fourth to be built in Philadelphia. The original building at 7th and Arch Streets was the first public building erected by the federal government. It was authorized by Congress on April 2, 1792. By the turn of the century only one million coins had been struck. Now, in only one hour, the U.S. Mint can turn out close to 1½ million coins. The mint currently makes five denominations for circulation—pennies, nickels, dimes, quarters and half-dollars. While on your tour you are likely to see at least some part of this money making operation.

The mint covers three city blocks. When you enter, signs direct you upstairs where a welcoming tape introduces you to the Mint and gets you started on your self-guided tour. You'll wind around the gallery which overlooks the work area below, listening to recorded messages and reading signs along the way. Although some of the preliminary work is no longer done at this location, you can watch the process from the blanking press, to the annealing and cleaning lines, through the upsetting mills and then to the actual coining. On the last stop, the coins are inspected, counted and bagged.

Along the gallery walls you see displays on coins and medals minted over the years. There is a collection of military medals, including the Congressional Medal of Honor. Plaques, marble relics and the first coining press from the 1792 mint remind visitors of the three earlier mints.

A bit of minting lore can be gleaned from the display describing the Trial of the Pyx. A pyx is a locked box with a slotted top. It was used to store test coins, which were randomly selected and inserted through the slots. The pyx was opened only in the presence of the assay committee who tested the coins. You'll see an 18th-century Pyx which was given to the U.S. Mint by the Master of the Netherlands Mint.

After you complete your gallery-top survey of operations, you go to see the display of coins and minting equipment in the numismatic room on the mezzanine. Visitors frequently linger over the case filled with gold coins and seem glad to hear that coins and books on coin collecting can be bought at the gift shop. Also, there is a machine adjacent to the gift shop where they can make their own Philadelphia mint medals.

You can visit the United States Mint from 9:00 A.M. to 4:30 P.M. Monday through Friday during January, February and March. During April and again in October, November and December the mint is also open on Saturday. It operates on a seven-day schedule from May through September. You do not need to make reservations and there is no charge to visit.

Directions: From center city take Broad Street north to Market Street. Go around City Hall to Arch Street. The United States Mint is located at 5th and Arch Streets. There is street, metered parking around all sides of the Mint. There is also a municipal parking lot underground between Market and Arch Streets with entrances on 5th and 6th Streets.

Villa Pace

Though it sounds like a Hollywood creation the story of the debut of Rosa Ponselle, though dramatic, is true. She was discovered by the great Caruso while she was singing at the Palace Theater in New York. Accustomed to the vaudeville stage, Rosa Ponselle had no operatic training, and, in fact, had seen only two operas. Her lovely voice, however, so impressed Gatti-Cazazza, General Manager of the Metropolitan Opera, that he immediately engaged her to sing after barely a few months preparation for the premier performance of *La Forza del Destino*. When Miss Ponselle made her debut on November 15, 1918, (with Caruso) a star was born and history was made. She was the first American-born and trained artist to sing a major role at the Metropolitan.

If Rosa Ponselle's life were to be filmed, Hollywood might balk at the idea that she exchanged the drawing rooms of the reigning cinema stars Irene Dunne, Gloria Swanson and Joan Crawford for the relative obscurity of suburban Baltimore, Maryland. But in 1940 Miss Ponselle and her husband, Carle A. Jackson, the son of Baltimore's Mayor Howard Jackson, purchased a 71-acre tract in the Greenspring Valley. She built a beautiful hilltop estate that, through her generosity, is open today to the public as a Museum and Center for the Arts.

As you will discover when you visit, her home resembles the villas of the Tuscany region of Italy. It also reflects her deeply religious nature and her unparalleled operatic career. The estate is called "Villa Pace," from a famous aria in the Verdi opera in which she made her debut. [Pace is pronounced pā ché.]

The house is designed in the shape of a cross, and religious paintings and statues are an integral part of the decor. Also prominently displayed are mementoes from her legendary singing career. As you stand in the entrance foyer you will see the grand staircase, resembling nothing more than the perfect Hollywood set. In fact, Miss Ponselle liked a good entrance and she often greeted her guests from the staircase balcony with an exuberant song. Suspended from the ceiling in the center of a giant sunburst is a torchlight-like chandelier.

On one side of the foyer is the dining room where the massive furniture is all hand-carved. The walnut hand-painted coffered ceiling is a style frequently seen in churches and palaces in Italy.

Across the foyer is Miss Ponselle's favorite room where she did much of her musical entertaining, launching her numerous protégés who went on to earn illustrious careers of their own— Beverly Sills, Sherill Milnes, James Morris and Spiro Malas, to name just a few. RCA once brought an entire recording setup to this Music Room in order to make records with Miss Ponselle. There are beautiful sculptured figurines showing the costumes from some of Rosa Ponselle's best known roles. In addition to the wall-size 16th-century Belgian tapestry there are smaller pieces of needlepoint stitched by Rosa Ponselle while she was on tour. Again the ceiling is hand-painted. This room with its red and gold motif contrasts dramatically with the more somber dining room.

Another theatrical turn in Miss Ponselle's life to be included in any celluloid study centers around the library where on Christmas Eve in 1979 a fire almost destroyed all that Rosa Ponselle had spent years creating. It was a tragedy that her last years were spent trying to repair the ravages of this blaze. The house has indeed risen phoenix-like from the ashes. Her personal suite was badly damaged, but it was returned to its original appearance. The room is a very feminine carnation pink with mirrored and lucite furniture. Draped across a divan is a costume designed for Ponselle by Caramba to wear in *The Love of Three Kings*. It is gorgeous with spun gold threading, but it weighed 30 pounds and was too heavy for her to wear.

The adjoining dressing room would be a great place to raid if you were attending a costume party. Here in lacquered and painted cabinets, drawers and closets are costumes and personal gowns and accessories worn by Miss Ponselle. The room is striking because, like the bathroom, it is in the style of Pompeii. Black enamel fixtures set off the octagonal bathroom.

It is a genuine privilege to view the personal side of a star of the magnitude of Rosa Ponselle; one does not have to be an opera buff to enjoy this glimpse of the lifestyle of an illustrious diva.

Tours are available without appointment on Wednesday, Saturday and Sunday from NOON until 4:00 P.M. Group tours can also be arranged. On Tuesday, Thursday and Friday groups can enjoy an escorted tour and luncheon at Villa Pace. On Sunday afternoons groups can attend concert performances, as well as explore the villa. For information on these tours call (301)486-4616. Admission is charged.

Directions: From Philadelphia take I-95 south to the Baltimore Beltway I-695 and go west towards Towson. Use Exit 23, Jones Falls Road. Drive north on Jones Falls Road to the second traffic light. Turn left onto Greenspring Valley Road. Drive approximately two miles to Villa Pace which is on the left side of the road, directly across from the Villa Julie College.

Walt Whitman House

If your taste leans toward the literary, or someone in the family is studying American literary giants, a destination not to be missed is the Walt Whitman House in Camden, New Jersey, just across the Benjamin Franklin Bridge from Philadelphia.

Aspiring writers find comfort in the fact that Whitman was unable to find a publisher and financed the printing of his own book, *Leaves of Grass*, in 1855. He had previously written sentimental stories and poems for popular magazines and newspapers. Critics heaped abuse on his book, faulting its unconventional metrical style and subject matter. A few, among them Ralph Waldo Emerson, hailed it as the work of a writer with great promise.

Walt Whitman's journey to Camden can be said to have begun in 1862 when he traveled from New York to Virginia to nurse his brother who was wounded at the Battle of Fredericksburg. At

Chatham, a gracious estate overlooking the Rappahannock River, both Walt Whitman and Clara Barton nursed the Civil War wounded in the hastily supplied field hospital. Whitman remained in Washington, D.C., as a volunteer army nurse and later as a clerical worker for the government. His efforts led to fatigue and mental strain and he suffered a stroke in January 1873.

He was not the only family member to suffer ill health at this time. While still recovering from the effects of his stroke Whitman learned that his mother had become seriously ill while visiting his brother, George, in Camden. Whitman traveled to New Jersey to be with them. His mother's death in his presence in May caused him to suffer a serious relapse. This was the bleakest period of his life.

He never really recovered his health, nor did he leave Camden. He stayed with his brother until the 1881 printing of the seventh edition of *Leaves of Grass* unexpectedly proved economically successful. His royalties allowed Whitman to purchase the only house he ever owned. It was at 330, then numbered 328, Mickle Street. This modest two-story frame house that you can tour is filled with the furnishings, mementos and books used by Whitman from 1884 until his death on March 26, 1892.

The Walt Whitman House is open at no charge every day except Monday, Tuesday and holidays. Hours are Wednesday–Friday, 9:00 A.M. to NOON and 1:00 to 6:00 P.M.; Saturday, 10:00 A.M. to NOON and 1:00 to 6:00 P.M.; Sundays 1:00 to 6:00 P.M.

Directions: From Philadelphia take the Benjamin Franklin Bridge to Camden. Go south on Broadway to Cooper Street. Turn right on Cooper Street to 3rd Street. Then make a left on 3rd Street to Mickle. Turn right on Mickle Street to the Walt Whitman House at 330.

Washington National Cathedral and London Brass Rubbing Centre

It is said that when George Washington laid the cornerstone for the national Capitol building he also envisioned the construction of "a great Church for national purposes." Washington and Major Pierre Charles L'Enfant even found the location for the church; they envisioned it set on a ridge high above the newly laid out capital city.

It was to be 100 years before this early dream began to become a reality. It wasn't until 1891 that Charles Carroll Glover, a Washington banker and civic leader, renewed the movement to erect a national cathedral. In 1893 Congress gave the Protestant Episcopal Cathedral Foundation a charter for a "house of prayer for all people." The majestic treasure that is the **Washington National**

Cathedral has been under construction ever since. This staggeringly beautiful edifice will be completed in this decade. Under construction are the twin west towers of the Gothic church, the fifth largest cathedral in the world.

Washington Cathedral is actually named the Cathedral Church of Saint Peter and Saint Paul. The two remaining towers that are being added will be dedicated to the two saints in whose name the cathedral was built. The cathedral is in the 14th-century English Gothic style, and contains—in addition to the main part of the church—nine chapels in which 1,600 services are held each year. Services on weekdays are at 7:30 A.M., NOON, and 4:00 P.M. Sunday they are at 8:00, 9:00, 10:00 and 11:00 A.M., and at 4:00 P.M.

The vast nave of the cathedral is crossed by the transept, forming a cross which soars to more than ten stories at its apex. The towering arches and glowing stained glass windows add to the overall majesty.

All of the stained glass windows have their own themes, and each is a work of art. Visitors particularly enjoy the Space Window which contains an encapsulated sliver of moon rock given to the cathedral by the Apollo 11 astronauts. The two rose windows never fail to awe first-time visitors. In fact, the west rose window is called "the jewel of the cathedral."

Many of the windows honor famous Americans. Over the tomb of Woodrow Wilson are the lancet windows depicting the universal themes of war and peace which were of great concern to Wilson during so much of his presidency. Other windows depict episodes in the lives of Generals Robert E. Lee and Stonewall Jackson.

Statues, too, play homage to pivotal figures in our country's past. In the Washington Bay there is an heroic statue of our first president. Sculptor Lew Lawrie said, "I have tried to show not the soldier, not the President, but the man Washington, coming into Christ Church, Alexandria, pausing a moment before going down the aisle to his pew." Another important American, Abraham Lincoln, is shown as the young man who left Springfield, Illinois.

An interesting story about cathedral statues relates to the commission by the Washington Cathedral for a group of "lifesize" stone statues from an Italian sculptor. When the statues arrived the saints were all a scant five feet, one-inch tall. Confused by this, cathedral officials invited the sculptor to explain this determined consistency. When he arrived the explanation became immediately apparent: the sculptor stood five feet, one-inch tall.

It is not only the large carvings that deserve your attention. Be sure to observe the detail work, both interior and exterior. On the central tower under the balustrade you'll see a frieze of 96 angels, each with its own special countenance. Gargoyles and grotesques have not only an ornamental but a practical purpose. Water runs off their frightful visages, thus protecting the cathedral walls.

Whether you ascend to the heights, or descend to the depths of the church, there are many additional points of interest. From the Pilgrim Observation Gallery (490 feet above sea level) you'll have a stunning panorama of Washington and the countryside to the west of the city. This viewing gallery is just 55 feet lower than the Washington Monument and it offers an entirely different perspective of the city and its outskirts. On a clear day you can see the Catoctin and Blue Ridge Mountains. The gallery is open Monday through Saturday 10:00 A.M. to 3:15 P.M.; Sunday, 12:30 to 3:15 P.M. from mid-March to mid-November. The rest of the year it is open on weekends only for the same hours. A small admission is charged.

After going up to the gallery you can descend to the cathedral's crypt where the **London Brass Rubbing Centre** is located. Since 1970, when the first brass rubbing center opened in London, these specialized centers with their collections of facsimiles of old English church brasses have become increasingly popular. At the Washington Cathedral Centre there are over 70 brasses on display. In just an hour you can do a brass rubbing that can be matted and used as a handsøme wall hanging. Young and old can easily master the art of brass rubbing. Children like the chance to make gifts that can be paid for from their own allowances. (Some of the rubbings cost less than $5.00.) Adults like the more challenging options of black-on-white rubbings, or the sophisticated combinations of silver, gold and bronze wax on a single rubbing.

The brasses vary from saucer-size to life size. Details of medieval garb are clearly seen on these old brasses. The "Lace Lady" is popular because the brocade pattern of her gown is so beautifully captured. Many of the brasses were made to commemorate the Crusader knights. You will observe the difference between the armor worn into battle by knights and that worn for ceremonial occasions.

Brass rubbings make excellent Christmas gifts and imaginative valentines. There is a substantial collection of brasses with a romantic theme, as well as a zodiac series for birthdays. The reasonable cost of brass rubbings make them economical; the effort and thought that goes into choosing just the right brass make them highly personal. The centre is open daily from 9:30 A.M. to 5:00 P.M.

One last treasure of the Washington Cathedral that should not be missed is the Bishop's Garden, modeled on a 12th-century walled garden. As soon as you pass through the 800-year-old Norman arch you'll feel as if you have entered into an earlier epoch. Small Norman courts, a ninth-century herb garden, old sundials, a Wayside Cross and carved stone panels are enhanced by boxwood-flanked paths and ornamental roses. There is an ivy-covered gazebo built from stones taken from an early home of Grover Cleveland. After you descend the Pilgrim Steps you will see an equestrian statue of George Washington. He seems to be looking up towards the great cathedral on the hilltop, contemplating the fulfillment of his dream for a "great Church for national purposes." Thus, you have come full circle on your visit to this all too often-missed national church.

Directions: From Philadelphia take I-95 south to Washington. Take I-495, the Washington Beltway, toward Silver Spring. Take Exit 34, Wisconsin Avenue, south toward Washington. The Washington National Cathedral is at the intersection of Massachusetts Avenue and Wisconsin Avenue, just above Georgetown. Parking is available on the grounds. Telephone (202)537-6200 for information.

___Spring___

Andalusia

If great river houses with colonnaded porticoes suggest only Southern plantations, you have two lovely corrections in store. There are two such mansions you can visit right along the Delaware River in Bucks County, Pennsylvania. They are Pennsbury Manor, (see Autumn section) and Andalusia, perhaps the nation's finest example of 19th-century Greek Revival architecture.

It is not surprising that Andalusia is so highly regarded; it was the work of two of our country's most acclaimed architects. The main house was designed in 1806 by Benjamin Latrobe. He had made a significant contribution to the architecture of both Philadelphia and Washington, D.C., having designed the Bank of Pennsylvania and the Bank of the U.S. which eventually became the Philadelphia Custom House. He designed the South Wing of the Capitol, and after the British burned the Capitol during the War of 1812 he played a major role in its restoration and rebuilding.

Andalusia was built for the Craig family, prominent Philadelphians, who like so many of their contemporaries built their country homes on the cool banks of the Delaware River. Their daughter, Jane Craig, married Nicholas Biddle in 1811. When they acquired the house following Mrs. Craig's death, they hired the noted architect, Thomas U. Walter, to enlarge the house. He designed the Greek Revival additions to the main house. The Gothic "ruin" or grotto along the water's edge and a temple-like billiard room were also added at this time.

These renovations on their summer estate were taking place while Nicholas Biddle, President of the Second Bank of the U.S. and the new nation's most powerful banker, was locked in a struggle for control of the currency with President Andrew Jackson. Their battle was a classic confrontation between two strong-minded men, and it led the country into a depression. Jackson removed Federal deposits from the bank and Biddle retaliated by calling in bank loans. This created a series of bank foreclosures and business failures leading to personal bankruptcy on a wide scale.

Andalusia did not suffer. Still a private home and still owned by the Biddles [seventh generation] it evokes 19th-century elegance without a hint of economic strain. You can easily imagine the Biddles entertaining President John Quincy Adams, Daniel Webster, the Marquis de Lafayette or Joseph Bonaparte, the King of Spain and the brother of Napoleon.

The grounds have been maintained as an English park reflecting the popular landscaping fad of Nicholas Biddle's day. One 20th-century feature is the Green Walk, with its ornamental dwarf evergreens. Nicholas Biddle, in addition to being a financial wizard, was an experimental farmer. Andalusia was the first place in America to stock Guernsey cattle. Like Thomas Jefferson at Monticello, Biddle grew mulberry trees for silkworms.

One may enjoy the beauty within and without at Andalusia by appointment only. The peak visiting months are May and June. Groups of four or more can be accommodated. Admission is charged. To plan a tour call Cliveden estate at (215)848-1777, and they will book your visit to Andalusia.

Directions: From Philadelphia take I-95 north to the Academy Road exit. Bear right to Linden Avenue, which crosses above the railroad tracks and exits on to State Road just south of Grant Avenue. Turn left and take State Road for about two miles to the white gates of Andalusia on your right.

Annapolis

What onetime United States capital has the greatest concentration of 18th-century architecture in the country, and quite possibly a greater number of Georgian-era homes than you'll find in London? The answer is historical, nautical Annapolis, Maryland. Its manageable size—one-third square mile—makes it ideal for a leisurely walking tour.

This city, begun in 1649 just three decades after the Pilgrims landed at Plymouth, is designed around two circles—State and Church. The streets that radiate from these hubs have names redolent of the past. Merrie Old England is recalled by such streets as Duke of Gloucester, Prince George and King George. Then there are those names that suggest our colonial experience: Franklin, St. Mary's, Maryland Avenue and the cryptic Compromise Street. Reflecting nautical Annapolis you will find Fleet and Shipwrights Streets. One thing you should keep in mind is that since the sidewalks were laid so long ago they are decidedly irregular, and comfortable shoes are a must.

Thanks to the efforts of Historic Annapolis, Inc., much of the charm of this historic city has been reclaimed and restored. It is rightfully called "A Museum Without Walls." Probably the society's most dramatic success to date is the restoration of the gracious Palladian-influenced Georgian mansion of William Paca, signer of the Declaration of Independence. Allowed to fall into disrepair while being used as a 37-room adjunct to the Carvel Hotel, the house was slated for demolition when it was fortuitously rescued by Historic Annapolis, Inc. Five years of painstaking historical, architectural and archeological research was undertaken before any restoration work even started. It was decided to restore the mansion to its appearance in the years 1765–1780. The dwelling has also been furnished with a careful regard for historical accuracy, using detailed Paca family inventories. The William Paca House is open Tuesday through Saturday from 10:00 A.M. to 4:00 P.M., and on Sunday from NOON until 4:00 P.M. Entrance is on Prince George Street and admission is charged.

The ambitious Paca project was expanded to include reclamation of the terraced pleasure garden that once graced the old home. The two-acre Paca Garden includes a Chinese trellis-pattern bridge, a two-story pavilion, and a grand allee or walkway flanked by four parterres—rose, holly, boxwood and flower. At the end of the walkway you'll come upon a wilderness garden, a popular 18th-century conceit. The garden has its own Visitors Center where one can obtain horticultural information and a schedule of special events hosted by the William Paca House and Gardens. You can visit the garden Tuesday through Saturday from 10:00 A.M. until 4:00 P.M., and Sunday NOON until 5:00 P.M. Admission is charged. The Paca Garden entrance is at King George and Martin Streets.

In 1760 another Maryland signer of the Declaration of Independence, Samuel Chase, also decided to build a home in Annapolis. Chase was an outspoken advocate of independence, a radical member of the Sons of Liberty. The mayor of Annapolis called him "an inflaming son of discord." Unfortunately, his business sense was not as sharp as his tongue, and financial reverses necessitated the sale of his dreamhouse before it was completed. His name, however, still identifies this handsome house on the corner of King George Street and Maryland Avenue. Although it is now a home for elderly women the Chase Lloyd House is open to the public from 2:00 until 4:00 P.M. daily, except Sunday and Wednesday.

A third restored home directly across the street is the Hammond-Harwood House. This mansion was built by one of America's most famous 18th-century architects, William Buckland. Many authorities feel it is his best work. The delicate carved woodwork is clearly the result of skill and artistry. The house is open daily except Monday. Hours are Tuesday through Saturday from 10:00 A.M. to 5:00 P.M., and Sunday from 2:00 to 5:00 P.M.

From November through May the hours are Tuesday through Saturday, 10:00 A.M. to 4:00 P.M., and Sunday from 1:00 to 4:00 P.M.

While at State Circle you shouldn't miss the Maryland State House, the architectural focal point of the city. A number of significant events occurred here. For nine months in 1783–84 Annapolis was the capital of the new nation. On December 23, 1783, Washington resigned as Commander-in-Chief of the Continental forces. Three weeks later on January 14, 1784, the Continental Congress meeting here ratified the Treaty of Paris, thus officially ending the American Revolution.

Other spots of historical interest containing museum collections are the Victualing Warehouse, Tobacco Prise House and the Colonial Barracks. If you stop at Historic Annapolis, Inc. you can pick up a walking tour map or arrange to take one of the escorted tours.

The sea-going tradition of this port city is indelibly retained because of the presence of the United States Naval Academy. Visitors can explore the Academy "Yard" daily from 9:00 A.M. to 5:00 P.M. You'll enter Gate 3, at the bottom of Maryland Avenue. To your left is Worden Field where on Wednesday afternoons in the spring and fall the Midshipmen hold their dress parades. Your next stop should be the well-marked Naval Museum with its nautical exhibits and historical memorabilia. Finally, don't miss the Naval Academy Chapel. The stained glass windows depict biblical passages pertaining to the sea. In the chapel crypt is the sarcophagus in which John Paul Jones is entombed. The chapel is open daily. Visitors can also attend the 10:30 A.M. service on Sunday mornings and watch the Midshipmen march in, en masse.

If the nautical ambience makes you yearn to take to the sea, you'll find that easy to do at the Annapolis City Dock. The *Harbor Queen* leaves for a 40-minute tour on a regular schedule in the spring, summer and fall. The cruise is not expensive and gives you an interesting view of the Academy, Bay Bridge and harbor area. There is also a 45-minute cruise along Spa Creek and the residential areas of Annapolis on the *Miss Anne*; the 90-minute Severn River and Chesapeake Bay Cruise aboard the *Rebecca Forbush*; and the much longer 7½-hour "Day on the Bay" Cruise to St. Michaels, located on Maryland's Eastern Shore. Whether you're waiting for a boat or just watching the harbor action you can make a quick stop at the restored 1858 Market House and pick up a snack or make up a picnic lunch. A limited number of benches are available at the dock area, and across from the Market House is a kiosk where you can get brochures and maps of Annapolis. The city also boasts a growing number of boutiques and specialty shops, plus an array of taverns, inns and eateries. There is so much to see and do that you'll probably want to return. Check the calendar of events, as Annapolis hosts annual celebrations throughout the year.

Directions: From Philadelphia take I-95 south to the Baltimore Beltway, I-695, and go east over the bridge, rather than straight through the tunnel. From the Baltimore Beltway take Route 2 into Annapolis.

The Barnes Foundation

Fine art and the art of landscaping combine at The Barnes Foundation in Merion Station, Pennsylvania. A visitor will discover a world of beauty both indoors and out.

The art gallery at The Barnes Foundation has one of the world's finest collections of 19th- and 20th-century paintings. You'll see the work of Renoir, Cezanne, Manet, Degas, Seurat, Rousseau, Picasso and Matisse in a staggering array massed from floor to ceiling. Over 150 Renoirs in the collection give a viewer a chance to observe the many facets of the artist's creative career.

Included in the collection are works by the old masters such as Titian, Tintoretto, El Greco, Daumier, Delacroix and Corot and the modern painters Soutine, Modigliani, Klee, Miro, Rouault are also represented. Less familiar works from China, Persia, Greece, Egypt, India and Africa as well as American Indian art and a comprehensive selection of antique furniture and wrought-iron objects round out the collection.

The grounds of The Barnes Foundation leave no doubt that landscaping is also an art. There is a 12-acre arboretum that contains a collection of more than 290 genera of woody plants. Not all the specimens are from the northern hemisphere. Trees from the Orient include the Chinese fringe tree, paperbark maple, Korean boxwood, bee-bee tree, raison tree and beauty bush. The dove, or handkerchief tree is an Oriental species rarely found in this country. The best time to see this tree is in early May when the tree looks like it has a bad cold. Beneath the tree the ground is littered with white Kleenex-like flowers. A visit in late May will let you catch the tree peonies in bloom. During the summer months you can enjoy the Rose and Rock Gardens.

Although a limited number of visitors are admitted on a walk-in basis—100 people on Fridays and Saturdays and 50 on Sunday afternoons—it is best not to rely on this speculative option. Therefore make a reservation by calling (215)667-0290 or by writing The Barnes Foundation, Box 128, Merion Station, PA 19066. You must include the full name and complete address for each person for whom a reservation is requested. No children under 12 are admitted and children 12 to 15 must be accompanied by an adult.

The art collection is open Friday and Saturday from 9:30 A.M. to 4:30 P.M. and Sunday afternoons from 1:00 to 4:30 P.M. It is closed on legal holidays and during July and August. A nominal admission is charged. Visitors must check coats, cameras and even handbags before entering the galleries.

There is no charge to visit the arboretum but again you do have to make an apointment. The arboretum is open year round from 9:30 A.M. until 4:00 P.M. Monday through Saturday and on Sunday from 1:30 to 4:30 P.M.

Directions: From city center take Route 1, the Roosevelt Boulevard across the Schuylkill River. Then go south on Route 1, City Line to Merion. At 54th Street turn right and go up to North Latch's Lane and make a left. The Barnes Foundation is at North Latch's Lane and Lapsley Road.

Brandywine Valley

America's artistic and historic pasts merge in one of the loveliest areas in the Middle Atlantic region, at Chadds Ford, the most famous point on the Brandywine River.

This Pennsylvania valley served as the inspiration linchpin of a world-famous group of American artists who painted in a style called "The Brandywine Tradition." The Howard Pyle School of Art, begun during the summer of 1897 in Philadelphia by illustrator Howard Pyle, soon moved to this valley, spreading the fame of the area and that of the artists. Today in the 19th-century Hoffman grist mill, itself a work of art, you can see the scope of their accomplishments. One of the aims of the Brandywine River Museum has been to amass a collection of three generations of Wyeths. N.C. Wyeth, patriarch of the family, was a book illustrator and artist. Visitors may be surprised to see colorful paintings he did for some of their old favorites like *Treasure Island* and *Kidnapped*. Paintings by his well-known son, Andrew Wyeth, are represented to such an extent that this is the world's largest museum collection of his work. The work of Jamie Wyeth and other members of the Wyeth family is also displayed.

The museum galleries, with their old beamed ceilings and pine floors, include a wide range of work by other American painters, sculptors and illustrators. Visitors climb from floor to floor in a striking glass tower with brick terraces that provide a panoramic view of the beckoning Brandywine River. James Michener, popular novelist, regards the Brandywine River Museum as one of the three best-designed museums in the country. Added in the fall of 1984 is a second tower containing a restaurant, a new art gallery and a new museum gift shop.

The shop sells not only framed and unframed prints and art books, but also books on natural beauty. Available, too, are wild-flower seeds that volunteers of the Brandywine Conservancy have collected from the colorful gardens surrounding the museum. With these seeds you can grow your own bluebells, sundrops, black-eyed susans, New England asters, cardinal flowers and daylilies. Picnic tables line the riverbank. If, as you sit enjoying the river it looks particularly inviting, you can head upstream to Lenape and rent a canoe for yet a different perspective.

The Conservancy also maintains a mile-long nature trail that starts at the museum and wanders along the riverbank. A bonus will be yours if you take a hike in the spring, as there are wildflowers blooming along the woodland trail. Elevated crosswalks help avoid the marshy areas; trail markers eschew the normal Latin botanical names for commonsense pointers. Signs alert you to animal tracks or poisonous plants, like the stinging nettles whose leaf hairs cause a burning sensation when touched.

The trail leads to John Chad's stone farmhouse, open for a small fee Friday through Sunday from Memorial Day to Labor Day, from NOON to 5:00 P.M. On Sunday afternoon bread is baked in the old beehive oven. Chadds Ford was named for this early ferryman and tavernkeeper. The two-story spring house next to Chad's farm was used in the 19th century as a one-room school.

Your next stop should be the tiny village of Chadds Ford known for its crafts. The Chadds Ford Barn Shops, built around an open courtyard, offer an array of artisans. The place for lunch is the Chadds Ford Inn. It has been serving travelers since 1736 when colonists would stop after fording the Brandywine River. Some of Washington's troops also dined here before the Battle of Brandywine. Luncheon fare features fish and veal on weekdays, from 11:30 A.M. to 2:00 P.M. Dinner is served from 5:30 to 10:00 P.M., except on Friday and Saturday evening when times are 5:00 to 10:30 P.M. On Sundays the inn is open from 2:00 until 8:00 P.M. For reservations call (215)388-7361.

Picnickers can lunch either outside at the Brandywine River Museum or at the 50-acre Brandywine Battlefield Park. To put this battlefield into perspective stop first at the Visitors Center to see the 20-minute audio-visual show. General Washington might well have wished for a similar clear picture of what was happening, as he led his men on that fateful September 11, 1777. Washington kept receiving conflicting reports on the position of the 15,000 British soldiers under General Howe. The 14,000-member American force, although lacking in equipment and experience, still managed to retreat rather than surrender—thus saving the Continental force to fight another day. From this encounter the

British moved to their comfortable winter quarters in Phila-delphia, while the Americans endured the privations at Valley Forge.

Within the park the houses used as headquarters by Wash-ington and Lafayette have been restored. The Benjamin Ring farm, General Washington's base, has had to be completely re-built, for the original structure burned to the ground. The farm is again furnished to look as it did in 1777.

The Marquis de Lafayette stayed at the more modest farm of Gideon Gilpin, who later received permission to operate a tavern in recompense for the expenses he incurred during the Battle of Brandywine. At this location there are restored dependencies: a rootcellar, a barn, and a carriage house whose adjacent shed contains an original Conestoga wagon. Few people realize that this wagon was developed in the upper Brandywine valley. An operable forge is demonstrated by a blacksmith in a colonial regimental uniform on weekends when special events are sched-uled.

Brandywine Battlefield Park is open daily 9:00 A.M. to 5:00 P.M., except Mondays and state holidays. The Visitors Center may be visited daily from 9:00 A.M. until 5:00 P.M. On Sunday, how-ever, it doesn't open until NOON. Tours of the historic buildings are given upon request from October to May. On weekends and during the summer months they are open on the same schedule as the Visitors Center. There is a nominal admission charged.

Directions: Chadds Ford is 28 miles from Philadelphia. Take U.S. 1 south and look for signs for all these attractions which are found directly off U.S. 1.

Cape May

What do Robert E. Lee, William Sherman, P.T. Barnum, John Philip Sousa, Abraham Lincoln, James Buchanan, Franklin Pierce, Ulysses S. Grant and William Harrison have in common? Well, only the last five were presidents, so that's not it. Give up? They all enjoyed vacationing at the "nation's oldest seashore resort," Cape May, New Jersey.

The city of Cape May has been designated a National Historic Landmark City, one of only five in the nation. It boasts more late 19th-century houses than any other community in the United States. When Cape May offers visitors gingerbread, it is not cake with whipped cream. Rather, the city invites you to succumb to the delightful variety of the 600 wooden buildings erected from the ashes of the fire which swept through Cape May in 1878. From 1837 to 1901, when Queen Victoria ruled England, was a time of architectural excess. This "Gingerbread Era" was noted for all manner of embellishments—lattice, scroll, fretwork, bargeboard, brackets, dormers and a wide range of colors. The latter eccentricity makes the Pink House at 33 Perry Street a popular favorite with camera buffs.

To get an idea of the diversity of houses to be seen in Cape May you will need a walking tour map. One of your first stops, if you come via the Garden State Parkway, should be at Exit 11 where you'll find the Cape May Chamber of Commerce Information Center, open year-round. Another excellent place to obtain information is at the Cape May Welcome Center at 405 Lafayette Street. The latter has a hot line you can call to obtain information on accommodations, restaurants and marinas. During the summer months there is also a Visitors Information Booth at the Washington Street Mall.

The Welcome Center, with handy adjacent parking lot, is in an 1853 church whose onion-domed tower reflects the Victorian fascination with the Far East. Within the center you'll find rocking chairs so you can relax while you have a cup of tea or coffee and plan your day. If you stop at the Washington Street Mall Information Booth you will learn that many of the guided walking tours begin at this location. These 1½-hour walking tours cover the history and gossip of the old seaside resort. Tours are given Saturday, Sunday and Wednesday at 10:00 A.M.; Monday, Thursday and Friday at 7:00 P.M. Advance reservations are not necessary. Tickets can be purchased immediately prior to the tours.

One house you should certainly plan to see is the Emlen Physick House and Estate at 1048 Washington Street. Forty-five-minute tours cover three of the eight buildings on this eight-acre estate. The Main House was built in 1881 in the stick style. (You'll notice as you view the houses in Cape May that each one has an original, distinctive decor. The status-conscious millionaires who built here wanted their summer homes to be unique.) The Emlen Physick House, designed by Frank Furness, features elaborate chimneys and hooded dormer windows. It is now a museum containing furniture, costumes and toys of the Victorian period.

The Cape May County Art League has its headquarters in the second estate building open for tours. Though horses were once stabled here the Carriage House has beautiful wood paneling and interesting iron grillwork in the stalls. The third building, the Small Barn, houses a growing collection of 19th-century tools.

Tours of the Physick Estate are given in the summer daily from 10:00 A.M. to 4:00 P.M., and from 7:00 to 9:15 P.M. The rest of the year it is open only on weekends. Admission is charged.

If you are in Cape May on a Wednesday evening during the summer you may want to take the "Mansion by Gaslight Tour" starting at the Physick House and covering the interior of four

Victorian homes. Purchase tickets at 7:30 P.M. The houses are open from 8:00 to 10:00 P.M. On Monday evenings there are "Cottage at Twilight Tours" that start at the Dr. Henry Hunt House, 209 Congress Place. Four cottages can be visited from 8:00 to 10:00 P.M.

A special daylight tour is given at 4:30 P.M. on Mondays and Fridays at the Chalfonte Hotel, 301 Howard Street. This hotel has been open every summer since it was built in 1876. Colonel Henry Sawyer, who built it, was a Confederate prisoner during the Civil War and was exchanged for Robert E. Lee, Junior. Tours of this elegant Cape May hotel begin on the porch and end with a glass of wine in the Victorian lounge.

There are many more historical and architectural buildings in Cape May that deserve your attention. One novel way to explore the city is to take either the East or West End Trolley Tours. The former leaves from the Trolley Station on Beach Avenue and Gurney Street daily during the summer, at 45-minute intervals, from 9:00 A.M. to 1:30 P.M., and again from 3:30 to 8:30 P.M. The West End Tour departs from the front of Congress Hall at Perry Street and Congress Place. These tours leave every 45 minutes from 9:00 A.M. to NOON, and 4:00 to 7:00 P.M.

Historians, antique buffs and architecture enthusiasts aren't the only ones who will find plenty to interest them in Cape May. This area also appeals to naturalists, botanists, bird watchers, fishermen and beach buffs.

Cape May is an Auduboner's paradise. Whether you're a novice or an experienced birder you'll want to explore the Stone Harbor Bird Sanctuary and the Cape May Point State Park with its two well-known birding spots.

Stone Harbor Bird Sanctuary is a unique 21-acre heronry with 6,000 birds during the height of the season in May and June. Stop at the pull-off where handy pay-binoculars are available. (It helps if you remember to bring your own.) You'll see a variety of herons: the green heron, Louisiana heron, black-crowned heron and the yellow-crowned heron are just some you might spot. Egrets are also found in abundance. Species include the American or common egret, snowy egret and the cattle egret. The third most common species in the sanctuary is the glossy ibis. Spring is a good time to visit because the birds are nesting and the nestlings are never left unattended. Fall offers its own spectacular vision when thousands of birds take to the air on their annual migration south. The sanctuary is located on Ocean Drive at the southern end of the town of Stone Harbor, 30 miles from the city of Cape May. Stone Harbor is also the location of the Wetlands Institute where you can see a variety of shore and marsh birds.

Cape May Point State Park has observation platforms from which to spot the many unusual birds that frequent this area. There is even a 24-hour bird hot line, (609)884-2626, that will let you know what birds have just been sighted. From September through November hawk watches are kept by the Cape May Bird Observatory; as many as 90,000 migrating birds of prey pass over this area every fall. Within this state park there is a 180-acre Cape May Migratory Bird Sanctuary.

If you are interested in plants you may want to visit the Yearick Hedge Gardens. Started some 50 years ago, these gardens contain over 75 different hedges shaped and trained in patterns to delight young and old. Hedge designs include a baseball game in perpetual progress, Santa Claus, biblical scenes, the Statue of Liberty, animals and ships. You find the hedge gardens by following the signs to the Cape May County Airport and turning south on Breakwater Road at the airport entrance blinker. Small donations are solicited and the gardens are open from 9:00 A.M. to dusk.

Another spot you won't want to miss if you like flowers is the Leaming's Run Botanical Garden, north of Cape May, up Route 9 in Swainton. There are 25 specialty gardens including the English cottage garden, corner shade garden, reflecting garden, celosia garden, serpentine garden, houseplant garden and others featuring one or two colors like the yellow garden, the red and blue garden, the orange garden and the white and red garden. The gardens are open daily from 9:30 A.M. until 5:00 P.M., mid-June to mid-October.

Bennett Bog is another botanical charmer. This wildflower preserve is owned by the New Jersey Audubon Society and is particularly enjoyable in the spring when most of the wildflowers are blooming. Popular with both birds and tourists, the bog is located on Shunpike Road near the County Airport, just three miles north of Cape May city.

If your interest in nature leans towards geology, you will want to try your luck at finding a Cape May "diamond." These semiprecious quartz stones are found only along this part of the Atlantic coast. They range in color and size. The largest ever found weighed almost half a pound and rather resembled a chicken egg; most, however, are the size of walnuts or peas. Cape May "diamonds" can be picked up along the beaches from Higbee's Beach to Cape May Point. One of the best places for spotting these delightful souvenirs is Sunset Beach at the end of Sunset Boulevard, at Cape May Point.

At Sunset Beach you'll also find the sunken remains of the experimental concrete ship, *Atlantis*. This wreck testifies to the failure of the idea of using concrete rather than steel in shipbuilding. Another wreck of an even earlier vessel can also be seen in the area. The British sloop of war, *Martin*, which block-aded Delaware Bay during the War of 1812 was discovered in 1954, beached in the sand. Salvaged and mounted on the beach at the lower end of Lighthouse Avenue for the public to see, the *Martin* again stands watch over the bay.

Fishing and crabbing are also popular Cape May activities. Of course the fine white sandy beach is the primary reason visitors have been coming to Cape May for so many years.

As you can see, Cape May offers too much to do and see in one day. But with a driving time of only two hours from Phila-delphia, you can return many times to sample the gingerbread city.

Directions: From Philadelphia take I-95 south to I-295 and cross the Delaware Memorial Bridge. Take Route 40 south to the Garden State Parkway. Follow the parkway south to Cape May, New Jersey.

Chestertown

On May 23, 1774, the irate citizens of Chestertown, Maryland, were riled up over the unjustly high tea tax imposed by the British. In sympathy with their Boston compatriots, they marched down to the Chester River, boarded the brigantine *Geddes*, and dumped the cargo of tea—as well as some of the crew members—into the water.

Surprisingly, more than 200 years later they're still at it. Each year on Memorial Day weekend they hold the Chestertown Tea Party Festival. The highlight of the festival is the reenactment of the historic tea party. Music, crafts, historic walking tours, a sound and light show and dancing in the street all add to the fun of this special event.

Although this May weekend is undoubtedly the best time to visit Chestertown, the town merits attention on its own. You will discover that Chestertown is as rich in charm as it is in history. You can obtain a "Walking Tour of Old Chester Town" brochure from the Kent County Chamber of Commerce located in the Chestertown Municipal Building on South Main Street. This brochure includes a map and information on the many lovely Georgian and Federal houses constructed in pre-Revolutionary times by the town's rich merchants. Most of them are not open to the public. On Saturday afternoons from May through October, from 1:00 to 4:00 P.M., you can, however, tour the Geddes-Piper House at 101 Church Street. This 3½ story, 18th-century house was the home of William Geddes, owner of the brigantine whose cargo was so unceremoniously offloaded. It is therefore appropri-ate that on display in this carefully restored and decorated home is Mr. Geddes's collection of teapots.

Operating on the same schedule is the Buck-Bacchus Store Museum. During the 18th century this was both a store and residence. It has been restored and now includes an 18th-century living area and a 19th-century general store.

If you want to sustain the mood of Chestertown, why not stop in at the White Swan Tavern for a cup of tea? This popular tavern where George Washington often stayed is now a bed and breakfast inn. Tea is served Monday through Thursday, from 3:00 to 5:00 P.M. Tours of the tavern are conducted at 2:00 P.M. If you are interested in overnight accommodations call (301)778-2300. You might want to consider the third Saturday in September, as that is when the annual Candlelight Walking Tour takes place.

After exploring this quaint old town you may want to stop at one or both of the nearby natural sites. Owned and operated by the Remington Arms Company, Inc., Remington Farms is a 3,000-acre wildlife research and demonstration area. There is a waterfowl sanctuary and a wildlife habitat area. The waterfowl sanctuary is open year-round, from dawn to dusk. Your best chances of seeing a wide range of ducks and geese is from October through March. (Remember your binoculars.) Part of the acreage is farmed and the corn is used to help feed the waterfowl that winter here. Within the wildlife habitat area you may see deer, red foxes, rabbits, and both game and songbirds. This area is closed for the hunting season from the middle of October through January.

Also nearby is the 2,300-acre Eastern Neck Wildlife Refuge. From the observation platform you can see the thousands of Canadian geese that stop here on their migratory flights. Like Remington Farms there is both a marshland area and a woodland habitat. A well-marked nature trail through the woods is available, if you have time for a hike. There is no charge at Eastern Neck or Remington Farms.

Directions: From Philadelphia take I-95 south past Wilmington and then continue south on Route 301. Turn right on Route 291 for Chestertown. At Chestertown turn left on Route 20 and proceed to Remington Farms, the tour route will be well marked. For Eastern Neck continue south via Route 20 to Rock Hall and then go south on Route 445 to the refuge.

Cliveden and Upsala

A painting by E. L. Hunt of the Battle of Germantown hangs at **Cliveden** on the very same walls that still bear traces of the perilous moments, in 1777, when the Americans tried valiantly to breach the sturdy stones and defeat the British. You will see reminders of this historic October 4th confrontation when you tour Cliveden (pronounced cliv-den) and Upsala. They face each other across this old battleground.

Benjamin Chew, who built Cliveden ten years earlier and still owned it, was being held under arrest in New Jersey because of his suspected British sympathies. As Chief Justice of Pennsylvania, he had scrupulously endeavored to uphold the law—British law. This led to his arrest in the summer of 1777 and he did not see his war-ravaged house until the following spring. It was "an absolute wreck, and materials not to be had to keep out the weather." Chew's despair was all the deeper because he had taken such an active role in the designing of his countryseat. It had taken four years to build the mid-Georgian 2½ story house. Particularly pleasing to him were the five urns that adorn the roof, each on its own ornamented pedestal.

Another Henry painting that you will see when you tour Cliveden is of the Lafayette Reception held in 1824 when the Marquis de Lafayette returned to America to celebrate the Revolutionary victories. The painting hangs in the front entrance hall and replicates the two portraits and the Tuscan columns that are still there.

In Mrs. Chew's sitting room you will see a silhouette of Benjamin Chew. It is the only likeness that exists because, although he was read out of the Quaker meeting for defending his Maryland home, he did continue to follow Quaker beliefs which meant that he would never sit for a portrait. One portrait was made later from the silhouette, however, and it hangs in the parlor. While observing the lavish furnishings look for the names of earlier guests to Cliveden. Their names are not in a guest book but are inscribed on the window panes with a diamond point stylus. The ornate parlor mirrors were used to decorate the tent walls when General Howe's junior officers gave an elaborate party, or *fête champetre*, in his honor before his return to England.

As you move to the second floor you will pass the window that once looked out on the rear court. An 1856 addition to the main house has been artistically camouflaged so that visitors do not lose the original ambience. Upstairs the 13½-foot-high ceilings reminds us of the lavish construction associated with an earlier era. Of course, nothing smaller could accommodate the Philadelphia mahogany high-post bed made between 1760 and 1790.

Antique lovers and history buffs will appreciate the many fine pieces of family heirlooms. Cliveden, with the exception of an 18-year period after the Revolution during which it was owned by a wealthy Irish merchant, has always belonged to the Chew family. It was acquired by the National Trust for Historic Preservation from the Chew family in 1972.

You can visit the six-acre Cliveden estate at 6401 Germantown Avenue from April through December on Tuesday through Saturday from 10:00 A.M. until 4:00 P.M. The tours are given on the hour with the last tour at 3:00 P.M. Sunday hours are 1:30 to 4:30 P.M. Admission is charged.

If you visit Cliveden on Tuesday or Thursday you can also visit **Upsala** across the road. It is open from 1:00 to 4:00 P.M. This too, although built 30 years later, was in the style of an English countryseat. In 1798 on 5½ acres that had already been in the family for four generations, John Johnson built this Federal mansion. It is not as grand as Cliveden but there are a number of similarities. Both are 2½ story dwellings with dormer windows and a central door which is balanced by two windows.

The interior furnishings will bring back the days of elegant colonial entertaining. The library is one of the most attractive rooms with its unusual color scheme of peach, mustard, maroon and white. Upsala has never been altered and has all the original woodwork and mantels. Many fine Philadelphia pieces adorn this gracious old house.

Together Cliveden and Upsala open windows on fine living and the impeccable taste of the past. They are just two reasons why Germantown is considered Philadelphia's best kept secret. While you are in the area, check out the other Germantown attractions included in this book: the Ebenezer Maxwell House, Germantown Historical Society Museum, Wyck and the Deshler-Morris House.

Directions: From center city take East River Drive which becomes Wissahickon Drive. Take this to Lincoln Drive. Continue on Lincoln Drive through three traffic lights to Johnson Street. Make a right on Johnson Street to Germantown Avenue. Turn left on Germantown Avenue and you will see the grounds of Cliveden on your right and Upsala directly across the street.

The Ebenezer Maxwell Mansion

The concept of commuting can be traced to the advent of rapid transportation. By the 1850s one of America's earliest commuter railroad lines had linked downtown Philadelphia with rural Germantown and what had been primarily a summer retreat became a year-round green suburb.

One of the prosperous Philadelphia businessmen who built in Germantown was Ebenezer Maxwell. His Norman Gothic villa would make a perfect set for the vintage television series, "The Adams Family." The stone house is built of local Wissahickon schist and red sandstone. Following a popular building practice of that day, coal dust was added to darken the mortar; and sand was added to the paint to give texture to the wooden window frames. A gingerbread tower soars over elaborate Flemish cornices, a patterned mansard roof and seven different shapes of windows, many of them set with stained glass.

When the Maxwell house was finished in 1859 it incorporated all the latest conveniences—running water, gas lights, central hot air heating and even vents to allow the vitiated (used or polluted) air to escape. These new-fangled ideas were viewed with caution. That explains why the children's room was heated by a fireplace to avoid any possible ill effects of the new heating system. The "modern" bathroom was put in the servants wing because it too was viewed with skepticism.

New decorating techniques allowed the middle class Maxwells to imitate the homes of the wealthy. Thus you'll see that the fireplace has marbleized slate and even the wallpaper is made to look like marble. The linoleum entrance way was designed to resemble tile, and the wood-graining also creates a monied appearance.

It is hard to imagine how anyone could have considered demolishing this wonderful period piece, but it came close to the wrecker's ball. It is fortunate that it was saved because the Maxwell mansion is the only Victorian house museum in the Philadelphia area.

Two time periods are reflected in the interior. The first floor furnishings are of the 1850s and 1860s, the second floor, the 1870s and '80s. The Maxwells lived here fewer than three years before moving to a house they had built next door. The rooms appear to be wrapped in brocades, velvets and feathers. The beds are massive and elaborately carved. Ceilings, walls and doors that were painted in intricate patterns in the 1870s are being carefully restored. From the entrance hall you can see three different floor patterns. The decor very nearly assaults the senses.

Though it must have been difficult to live in such a busy environment, it's fascinating to visit. Even the garden continues the dual ambience achieved by the interior. The front yard captures the landscaping of the early 1850s while the ribbon garden and hemlock arch at the back represent the 1880s. The yard is still enclosed by the original iron fence.

While you are at the Ebenezer Maxwell Mansion pick up a walking tour map for "Maxwell's Neighbors—The Houses, The Gardens and the People of West Tulcehocken Street and West Walnut Lane." A six-block walk will introduce you to some 40 interesting structures.

You can visit the Ebenezer Maxwell Mansion on Wednesday, Friday or Saturday from 11:00 A.M. until 4:00 P.M. and on Sunday from 1:00 to 5:00 P.M., April through December. Admission is charged.

Directions: From center city take Broad Street, Route 611 north to Route 1, Roosevelt Boulevard. Go left for just a short way to Route 422, Germantown Avenue. Follow Germantown Avenue into Germantown proper and then go left on Tulpechocken Street to the Mansion. You can also take the Schuylkill Expressway, Route 76, west to the Lincoln Drive exit. Follow Lincoln Drive to Harvey Street. Turn right on Harvey Street. Follow Harvey to Greene Street and turn left. The Maxwell Mansion is on the corner at 200 West Tulpechocken Street.

The Franklin Mint Museum

It is frequently assumed that the **Franklin Mint Museum** is an adjunct of the U.S. Mint in downtown Philadelphia. People pass it along Route 1 and think it has nothing to offer but walls of coins and medals. Nothing could be farther from the truth. This is a great place for collectors—of just about anything—to visit. It is actually the world's largest private mint. It issues commemorative coins, medals, first editions and an impressive array of artworks suitable for display.

Anyone who has read the Sunday supplement ads will recognize many of the porcelain and pewter plates, figurines, bells, pillboxes and cups and saucers on display in this artistic museum. The pieces are arranged according to their subjects. The first grouping focuses on birds and flowers. As you peruse these lovely creations you will hear in the background the twittering and chirping of birds. The displays create a flower bower with the colorful blossoms appearing on porcelain plates, cups and saucers, thimbles, bells and pillboxes. Three dimensional boughs support birds and flowers. Butterflies are also abundantly depicted. Vivid enameled flower baskets designed by Gloria Vanderbilt capture the distinctive appeal of each season.

Since this museum is in the Brandywine Valley it is not surprising to see the work of the multi-talented Wyeths. A handsome porcelain bowl decorated with apple blossoms was created by Andrew Wyeth.

The next grouping depicts children. While you hear young voices singing you can trace, from rough sketch to finished figure, the creation of one of the porcelain figures done by Carol Lawson for the U. N.'s International Year of the Child. The complete collection of figurines showing children from around the world is in a nearby showcase. You'll also see plates illustrating Grimm's fairy tales and the stories of Hans Christian Anderson. White bisque Norman Rockwell children seem to step from·the pages of his *Saturday Evening Post* covers.

To the refrains of old western ballads you'll view pewter cowboys and Indians. Some depict the violent action of the Wild West. A pewter overland stage coach holdup would certainly be a striking coffee table center piece. In line with the diverse nature of the Franklin Mint Museum there is also a gun collection. One model is an authentic reproduction of Wyatt Earp's 44 calibre six-shooter which he used in the gunfight at O.K. Corral.

In this eclectic museum you can also see a selection of signed editions from the Franklin library, items from the Franklin historic furniture display and first edition stamps.

A darkened mirror-accented room provides the perfect setting for the finely etched crystal pieces. A collection of aquatic designs embodies the natural beauty of the undersea world associated with Jacques Cousteau. Others reflect the world of ballet including the lovely wine glass, Pavlova, created by Igor Carl Fabergé. Another beautiful piece depicts a skater on a crystal lake.

After passing through a room devoted entirely to miniatures you'll see the coins, ingots and medals. A theater presentation will acquaint you with the technique used by the skilled artisans to create the coins and medals so closely associated with the Franklin Mint. The art of minting is described from the artist's first sketch to the finished product. At the Franklin Mint Gallery you can purchase many of the pieces you've seen at the museum.

The Franklin Mint Museum is open Tuesday through Saturday from 9:30 A.M. until 4:30 P.M. Sunday hours are 1:00 to 4:30 P.M. It is closed on Mondays and major holidays.

While in the area you may want to stop at **Linvilla Orchards**, one of the largest working farms in the Philadelphia area. In the 1889 octagonal barn you will find seasonal fruits and vegetables on sale plus a variety of baked goods, preserves, cider, candy, ice cream, honey and decorations for your home. If you want to get in on the action you can pick the strawberries, raspberries and peaches yourself. In the fall you can find the perfect pumpkin in Linvilla's Pumpkinland. Family fun on this farm can include fall weekend hayrides and a chance for children to climb into the loft and jump into the soft hay or to feed the animals. A picnic area is available if the pastries and fruit prove irresistible.

Linvilla Orchards at 137 W. Knowlton Road in Media is open in the spring, summer and fall. May through July, the hours are Tuesday through Sunday 10:00 A.M. to 6:00 P.M. Closed on Monday. During September and October it is open Saturday through Wednesday from 10:00 A.M. to 6:00 P.M. and on Thursday and Friday until 8:00 P.M. During August, November and December the farm is open daily from 10:00 A.M. until 6:00 P.M. For additional information call (215)876-7116.

Directions: From Philadelphia take I-95 south to Chester and exit on Route 352. Go north on Route 352 to Knowlton Road and make a left on W. Knowlton. You will see Linvilla Orchards on the right side after about one-half mile. The Franklin Mint Museum can be reached by continuing up Route 352 to Route 1, the Baltimore Pike. Head south on Route 1 and the museum will be on your left after a few miles.

Gettysburg National Military Park and Eisenhower National Historic Site

History has been made at Gettysburg—and notable historic figures have traveled to this rural Pennsylvania town to reflect on that past. You should do likewise!

The conflict between the Southern forces under General Robert E. Lee, and the Northern Army of the Potomac under General George Meade cost more American lives than any other single battle in our history. It proved to be the turning point of the Civil War.

Gettysburg National Military Park has been called the world's largest outdoor open-air museum. An estimated 2,500 markers and monuments tell the story of the three tumultuous days in July 1863. Obviously, the scope of this historic park is daunting. It is important to understand the significance of what you will see. It isn't enough just to trudge along the fields and woodlands of Gettysburg. You need to people the countryside with the young men and their gallant leaders who fought here. An electric map orientation program at the Gettysburg National Military Park Visitor Center will provide the background you need. Augment the map program with the free movie shown at the adjacent Cyclorama Center. For a small admission fee you can also see the sound and light program in the circular auditorium built to display the 356-foot cyclorama painted in 1881 by Paul Philoppoteaux. This is one of only three of these once-popular cycloramas still to be seen in the United States.

Once you have some background information you can obtain park maps with a well-marked auto tour of the battlefield, which will take between two and three hours to complete. You should try to explore at least one of the foot trails, as you will get a more personal feeling if you literally follow in the footsteps of the soldiers who fought and fell here. Park roads (including bicycle and horse trails) are open from 6:00 A.M. until 10:00 P.M. The Visitor Center is open 8:00 A.M. to 5:00 P.M.; the Cyclorama, from 8:30 A.M. until 5:00 P.M.

Just a few short months after the July encounter, on November 19, 1863, Abraham Lincoln came to Gettysburg for the dedication of the Soldier's National Cemetery. Lincoln's brief two-minute address after the two-hour main speech is the perfect example of "less is more." His simple message of national purpose still speaks to the heart of our country's enduring pride. The Soldier's National Monument was the first of many memorials to be built at Gettysburg; it stands near the spot where Lincoln stood to deliver the Gettysburg Address.

Another American president, Franklin Delano Roosevelt, was on hand in 1938 for the 75th anniversary of the Battle of Gettysburg, to dedicate the Eternal Light Peace Memorial.

This land, once so battle-scarred and bloodied, was quiet, rolling farmland both before and after the battle. Gettysburg still provides a look at farms that represent the now and the then; there are 1860s farms and one that reflects a very special family of the 1950s. During the summer months, one of these "then"farms—Granite Farm—is open to the public. There, park rangers discuss with visitors the rigors of rural 19th-century life and the effects of the war on civilians. You can visit Granite Farm from mid-June until Labor Day.

Some of the famous visitors who have trooped to Gettysburg, Pennsylvania, within more recent times were guests at the farmhouse of Dwight and Mamie Eisenhower, now open as the **Eisenhower National Historic Site**. The farm, built in the 1840s, was acquired by the Eisenhowers while Ike was president of Columbia University. Later, when Eisenhower became NATO Commander and spent two years in Paris, Mamie spent her time planning the major reconstruction of their Gettysburg farm. The modified Georgian farmhouse, with 18 rooms and eight baths, became their weekend retreat and sometime-White House when Mr. Eisenhower was President. When he left office on January 20, 1961, he retired to this haven and spent his last years here.

One of the nice things about visiting this farm is that it really does seem like a home. You'll get no museum feeling when you tour. Homey touches abound—like Ike's faded blue rocker and much-used easel. There are seven of his oil studies on an upstairs wall. Mamie, too, had her pictures: family photographic portraits are framed and massed on the grand piano, indicating her close family ties. The open door in Mamie's pink and green bedroom and the General's robe and slippers on the bed where he often napped give an illusion that the Eisenhowers have just stepped out and will soon be coming home.

One can imagine such distinguished guests as Winston Churchill, Charles de Gaulle, Nikita Khrushchev and Jawaharlal Nehru getting a genuine look at real life in America while visiting the Eisenhowers at Gettysburg. A warm and friendly atmosphere still makes itself felt here.

Tickets to the farm can be obtained at the Eisenhower Information Center, located in the Gettysburg National Military Park Visitor Center. Buses transport visitors from the center to the farm for a nominal fee. The lack of on-site parking and the restrictions on crowds within the farm necessitate obtaining tickets early in the day to reserve a tour.

Directions: From Philadelphia take Route 202 to the Lincoln Highway, Route 30. Go west on Route 30 past Lancaster and York to Gettysburg. Route 30 will become York Street. Continue on it one block past Lincoln Square and then turn left on Route 134 south, which is called South Washington Street. This becomes Taneytown Road and the Visitor Center will be on your right.

The Grange

During The Grange's 300-year-old history it has had at least ten owners, three names and numerous architectural revisions. It is this layering effect that makes the place so interesting historically, architecturally and horticulturally.

The present estate is just a small part of the 500 acres claimed in 1682 by Henry Lewis, a Welsh Quaker and one of the first three European settlers in this area. He named his new home after the area he left in Wales—Maen Coch—which is Welsh for Redstone. It is not his house that endures but a later one built by his son Henry Lewis, Jr., circa 1700. The son's house forms the drawing room of The Grange and the rooms directly above. The part that is now the library and stair hall were added in about 1730.

In 1750 the house acquired a new owner, a new name and a new look. Captain John Wilcox named it Clifton Hall and made the house more formal by adding a large room for entertaining. After only 11 years he sold out to Charles Cruikshank, a Scot. Cruikshank did not support the American Revolution, and left the country when the colonists won the war. He sold the estate in 1782 to his daughter's husband, John Ross. Ross, a major financier of the patriot's cause, must have been unpopular with the father-in-law. He procured clothes, arms and gunpowder for the army. Like so many who supported the impecunious Continental Army he often paid out of his own pocket. When Ross purchased the Cruikshank estate, he renamed it The Grange after Lafayette's French home.

Lafayette, Washington and many members of his cabinet enjoyed the hospitality of John Ross. Entries in George Washington's diary refer to such visits as the one on June 17, 1787: "Went to church.-After wch rid 8 miles into the country and dined with Mr. Ross in Chester County. Retd. to town about dusk."

Today when you visit you see as well as the house, the dependencies, or outbuildings, so essential to an 18th- and 19th-century gentleman's country home and grounds. Ten acres of woodland contain many trees of record size. One of the last owners of The Grange, Benjamin R. Hoffman of Philadelphia, greatly enhanced the gardens. The terraced gardens are not to be missed. Blooming from early spring to late fall these boxwood-enclosed beds offer nearly continuous color. Closest to the mansion are a rose garden, an herbal bed with more than 50 different herbs and an old-fashioned knot garden. In the spring daffodils and narcissus brighten the woodland trails.

The English Gothic appearance of the house is the result of alterations made from 1850 to 1863. It is this period that is reflected in the interior furnishings.

You can enjoy guided tours of the mansion, gardens, outbuildings and woodlands from April through October on Saturday and Sunday from 1:00 to 4:00 P.M. You may make an appointment to tour at other times throughout the year by calling (215)446-4958. Admission is charged. Special evening tour hours are scheduled during the summer and during the first two weeks of December.

Directions: From center city take Broad Street or the Schuylkill Expressway north to U.S. 1. Take U.S. 1 south about four miles to Earlington Road and turn right. Following Grange signs from Earlington, turn right on Bennington Road, then left on Myrtle Avenue. Make a right into the Grange entrance at Warwick Road next to St. James Church, which was once the Grange barn.

Green Hills Farm

In *My Several Worlds* Pearl Buck wrote, "I decided on a region where the landscapes were varied, where farm and industry lived side by side, where sea was near at hand, mountains not far away, and city and countryside were not enemies." It was her Bucks County home she was describing, but it could easily have been the "good earth" of China where she spent her early years.

Pearl Buck throughout her life served as a bridge between East and West. They meet at her homey Pennsylvania farm. Pearl Buck and her second husband, publisher Richard Walsh, purchased this 1835 farmhouse with its dependencies and 48 acres of land during the Depression for $4,100. Pearl Buck legally adopted seven children and cared for many more either at her home or through her foundation for needy children. She still found time to write more than 100 novels, children's books and non-fictional works at Green Hills Farms.

A tour of this National Historic Landmark begins appropriately in the oversize kitchen of the rambling old house. The kitchen was added by Miss Buck to accommodate her large brood. Like so much of the house it is a blend of the old and the new. Modern appliances share space with an old Franklin stove, and the large table was her husband's desk when he was at John Day Publishing Company.

The original kitchen is now the dining room. It's childproof brick floors were appreciated by Miss Buck who didn't worry about children's spills. The antique Pembroke table that Miss Buck used for morning and midday meals is perfectly at home amid the Chinese porcelains, paintings and pewter that adorn the room.

Four rooms were combined to form the expansive living room and entrance way. The elements that made this farmhouse so appealing to Miss Buck—the stone walls and sturdy wood—are much in evidence in this striking living area. The huge stone fireplace and hand-hewn ceiling beams are balanced, not in size but in eye-appeal, by the artistic treasures of the East. On the console table you'll see the small figure of a 500-year-old Buddha. Another treasure is the Tibetan embroidered wall hanging that was a gift from the Dalai Lama.

From the living room the tour goes upstairs to Miss Buck's bedroom which has not one but two fireplaces. In an anteroom, which has become known as the Treasure Room, glass cases hold the carved sea-green celadon, rare fans, inlaid chests and the lovely silk ceremonial robes that she collected in China.

In the main library downstairs is the box-like desk Miss Buck used in China when she wrote *The Good Earth*, her Pulitzer Prize winning novel. The Chinese wooden chair looks more decorative than comfortable; its unyielding lines were good "for discipline," according to Pearl Buck. Both the library and the adjacent reading room are filled with books. Guides will tell you that no one, not even Miss Buck, was permitted to take books out of the reading room.

Pearl Buck did not use the library as her office; she worked in the attached cottage added in 1938 along with the country kitchen. Here you'll see the typewriter desks she used during 38 prolific years of writing at the farm, also some of her own sculptures. She sculpted and also painted in the cottage loft.

Pearl Buck died at Green Hills on March 6, 1973. Her humanitarian work lives on from the headquarters of the Pearl S. Buck Foundation which is located in the old 1827 red barn at Green Hills Farm. From here Amerasian children in six Asian countries are supported in keeping with the work Miss Buck began when she founded Welcome House in 1949.

You can tour Green Hills Farm year-round on Monday through Friday at 10:30 A.M. and 2:00 P.M. From May through September tours are also given on Sunday afternoons at 1:30 and 2:30 P.M. The grounds are open daily until 5:00 P.M. Picnic tables are available. Admission is charged.

Directions: From center city take Broad Street, Route 611, north to Doylestown Bypass. Exit at Dublin. Turn left to Route 313. Continue on Route 313 to the second traffic light in the center of Dublin. Turn left at the light onto Maple Avenue. This changes to Dublin Road after leaving the boro limits. Green Hills Farm is one mile from the intersection on the right.

John Bartram's House and Gardens

If you have trouble rounding up the family for an outing to a spot just a few miles from your home, you can appreciate the extent of John Bartram's enthusiasm for the natural world. In the days when travel was far more difficult than it is now he would eagerly pack up and undertake an arduous trip of a hundred miles to learn more about a new plant discovery.

John Bartram's interest in botany began as a young boy. Though he was a farmer, he would frequently leave his fields to explore the still-virgin North American continent. In 1743, just 13 years after he had settled at his Kinsessing farm on the Schuylkill River, Bartram undertook a journey to visit the Indian tribes of the League of Six Nations and explore the wilderness north to Lake Ontario in Canada. He published an account of this trip in 1751. In 1769 a companion volume revealed his observations on a later tour of Georgia and eastern Florida.

From all his trips John Bartram returned to his Pennsylvania farm with cuttings, seeds and roots. He created what has become America's oldest botanic garden still in existence. Naturalists and botanists in London were keenly interested in obtaining seeds and roots from the New World. Peter Collinson, a London wool merchant, engaged Bartram as a plant collector and for 35 years they corresponded. Bartram shipped many of his discoveries to England; he is credited there with introducing more than 200 North American plants. This is certainly a significant contribution when you realize that in 1753 there were only 889 known species from the entire North American continent. Bartram's fame spread, and in 1765 King George III named him botanist to the king for the American colonies.

It is fortunate that two of Bartram's 11 children, William and John, Jr., were also interested in botany. William, called by his father "my little botanist," followed in his father's footsteps, continuing the botanical explorations and bringing specimens back to the Pennsylvania garden. John, Jr. inherited the garden from his father and together with William started a nursery and published the first seed plant catalog. It was their joint efforts that helped preserve this garden so that today we are able to enjoy it just as George Washington, Thomas Jefferson and Benjamin Franklin once did. Although Washington did comment that the garden looked like it was "jumbled around in heaps," Carl Linnaeus; noted Swedish scientist, called the senior Bartram "the greatest natural botanist in the world."

In addition to exploring the garden you can also tour the 18th-century stone farmhouse. John Bartram made a number of changes to this already old farm when he acquired it in 1728. As an amateur architect he added a stone pillared porch and carved stone window frames. From the rocky river bank he also cut a stone cider mill and press.

The garden is open daily during daylight hours, year-round. The house is open from April through October on Tuesday through Saturday from 10:00 A.M. to 4:00 P.M.; from November to

March it is open only Tuesday through Friday. There is no charge to see the garden, but you may want to pay the nominal fee for a self-guiding tour map. There is a small admission charged for the house tour.

Directions: From downtown Philadelphia take Island Avenue to Lindbergh Boulevard. Travel north on Lindbergh to 54th Street. The John Bartram House and Gardens are at 54th Street and Lindbergh Boulevard.

Longwood Gardens

If you stopped visitors randomly as they left Longwood Gardens you would undoubtedly find the same comments repeated again and again. Most first-time visitors are amazed to discover such a perfectly splendid garden. They are delighted it is located where it is, rather than in some far-distant country, and they vow to come back again. Indeed, Longwood seems to induce an evangelical fervor; visitors want to tell everybody they know about the wonder of Longwood.

Longwood Gardens should be visited during every season to appreciate fully the scope and beauty of its many attractions. A visit during the harsh winter months brings perhaps the most solace. Even if you close your eyes and don't partake of the visual splendor in the four-acre conservatory the smell of the delicate blossoms is worth the trip. Suddenly, it is springtime and the snow and slush that may be as near as the other side of the door seem far away. January's display, featuring hyacinths and daffodils, creates the illusion of April in January. The conservatory's great height is utilized by having the large columns entwined with creeping fig and bougainvillea. Hanging plant chandeliers pick up the flower motif of the display. It provides a breathtaking vista and cameras are always much in use.

Year-round favorites can also be enjoyed in this glassed-in garden. There is a special orchid room where the display is changed every week. Rare specimens are shown in an amazing array seldom duplicated, and certainly not surpassed anywhere. The same can be said for the rose collection where row after row of your favorite summer bloomers bask in the winter sun. The conservatory has some unusual plants like the insect-eating plant, the air plant and a 400-year-old bonsai. Other areas feature succulents, house plants, and plants of economic value such as cocoa, vanilla and bananas.

If winter delights visitors by its contrasts, spring at Longwood Gardens is overwhelming because of the sheer scope, size and variety of flowers on display. If you were forced to pick just one season in which to visit it would have to be during April or May, when both indoors and outdoors are a riot of color.

Along extended walkways there are rows of flower gardens with spring bulbs. A wisteria-topped arbor is particularly appealing in late spring. The walkway leads to the lake where blossom-laden trees are reflected in the still surface of the water. A romantic gazebo provides a perfect focal point for photographers. A wooded trail flanked by azaleas and rhododendron skirts the lake.

At the far end of the lake there is a very special treat—the Italian Water Gardens. An overlook is flanked by a water staircase leading to this garden designed to resemble the one at the Villa Gamberaia in Florence, Italy. Blue-tiled pools have parallel sets of fountains. This charming conceit is not the only fountain area at Longwood.

Directly in front of the conservatory is the main fountain display where you will see dozens of large fountain groups. It is during summer that this fountain area can be enjoyed to its fullest. On Tuesday, Thursday and Saturday evenings there is an illuminated fountain program. It's well worth staying late to catch a performance, for this aquatic extravaganza delights both young and old. The Terrace Restaurant, an indoor-outdoor eatery, stays open on evenings when performances are scheduled. Other shows are presented at the Open Air Theater, one of the few theaters anywhere to boast a six-foot-high water curtain. Here, too, there are colored fountains used to great effect during many of the musical concerts.

Roses, wildflowers, vegetables and waterlilies are the seasonal pick of the summer months. There are garden walkways with trellised climbing roses, and many of the beds are planned around the rose bushes. Visual delights are also plentiful in the hillside garden leading to the chime tower. Along the banks of a sparkling waterfall ferns grow in profusion. This is another scenic spot from which to take photographs of Longwood.

A special feature much visited in summer is the Idea Garden. Here you will see an array of perennials, annuals, vegetables, herbs and fruits you may want to add to your own yard. Like many of the specimens grown at Longwood these could actually discourage some amateur gardeners because everything at Longwood grows bigger and better. Savoy cabbages are bigger than bowling balls; the conservatory delphiniums which come in a staggering assortment of colors are so tall they dwarf most visitors; and the waterlilies have pads that are the size of a large truck tire and can support a hundred pounds.

Many hobbyists get quite green with envy when they see the November conservatory display of giant chrysanthemums. The enormous mums—some as big as dinner plates—appear in massed arrays, cascades, baskets and pillars. Fall is also a good time to catch the last big rose display before frost.

Ending the year is the Christmas conservatory display with thousands of poinsettias. Longwood is bedecked with 35,000 colored lights at this festive time of year. Many families have made a visit to Longwood part of their holiday calendars.

Of course, the Topiary Garden, with its whimsical collection of shrub creations, can be enjoyed in any season.

If you want to discover how this lovely garden got started make sure you tour the Peirce-du Pont House. This land was originally purchased from William Penn in 1700 by a Quaker farmer, George Peirce. (One of the earliest battles of the American Revolution, the Battle of Brandywine, was fought within earshot of this property.) It was Peirce's grandsons who turned the land toward horticultural uses when they planted an arboretum of evergreen trees and called the place Peirce's Park. In 1906 Pierre Samuel du Pont purchased the land and began developing formal gardens on his new estate. Today there is still a mixture of natural spots and carefully planned garden areas. The house, too, reflects this dichotomy. The South Wing was the home of the original Quakers who farmed this land; furnishings go back to the 1730s. The North Wing was the early 20th-century addition of Pierre Samuel du Pont; it represents the relatively modest decor of an industrial prince who spent much more money on his gardens than on his house. There are guided tours.

Longwood Gardens is open 9:00 A.M. to 6:00 P.M. daily, except during the winter months, when it closes at 5:00 P.M. The conservatory opens one hour later and closes at 5:00 P.M. Fountain performances are given from mid-June through Labor Day. Admission is charged. Longwood has a self-service café, as well as the Terrace Restaurant. It is always a good idea to get reservations if you want to enjoy the restaurant. Call (215)388-6771.

Directions: From Philadelphia take I-95 south to Route 322 west. Follow Route 322 until it intersects with Route 1 at Concordville. Turn left, south, on Route 1 and continue eight miles to the Longwood Gardens entrance. Longwood is three miles northeast of Kennett Square, Pennsylvania.

Mill Grove

Only 20 miles away from Philadelphia you can experience the natural beauty that inspired John James Audubon. As you walk along the woodland and meadow trails of Mill Grove, the only surviving Audubon home in America, you will appreciate why the 19-year-old Audubon was enchanted with the birds he discovered in the new world.

Audubon had been sent to America from France by his father. The senior Audubon had purchased Mill Grove in 1789 as an investment with the money he had managed to bring out of revolution-torn Santo Domingo in the French West Indies. The Audubon family had never lived at Mill Grove before John James was sent to work its small lead mine and thereby improve the family's fortunes. Once the young nature lover saw the abundant bird and wildlife, he dismissed any idea about working the mine and spent each day outside collecting birds or inside his studio drawing.

John James Audubon had begun painting birds while still in France. His technique changed in Pennsylvania, however. Artists usually depicted birds in a static profile perched on a wooden twig, but Audubon felt this failed to portray the birds as he saw them here. In order to fill his drawings with life and movement he used wires to arrange the specimens into real-life attitudes. He would then do the picture in a single session.

The house on this 130-acre estate sits on a high hill overlooking the Perkiomen Creek. From the wide front porch Audubon could watch the birds in the nearby woods and at the small pond. The house itself was built in 1762 by James Morgan. Today it serves as a museum displaying all the major works of John James Audubon. Highlights of this display are 24 of the oversize or elephant folio prints for *Birds of America*. In all, Audubon did 435 watercolors for this set! The first edition was published in London between 1826–38. His wife Lucy Bakewell, whom he had met while at Mill Grove, gave him her savings so that he could get the pictures published. The museum at Mill Grove has a series of murals depicting Audubon's life plus a collection of Audubon memorabilia. The attic has been restored to a studio and taxidermy room with stuffed birds and small animals informally displayed as they once may have stood during the two years Audubon worked here.

It is outside that visitors get the most immediate sense of Audubon and what he called this "blessed spot." More than 175 species of birds have been identified at the Mill Grove Wildlife Sanctuary and 400 species of flowering plants. Each season has its special charm and its unique birds in residence. This is a perfect place to banish such remarks as, "I saw a red bird" or "a blue bird" and replace them with correct identifications. At Mill Grove you can become genuinely acquainted with the lively, colorful creatures that were the focus of Audubon's life.

Mill Grove is open at no charge Tuesday through Sunday from 10:00 A.M. until 5:00 P.M. It is closed New Year's Day, Thanksgiving and Christmas.

Directions: From Philadelphia take the Schuylkill Expressway west to the Route 202 exit. Go south on Route 202 towards Paoli. After just a short distance on Route 202 watch for the sign to the Betzwood Bridge and take that exit. Follow the County Line

Expressway for about 1¾ miles, then take the exit for Trooper and Route 363 north. This exit will immediately follow the Betzwood Bridge crossing of the Schuylkill River. Take Route 363, which will become Trooper Road, to the first traffic light where you will turn left onto Audubon Road. It dead-ends after a mile in front of the Mill Grove entrance on Pawlings Road.

Morris Arboretum

One of the main objectives of the American well-to-do has generally been—and still is—to be able to afford the best of Europe.

It was an eclectic but fashionable blending of the best of English and Italian, plus Oriental that John Morris and his sister Lydia assembled at Compton, their baronial Chestnut Hill estate. Now open to the public, the Morris Arboretum is a garden of compartments, or special areas, which are enhanced by a selection of outstanding specimen trees—many the largest known representatives of their species.

A splendid range of garden delights is provided by the combination of winding paths and a majestic oak allee, formal parterres and spacious English Park, a hidden grotto and a Tuscan Love Temple, formal Rose Garden and natural woodland.

Water adds visual appeal within the arboretum. Quiet Swan Pond mirrors the Love Temple on its banks. Thanks to a tercentenary gift to Philadelphia from Ottawa, Canada, the pond now has two mute swans. This scene is a photographic gem which challenges both amateur and professional shutterbugs. From the temple there are stone steps to the water's edge. Leading from the pond to the stream below is a naturalistic waterfall which draws the eye from one garden compartment to another like the flowing water.

Both John and Lydia Morris were conscientious in their desire to achieve authenticity in the gardens they created; no ersatz design was tolerated at Compton. To assure a correct Oriental effect the Morrises brought a Japanese gardener to the estate. They were also interested in the expeditions of plant explorer, E. H. Wilson, who brought to them from the East rare and exotic plants. One of the most striking of Wilson's contributions was the Katsura, which stands at the end of the Oak Allee. Its 100-foot canopy makes this another favorite with visiting photographers. The Katsura is even an impressive artistic subject when the limbs are bare in the winter months.

This is by no means the only special tree to be found at the Morris Arboretum. Other rare specimens include the Siberian and Chinese elms, European weeping beech, Bender oak, blue

Atlas cedar, Henry and Trident maples, lace-bark pine and tartar-wing celtis. These are only some of the notable varieties that comprise the collection of 3,500 different trees and shrubs.

Each season has its charm at the arboretum. The azalea meadow and magnolia slope offer a spring treat you won't want to miss. The Katsura with its blossom-laden branches is also splendid at this time of year. The meadow, too, is abloom with daffodils, those cheerful harbingers of spring. Somewhat later in the season the alpine plants in the rock, or wall garden provide a cascade of blooms. You will find this garden laid out below the hilltop where the mansion once stood.

Summer is the time to see the All-American roses in their parterre setting augmented by balustrade and fountain. In the open garden areas wildflowers still bloom in profusion and the butterfly bushes live up to their name by attracting their winged companions.

As so much of the arboretum is natural woodland the fall foliage presents an array of color that not even the blooms of spring can equal. Berries, nuts and fruits can be found in abundance. There are even some blooms remaining on the Franklin tree and the Chinese elm, and the very last flowers on the grounds are usually on the common witchhazel.

In winter it is the pattern of the trees that attracts the visitor's attention. Also a pleasure at this time of year is the tropical environment of the indoor Victorian-style fernery designed by John Morris.

The Morris Arboretum is open daily from 10:00 A.M. to 5:00 P.M. During June, July and August it is open until 8:00 P.M. on Thursdays. From November through March they close one hour earlier. They do charge admission.

Directions: From downtown Philadelphia take Broad Street north to Stenton Avenue. The Morris Arboretum is on Hillcrest Avenue between Germantown and Stenton Avenues.

Nemours

If you were to imagine a modern treatment of the Cinderella story, it could easily be set in the du Pont's fairytale fiefdom, Nemours. In this version of the tale an industrial prince built a French chateau in 1910 for his bride, Alicia Bradford. The couple did not live happily ever after in their fairy tale palace, however, for it is said Alicia didn't really like Nemours and only occasionally stayed there before her death in 1920.

It boggles the mind to think that someone would not want to live in this sumptuous 77-room chateau. Though no expense was spared in decorating it with treasures from around the world, there are enough personal memorabilia to make it feel like a home. The personal touches make touring Nemours fascinating; the formal touches make it impressive; and the gracious touches make it an elegant experience.

Few attractions take such pains to draw guests into the environment of the estate. At Nemours you are greeted by a hostess who will present all the guests in your tour group with a flower. In pleasant weather the hostess leads the way to the veranda where you can enjoy a refreshing glass of fruit juice while listening to the history of the du Pont family and the building of Nemours.

When you explore these surroundings, you feel you begin to know Alfred Irénée du Pont, a genuine Renaissance man. His range of interests and abilities is staggering, and his personality is firmly stamped on his home. Many of the furnishings remind one of the du Pont family's early association with Louis XVI and Marie Antoinette.

Alfred du Pont's great-great grandfather was the patriarch of the family. He had fled his native land after the French Revolution because his then recently created title and position in the cabinet of Louis XVI made it unsafe for him to remain.

The two marble sphinxes on the front terrace at Nemours were a gift from Louis XIV to one of his ministers, Jean Baptiste Colbert. These portrait sphinxes bear the likeness of Louise de la Valliere, who bore four children by Louis XIV.

Exterior decoration is not limited to the French period. The estate is flanked by massive gates—at one end, the English gates and at the other end the Russian gates, both made for royal Catherines. The English gates were made in 1488 at Henry VIII's request for Wimbledon Manor, the estate he presented to his sixth wife, Catherine Parr. Balancing these are the gates made for Catherine the Great's palace outside St. Petersburg.

You'll realize the grand manner in which this mansion is appointed as soon as you enter the Reception Hall, a room crammed with portraits and objets d'art. The hall clock is only one of the hand-crafted pieces with a very special provenance you will see. It once belonged to Marie Antoinette, and on the hour it plays an 18th-century tune. The chandelier in the dining room is also a family piece associated with Marie Antoinette as it hung in Schoenbrunn Palace, her girlhood summer home· in Vienna. Both the victim and the hero of the French Revolution are remembered, for another chandelier in the hallway once hung in Lafayette's home. The American Revolution is also brought to mind by an original chair from Mount Vernon.

The Music Room maintains a proper ambience with its lighted sconces in the shape of a lyre and the tapestry done with musical motifs. The Conservatory effects an Oriental style, with cages of finches and parakeets. The Master Bedroom also shows a Far Eastern influence; it contains Chinese Chippendale furnishings.

Surprisingly, it is the informal downstairs rooms that fascinate most visitors. These basement-level quarters most clearly evoke the presence of Alfred du Pont who gave free rein to his interests here. Projects include contrivances designed by du Pont himself to bottle his own spring water and another to make ice cream. The latter harkens back to the days when Alfred's father commented that if he were really rich he would spend his days on the veranda eating ice cream. Another section has a special custom-designed exercise area, complete with shuffleboard and both tenpin and duckpin bowling alleys. A billiard room and photographic lab reveal yet other interests, as do the trophies and pictures of the du Pont's sloop.

At Nemours even the boilerroom is interesting. Only here could one find a spanking clean layout, with two of everything—two boilers and two hot water heaters—just in case of an emergency. At Nemours you really see how much fun it would be to live in a house where money was never a problem.

At the end of the house tour there are other wonders to explore. You can either take a ride around the gardens on the tour bus or stroll down the impressive walkway into the gardens, which are often referred to as a mini-Versailles. As in those elaborate French gardens there are expansive vistas, reflecting pools, fountains and sculpture to enhance the plantings. At the midpoint in the garden's axis is the massive Colonnade which serves as a memorial to Pierre Samuel du Pont, the founder of the Delaware branch of the du Pont family and his son Eleuthère Irénée du Pont. The four massive sculpture groups dwarf visitors but seem perfectly balanced with the grand design at Nemour. In front of the Colonnade as you look towards the mansion there is a maze garden, and on the other side a sunken garden with additional sculpture and fountains leading down to a large pond with the Temple of Love at the far end of the garden expanse.

After you have explored the garden a bus will take you back to the visitors' reception area. One additional stop at the Garage and Chauffeur's House is made before your tour ends. Here you will see some vintage cars from the du Pont collection. One of the old Cadillacs with a 1924 body and a 1934 chassis was clearly designed to serve the rich. Here, style transcends function; the driver (who would surely never be the owner) had to enter through the back, then climb over the seat into the front. Other models include a 1912 Cadillac with a 1934 chassis, a 1951 Silver Wraith Rolls Royce, a 1960 Phantom V towncar, a 1933 Buick roadster and even a du Pont boat.

It is a fitting grace note that at Nemours even the water tower assumes a whimsical appearance. It, too, is pale pink with a gabled tower, more appropriate for Rapunzel than any utilitarian function.

You can visit Nemours from May through November. Reservations are a must and all guests must be over 16. Tours are held Tuesday through Saturday at 9:00 and 11:00 A.M., and 1:00 and 3:00 P.M. On Sunday the first tour is at 11:00 A.M. You will need to climb stairs as you move from floor to floor so wear comfortable shoes. When you write to obtain reservations give the day and time, plus an alternate date in case your first choice is already booked. Address your request to Nemours Mansion and Gardens, Reservation Office, P.O. Box 109, Wilmington, Delaware 19899. Phone reservations can be made by calling (302)651-6912. Admission is charged.

Directions: From Philadelphia take I-95 south to Wilmington. Exit on Route 202, the Concord Pike North ramp. On Route 202 get in the left lane so that you can turn left at the intersection with Route 141. Continue on Route 141 to the second light, Rockland Road. Turn left at Rockland Road and continue for a short distance until you see the sign for the Nemours entrance on the right. Signs will direct you to the parking area and reception center.

The People's Place and Amish Farm

It's said that Lancaster County, Pennsylvania can be easily recognized from the air because of its neatly laid out farms. As you drive through the area, the feeling of returning to a simpler era is enhanced by the county's extensive Amish and Mennonite population, which numbers approximately 29,000 (slightly less than 10 percent of the county's population) of which about 6,000 are members of the Old Order Amish just one of 20 different Amish and Mennonite groups.

The natural curiosity of visitors to this area and the Amish desire to protect their privacy and maintain their way of life can conflict. For example, the Amish believe that taking photographs violates the biblical injunction against graven images. But there are places to visit where you can gain an understanding of the lifestyle, beliefs and heritage of the Amish and Mennonites.

The best place to start is at The People's Place in Intercourse, Pennsylvania, a creative museum about the Amish and the Mennonites. A three-screen, 25-minute documentary film, "Who Are the Amish?", gives you more than factual background; it gives you the spirit and feelings of the "plain people" who are caught between seeking both perfection and humility. One of the delightful features of the film is that a tourist's voice is heard asking those questions that many of us think but wouldn't ask. If your questions are still not answered, you can query the knowledgeable staff at a "question and answer" session that follows the film.

This people-to-people interpretative center also offers what they call "An adventure into another world," in their Amish World exhibit. It deals with nine issues that demonstrate the tensions between the Amish and the mainstream, or "English" world as they would phrase it. One issue, the sense of time, is explored with a question box which reads: "Most Americans despise it, while most Amish choose it." Do you know what it is? You will after visiting The People's Place.

The Feeling Box has 14 items to touch and identify. As part of the transportation display you can sit in the front seat of a buggy and operate the signal indicators. A collection of summer and winter hats for men plus a group of women's bonnets leads to an area where youngsters may try on typical Amish clothes. Children may also want to sit in the small schoolroom and try a page of work; lessons are given for grades one to eight. Other issues covered in Amish World are mutual aid and barnraisings, social security and government aid, energy use and the important question of peace. The exhibit concludes with a collection of folk art.

The People's Place is open Monday through Saturday 9:30 A.M. to 9:30 P.M. except from November through March when it closes at 4:30 P.M. Admission is charged. There is a Book and Craft Shoppe and The Old Country Store which specializes in quilts and fabric. Just behind The People's Place is a collection of craft shops called the Kitchen Kettle Village. Amish buggy tours can be arranged here for either a 2½-mile ride along the country roads or a ten-minute trip around Intercourse.

When you leave The People's Place, drive along Route 772 (you'll find yourself sharing the road with numerous horse and buggies) to test your new knowledge of the Amish. See if you can spot the differences between the Amish farms and their neighbors'. Many of the Amish farms have produce and craft stands so you can purchase some of the homemade delicacies so popular in this area.

You may want to visit an Amish farm now and there are three alternatives: The Amish Homestead, The Amish Farm and House and The Amish Village. The Amish Homestead, a 71-acre working farm, is not owned by Amish but it is the only one of the three that has an Amish family in residence. This is also the only grossdawdy house, or grandfather house, with living areas for different generations. You will be given a guided tour of the farm's buildings and the house, and can take a buggy ride around the field. The Amish Homestead is at 2034 Lincoln Highway East, Route 30, in Lancaster. It is open daily at 9:00 A.M.; in winter it closes at 4:00 P.M., spring and fall at 5:00 P.M. and summer at 8:00 P.M.

The Amish Farm and House has a typical Pennsylvania-German stone farm house. You'll be given a conducted tour through the ten-room house after which you can explore the farm on your own. This look at a typical Old Order Amish home makes you appreciate the difficulties involved in living without electricity, telephones and automobiles. The Amish Farm and House opens daily at 8:30 A.M.; in winter it closes at 4:00 P.M., spring and fall at 5:00 P.M. and during the summer months at 7:00 P.M. Admission is charged. It is located six miles east of Lancaster on Route 30, at 2395 Lincoln Highway East.

At The Amish Village on Route 896 in Strasburg there is a guided tour of a typical Old Order Amish farmhouse. You can visit a one-room schoolhouse and an operational blacksmith shop and smokehouse. It is open daily 9:00 A.M. to 5:00 P.M. during the spring and fall and until 7:00 P.M. in the summer. It is closed in the winter. Admission is charged.

After any of these tours you may be ready to enjoy a hearty farm meal at a family style Pennsylvania-Dutch restaurant. You can try some of the "sweets and sours" that traditionally accompany the meals which usually include three meats and an assortment of vegetables and homemade breads. Amid the plenty be sure to save room for dessert. You'll want to try the shoo fly pie or the fruit cobblers and pies. Usually three or four choices are offered, and you are free to sample as many as you like. If you stop at the Pennsylvania-Dutch Visitors Bureau at 1799 Hempstead Road, you can pick up brochures on the many family style restaurants in Lancaster. It is safe to choose at random because all are highly regarded.

Directions: From Philadelphia take Route 30 west. At Lancaster exit at Hempstead Road. Make a stop at the Visitors Bureau in the cloverleaf off Route 30. You will be able to get a map that will make it easy for you to find all the attractions in the area. You may also want to see the 36 minute movie, "The Lancaster Experience," shown on the hour throughout the day.

Peter Wentz Farmstead

Did you ever stop to think that usually when you tour historical sites you are seeing the past through the patina of time? The quilt colors are faded, the upholstery frayed, the rugs well trod, and the furniture chipped and worn. This is not the case at the Peter Wentz Farmstead, and the exception demonstrates how much of the original we do lose over the years. Nothing has aged or dimmed at this colonial farm; its motto is "As It Was."

A slide presentation at the Reception Center takes you back to the year 1777, thus establishing the correct mood for your tour. The ambience is enhanced by the period dress worn by the guides. You'll quickly discern the difference this approach makes. The main house has shutters so sparkling they appear to be newly painted. Far from having mellowed with age, everything has a crisp brightness. The colors used here are not the subtle Williamsburg shades so popular in our modern colonial homes. In fact, the colors and manner of painting the walls at this farmstead must be seen to be believed. Knowing that visitors would be made incredulous by the bright stripes, spots, diagonals and squiggles on the walls, the restorers carefully left a small portion untouched as proof that what you see is "As It Was."

What exactly will you see? In the living room, downstairs hall, and upstairs bedroom the dado (lower wall border) is painted bright red with white dots. In the upstairs bedroom this design is further embellished by the addition of white diamond stripes with tadpole-like commas in the center of each diamond. The dado in the master bedroom is white with black dots, a design used for the entire wall in the winter kitchen.

It was decided to restore the farmstead to the way it was in 1777 because that was the year the Peter Wentz house had its brush with history. On two occasions George Washington, who made it a practice whenever possible to avail himself of the hospitality of the grandest home in the area, stayed at this farm. This distinction was fully appreciated and the rooms used by the General have remained structurally intact through the years. One of the rooms has been furnished as Washington's office; one of the upstairs chambers served as his bedroom. Another room at the farm, the winter kitchen, is also closely associated with the Washington visits. The story is told that Washington's fellow officers so feared for their leader's life that his cook was seldom permitted to leave the kitchen. To prevent poisoning, day and night the cook protected the food supplies served to the General.

The food preparation areas reflect Peter Wentz's German heritage. There is the traditionally designed five-plate heating stove in the dining room. The tile roof on the beehive bake oven also was a reminder of his native land. The farmstead has a German kitchen garden as well, laid out with a crossed path that forms four raised beds. There are over 100 different seasonal herbs, vegetables and flowers serving a variety of purposes: culinary, medicinal, olfactory and esthetic. Demonstration crops in the fields and an orchard complete the picture of a prosperous 18th-century farm.

In keeping with the goal of keeping the past alive there is an active crafts program at the Peter Wentz Farmstead on Saturday afternoons. Volunteers in colonial garb using authentic tools and oldtime techniques demonstrate a wide variety of colonial crafts. On a given weekend you may see such unusual crafts as "scherenschnitte" (scissor cutting), theorem painting, broom making or fraktur painting. More common highlighted crafts include spinning, quilting, weaving, candle-making, basketry, carving, block printing and cooking demonstrations using the hearth and the beehive oven.

The farmstead, considered by the Pennsylvania Travel Industry Advisory Council to be one of the top ten tourist attractions in the state, is open year-round. Hours are Tuesday through Saturday from 10:00 A.M. until 4:00 P.M., and on Sunday from 1:00 to 4:00 P.M. It is closed on Mondays, Thanksgiving and Christmas. In December there are candlelight tours of the main house. No admission is charged, but donations are used for the furnishing fund.

Directions: From Philadelphia take the Schuylkill Expressway, Route I-76 to King of Prussia; then take Route 363 north to Route 73. Turn right, east, on Route 73 one block, and then make a left into the farmstead parking lot.

Rockwood

Rockwood, the Shipley-Bringhurst-Hargraves Museum, has a style to match its name. The highlight of this Rural Gothic manor house is the newly restored conservatory, the oldest of its type on the east coast. This Victorian fancy has been carefully returned to its turn-of-the-century splendor, down to the original gingerbread plant stands that support the palms and ferns. Its unusual color scheme mixes five shades of beige with yellow; it sounds dreadful but it works.

Rockwood was built between 1851 and 1857 by Joseph Shipley, whose family helped found Wilmington, Delaware. His great-grandfather was the first Chief Burgess for the city. Shipley planned his Delaware estate to resemble his country home in Liverpool.

The tour includes 15 rooms filled with family treasures that combine furniture of the William and Mary period with decorative pieces from Europe and the Orient. One of the most stylistically interesting touches is the fanlight you see as you enter. Such cut glass fans were costly and almost always found over front doors where they could be admired by all who came to call. In the entrance hall you will also see the lovely wooden banister and raised ceiling which gives an illusion of great spaciousness.

Within this hall hangs a collection of portraits of the four generations who lived in this house over a 120-year period.

The drawing room has gold fabric walls, ornate gold cornices over the windows and huge gold scrolled mirrors. Even richer is the family's collection of overlay glass, which was popular during the Victorian era. It is one of the best collections on the east coast.

Upstairs the rooms are smaller and more intimate. In earlier periods it was not unusual for a lady to entertain in her bedroom while she continued her needlework, but by this time bedrooms were viewed as private sanctuaries.

Rockwood is the only estate in Delaware to employ a Gardenesque landscape design for the grounds. Essential to the Gardenesque concept was the unity of buildings and grounds. The gray Brandywine granite of the house blends with the boulders that were left on the 211 acres of grounds. The success of this goal is still evident today.

One hour tours are given Tuesday through Saturday from 11:00 A.M. until 3:00 P.M. and the house closes at 4:00 P.M. Admission is charged. To take a one hour grounds tour you must make reservations (call (302)571-7776). The grounds are open at no charge daily from dawn to dusk.

Rockwood hosts a nubmer of annual events: a "Spring's the Thing" Plant Sale in late April, an Old-Fashioned Ice Cream Festival in July and a Victorian Christmas celebration in December. Victorian reproductions and other gift items are available at Rockwood's shop.

Directions: From Philadelphia take I-95 south to the Wilmington area. Use Exit 9, Marsh Road. Turn left on Marsh Road and then right on Washington Street Extension. At the first traffic light make a right onto Shipley Road and you will see the entrance to Rockwood. It is located at 610 Shipley Road at the junction of Shipley Road and Washington Street Extension.

Schuylkill Valley Nature Center

A tranquil oasis of unspoiled natural areas can be found right within Philadelphia's city limits at the 300-acre Schuylkill Valley Nature Center. Six miles of trails meander through fields, woodlands and thickets skirting the ponds and streams where a visitor can see a variety of wildlife.

The message at Schuylkill—addressed to young and old—is that we are all the keepers of the earth, and we must understand and learn our role in this important partnership. Environmental education is fostered at the nature center in a myriad of ways.

Schuylkill calls the family "the ultimate everybody." Weekends are filled with activities geared to families. Guided walks, story telling, workshops and seasonal festivals are just part of the fun. Weekend activities geared especially for children include exploring nature through their senses, choosing favorites in the bug olympics or probing the mysteries of animal adaptation. The nature center believes it is imperative to communicate to the young the idea that we are all earthkeepers, so it also holds week long Sunship Earth programs for both public and private school groups.

Environmental theater has become a highly successful tool in the center's educational campaign. These performances pull the audience into the action. Few refuse to join the skits that are used to trace the cycles of the planet Earth. With the sun as conductor, the audience is transformed into a chorus of frogs, a thunderous storm or a forest full of animals.

Schuylkill's Widener Foundation is a pioneer in the development of a comprehensive environmental learning program for all kinds of handicapped learners. The program ranges from camping experiences to workshops and guided nature walks. A paved trail has been designed with an electronic, self-guiding system to enable disabled youngsters to explore.

Programs for senior citizens continue to grow at Schuylkill Valley Nature Center. Special walks and workshops are planned for them as well as programs in which they share experiences with one another.

Teachers, students and organized groups find the center an ideal ecological classroom, but certainly not in the traditional sense. If you are seeking an escape from the bustle of the city and suburbs, visit soon and discover its quiet appeal.

Schuylkill Valley Nature Center is open to the public Monday through Saturday from 9:00 A.M. to 5:00 P.M. and Sunday from 1:00 to 5:00 P.M. It is closed on holidays and on Sundays in August. Admission is charged. For information on special programs, call (215)482-7300.

Directions: From city center take East River Drive north to Ridge Avenue. Continue north on Ridge Avenue and turn left on Port Royal Avenue. Make a right on Hagy's Mill Road to 8480. It is only 12 miles from the center of Philadelphia.

Star-Spangled Banner House and Fort McHenry

Our flag was still flying over Fort McHenry at dawn on September 14, 1814. A worried young lawyer, Francis Scott Key, waiting aboard an American truce ship anchored outside Baltimore's harbor was so moved by the sight of the battle flag flying after a brutal 25-hour bombardment that he wrote the stirring words that were to become our national anthem.

The story behind this far-from-ordinary flag begins at the Mary Pickersgill House, now called the **Star-Spangled Banner Flag House and 1812 Museum**, at 844 East Pratt Street in Baltimore. Mary Pickersgill, her daughter Caroline, and her mother, Rebecca Young, moved to what is now the Flag House in 1807. Rebecca Young had been a flag and banner maker in Philadelphia. Some historians believe that it was Rebecca and not Betsy Ross who made the first American flag. At the request of George Washington Rebecca did make the "Grand Union" flag which was hoisted by the General in January 1776, at Cambridge, Massachusetts.

When Major Armistead, Commandant of Fort McHenry, wanted to have a flag fashioned that would be seen by anxious Baltimore residents and any attacking British foes he turned to Mary and her flagmaking family. He requested that Mary make a giant flag. Mary, her mother and her daughter worked ten hours daily for six weeks to sew the largest battle flag ever designed. It took 11 men to raise the 80-pound flag that measured 30 feet by 42 feet.

When you visit the Star-Spangled Banner House, decorated in the Federal style popular when Mary Pickersgill was in residence, you will see the upstairs bedroom where the three women worked. The material used for their flag was purchased from Mary's brother-in-law who owned a dry goods store at nearby Fells Point.

Adjacent to the house is the 1812 Museum. One of the items on display is a copy of the receipted bill for $405.90 given to Mary by Major Armistead in payment for the flag. There is also a replica of the flag that Mary made. The tattered original is one of the prize exhibits at the Smithsonian Institution's National Museum of American History in Washington. Another copy of Mary's flag still flies over nearby **Fort McHenry**. At Fort McHenry National Monument and Historic Shrine a moving 15-minute film tells about the fierce battle waged here in September 1814. This valiant effort was made to save Baltimore from a similar fate to that suffered by the city of Washington when the British got past the defenses and burned major areas of the new capital. Although the invading British fired 1,800 rounds of ammunition at the gallant soldiers defending Fort McHenry, the colonials held fast. This successful defense is captured in the movie. At the film's conclusion while the national anthem is played, the curtains slowly part revealing the flag still flying—a dramatic touch that brings visitors to their feet with a sense of pride and a lump in the throat.

You'll want to walk around the "star" fort. (You'll see by its design how it got its name.) At the base of the walls are the remains of the dry moat that once encircled the fort. Just across from the entrance is what is called a ravelin. This underground magazine protected the entrance from direct attack.

The arched entrance, or sally port, is flanked on both sides by bombproof underground rooms where Confederate prisoners were held during the Civil War. This area faces the parade grounds and the flagpole site from which Mary Pickersgill's flag once flew. During the summer months costumed members of the Fort McHenry Guard perform drills and military demonstrations on the parade grounds. Cannons thought to have been used during the September 13-14 battle, including one with the monogram of King George III, are in or near the star fort.

Surrounding the greensward are guardhouses, barracks for the soldiers and a powder magazine. The quarters of Major Armistead have also been recreated.

From mid-June through Labor Day park rangers lead guided tours of the fort at 10:30 and 11:30 A.M. and at 12:30 P.M. On weekdays additional tours are given at 1:30, 2:30, 3:30 and 4:30 P.M.

If you have the time one of the best ways to see the fort is by boat. The *Baltimore Patriot* leaves from the *Constellation* dock for an 1½-hour narrated tour that will let you view Fort McHenry from the water, providing the same perspective that the attacking British once had. These tour boats operate spring through fall. From mid-April to the end of May they run at 11:00 A.M., 1:00 and 3:00 P.M. From June through September boats depart hourly from 11:00 A.M. through 4:00 P.M. In October they return to their spring schedule. Evening cruises are added during the summer months. Two additional vessels, the *Defender* and the *Guardian* ply between the Inner Harbor and the star fort from Memorial Day to Labor Day, 10:30 A.M. to 5:30 P.M. For more information call (301)685-4288.

During July and August there is a military tattoo on selected Sunday evenings at 6:30 P.M. In September a Defenders' Day celebration is held in honor of the Battle of Baltimore, with a mock bombardment, music, military drills and fireworks. Fort McHenry is open seven days a week from 9:00 A.M. to 5:00 P.M. From Memorial Day to Labor Day hours are extended to 8:00 P.M. The fort is closed Christmas and New Year's Day.

Directions: From Philadelphia take I-95 south. Just outside Baltimore exit for the downtown area on Route 40, the Pulaski Highway. This merges with Fayette Street which will take you into the city. Turn left on Calvert Street and left again on Pratt Street. Continue past Harborplace to 844 East Pratt Street on the corner of Pratt and Albemarle Streets. There is a parking lot adjacent to Mary Pickersgill House.

To reach Fort McHenry from the Star-Spangled Banner House go up to Lombard Street and make a right on St. Paul Street which will become Light Street after you cross Pratt. From Light Street bear left on Key Highway for one mile to Lawrence Street and turn right to Fort Avenue which leads to the gates of Fort McHenry.

Washington Crossing Historic Park and Bowman's Hill Wildflower Preserve

Washington crossed the Delaware in defeat. His men were beaten in battle, their clothes were in tatters and their stomachs were empty. Nobody—certainly not the celebrating Hessians—thought they would recross the ice-clogged river. The Hessian commander, Colonel Rall, was so confident of himself and so disdainful of the ragtag Continental force that he didn't even read an intelligence report about Washington's imminent attack. Rall's arrogance cost the colonel his life and his men the battle.

You can retrace the tumultuous events of December 25, 1776, when you visit **Washington Crossing Historic Park**. At the Visitors Center and Memorial Building, the best place to start your visit, you'll see a 30-minute movie on the historic events that occurred here. The Memorial Building has a copy of the huge painting by Emanuel Leutze of *Washington Crossing the Delaware.*

As you will discover when you visit the Durham Boat House and see the cargo boats used to transport the 2,400 men who finally made it across the river, the famous painting probably erred in the depiction of the boat. Although all types of boats were used, it is doubtful that Washington crossed in a boat like that in the painting. Further, Washington's standing pose, although typical of the artistic style of the 1840s, is unlikely to have been assumed during the hazardous crossing which was complicated by the blinding snowstorm and virtually iced-over water.

Within the park you will see the house from which Washington planned his unexpected aboutface, and the inn where he took Christmas dinner before his heroic crossing. The Thompson-Neely House, whose oldest stone section was constructed in 1702, was used by Washington's staff for conference. They usually met in the kitchen as it was the warmest room in the house. Costumed guides will answer questions about the period furniture and the colonial artifacts on display in the building. Before you leave this section of the park be sure to visit the grist mill. During the summer months it, too, is open for guided tours.

The McKonkey Ferry Inn, or Old Ferry Inn as it is also called, is another important restored colonial building in this park. Costumed guides are available to escort you through the authentically restored inn and help you to envision the tension that must have been present when Washington tried to enjoy his Christmas dinner.

On alternate weekends during the summer season the park conducts cooking and baking demonstrations in the restored 19th-century Frye and Hibbs houses. The Hibbs House Committee sponsors these interpretive programs. In the winter try to be on hand for the annual reenactment of the December 25th crossing. This is a novel way to spend Christmas day. On the weekend of George Washington's birthday hot gingerbread is served at the Thompson-Neely House.

In the upper section of the park, commanding the hilltop from which sentries once kept watch, is the Bowman's Hill Tower. A recent extensive renovation program made it possible to reopen the tower. Beneath this picturesque tower is the 100-acre wildflower preserve dedicated to the brave Revolutionary soldiers serving under Washington who once camped here.

There are 26 trails and habitat areas in the **Wildflower Preserve** to be explored. The best time to plan a visit is April or May, but during the summer months the field flowers offer visitors a colorful vista. Actually there is something to see in every season. Pick up a self-guiding trail map, plus a monthly blooming list at the Wildflower Preserve Headquarters Building. The garden outside this building displays plants most suitable to backyard gardens in this area. Altogether there are more than 1,000 different kinds of native trees, shrubs, vines and wildflowers preserved in this park. There is also a pond for flowering aquatic plants, and a bog for those requiring a swampy terrain.

Washington Crossing Historic Park is open Monday through Saturday from 9:00 A.M. to 5:00 P.M., and Sunday from NOON to 5:00 P.M. There is a small admission for some of the historic buildings.

Directions: From Philadelphia take I-95 north to the Yardley Interchange. Signs will direct you north on Route 532 to Route 32. Washington Crossing Historic Park is located on both sides of Route 32.

The Wharton Esherick Museum

Wharton Esherick was a native Philadelphian who studied art at the Philadelphia Museum School of Industrial Art and the Pennsylvania Academy of Fine Arts. In 1913 he left the city, finding his artistic vision better inspired by the countryside around his stone farmhouse near Paoli, Pennsylvania.

The wooded hills proved to be a source of material as well as an inspiration. It was here he had what he called his "conversations with wood." In 1920 he began carving decorative wooden frames for his paintings. He next worked on woodcuts and then wooden sculpture. His innovative pieces gained him a reputation in the front ranks of modern American sculptors.

He was not satisfied with art for its own sake but sought to make it part of the practical side of life by designing sculptured furniture and furnishings. He worked for 40 years building and decorating his studio. Every aspect of it reflects his attention, even the wooden coat pegs which are carved as caricatures of the workmen who helped him build this visionary place.

Wharton Esherick died in May of 1970 but his studio survives like "a joy forever." It looks as it did when he lived and worked here. On display are more than 200 examples of his paintings, prints, woodcuts, sculpture, furniture and utensils. There are no signs and no museum-like displays. The studio has retained the look of a working environment and is described verbally by guides.

Because of the size of the studio, reservations are needed for the one-hour guided tour. The hours are 10:00 A.M. to 5:00 P.M. on Saturdays and 1:00 to 5:00 P.M. on Sundays. Special arrangements can be made for weekday tours. Call (215)644-5822 or write The Wharton Esherick Museum, Box 595, Paoli, PA 19301. Admission is charged. The museum is closed during January and February.

Directions: From Philadelphia take the Schuylkill Expressway, I-76, north. Take the Route 202-Paoli South exit to the Devon exit. Then follow Route 252 north, through Valley Forge Park to the covered bridge. Cross the bridge and go about 2½ miles. Before the turnpike overpass you will come to Diamond Hill Road on your right. Take Diamond Hill Road and go up the hill. At the crest bear right and take the first road on the right, and then the first driveway on the right for the Wharton Esherick Museum.

Wheaton Village

Step back into the Victorian era at Wheaton Village, a reconstructed south Jersey glassmaking town, circa 1888. It's all there on 88 pine-covered acres—the gingerbread architecture, the picturesque 1876 Central Grove Schoolhouse, the General Store with penny candy and a nickelodeon, the village green, the oldtime crafts and the "patent medicine" show. You'll also be able to visit a working glass factory and see a collection of glass unlike any you have seen before.

At the Museum of American Glass, which is customarily the first stop after entering Wheaton Village, you will see what is billed as "the world's largest collection of American glass." A guide to the museum is available in the Great Foyer. The provenance of several pieces in the foyer are included: the ornate chandeliers were once in the old Traymore Hotel, the brass wall sconces came from the Waldorf Astoria. Much of the collection is arranged in period rooms like the ornate dining room with its elegant stemware, or the kitchen containing glass objects dating from the 1880s to the 1920s.

The first glass objects were strictly utilitarian, as they were made to store medicinal properties and culinary supplies. But as the artisans became more proficient (around the middle of the 19th century) they began turning out highly decorative pieces. One room introduces you to the popular art of paperweights. The beauty and variety of these pieces is astonishing. (The Arthur Gorham Paperweight Shop nearby offers a wide range of these collectibles for sale.)

Once you have seen everything glass from Mason jar to missile nose cone, you will be ready to see how they were made. Using 19th-century techniques the skilled journeymen at the 1888 Glass Factory turn out pitchers, bottles, vases and paperweights that are sold at Wheaton Village. Special narrated demonstrations on the technique of glassblowing and paperweight making are given at 11:00 A.M. and 1:30 and 3:30 P.M. You can watch how the shapes are blown and molded and how color and bubbles are added to the glass.

This is not, however, the only craft to be demonstrated at Wheaton Village. In the Crafts and Trades Row potters, weavers, lampworkers, woodcarvers and tinsmiths are hard at work. All of this takes place under one roof, and kids will get a good overview of the type of hand-worked products made in the 1880s.

Several other areas at Wheaton Village have particular appeal to youngsters. At the 1880 Palermo Train Station they can ride the miniature train whose open-sided cars give passengers a good view of all the activity going on at Wheaton. There is a 100-year-old one-room schoolhouse and a playground. Visitors of all ages love the homemade ice cream in the sodas and sundaes at the Pharmacy, the turn-of-the-century drugstore that serves these treats from May through October.

The evocation of Victorian life wouldn't be complete without a traveling medicine show like the ones that used to stop in the small towns across America. At Wheaton Village, Professor Fester's medicine show is given at 1:00 and 3:00 P.M. He generally grabs visitors' attention by riding on a high-wheeled bicycle along the village green promenade. (That's one of those with the oversize front wheel and the little wheel on the back.) Once he hooks his audience he climbs on the platform of his buggy and begins his spiel on the magic properties of his elixir. It's all a lot of fun and though they may not really have been the "good old days" in '88, you are certain to have a good day at Wheaton Village.

Throughout the year there are special events planned at Wheaton Village. In June the annual Victorian Fair is held, with even more crafts and period entertainment than usual. During the month of December there is the Grand Christmas Exhibition with special seasonal displays in the Museum of American Glass. Dolls, antique toys, miniatures and period costumes are all part of the display. Seasonal decorations bedeck the village. This is an excellent time to visit and a good chance to pick up unusual gifts. Hours are 10:00 A.M. to 5:00 P.M. daily year-round, except for a somewhat earlier closing during the inclement weather of January, February and March. Wheaton Village is also closed Thanksgiving, Christmas, New Year's Day and Easter. Admission is charged.

Directions: From Philadelphia take the Schuylkill Expressway, I-76, south and cross the Walt Whitman Bridge. At I-295 go south to Route 47. Continue on Route 47 to Millville. Wheaton Village is located at 10th Street and "G" Street in Millville.

Winterthur Museum and Gardens

When you take a woodland walk and spot a blooming wildflower, do you get a special thrill? If so, you will find Winterthur a veritable paradise. Here, the natural Delaware woodland has been retained, and also, beneath the indigenous beech, hickory and tulip trees, you'll see hundreds of glorious azaleas. You won't have to search to spot a single wildflower in bloom. Instead you'll see a carpet of Spanish bluebells, trilliums, anemones and primroses.

Although Winterthur is a 200-acre naturalistic garden, careful attention has been given to achieving a felicitous blending of colors and species. Even the height of the bushes is controlled to maintain the panoramic vistas within the garden. Just one example of the concern for exactly the right backdrop is the placing of the Empress tree with its fragile purple blossoms against the dark green of the conifer.

The 13 focal points of the garden tour include the Quarry Garden, Azalea Woods, Peony Garden, Pinetum, Sundial Garden and the Glade and Pool Gardens. The last two are the only ones that can be considered formal. The Sundial Garden was once Henry Francis du Pont's tennis and croquet lawns. Now boxwood hedges and conifers form a backdrop for the flowering shrubs. The Glade and Pool Gardens, close to the Winterthur Museum, feature such ornamental touches as statuary, fountains and a swimming pool among spring-flowering bulbs and summer annuals.

You should allow between one and two hours to explore the 2½ miles of gardens. A 45-minute motorized tram tour is available spring, summer and fall. You can take this tour to get an overview and then set out on foot for a closer look at areas of special interest.

The gardens alone are worth a visit but Winterthur also offers the Henry Francis du Pont Winterthur Museum. In 1927 Henry Francis du Pont started adding woodwork to this 1839 country home, removed from houses along the eastern seaboard from New Hampshire to Georgia. He collected decorative American arts from the 17th century to the early 19th century—1650 to 1850. As his collection grew he added to his home until he had 196 period rooms representing the entire scope of the American domestic scene. There are drawing rooms, parlors, dining rooms, bedrooms, kitchens and simulated outdoor settings. You can see more than 71,000 examples of domestic architecture, furniture, silver, pewter, paintings, textiles and ceramics. The museum was first opened to the public on October 30, 1951. It has been a popular attraction ever since.

A number of tour options are available at Winterthur, depending on the time of your visit. The museum and gardens are open year-round. General admission throughout the year includes various tour components.

During the Winterthur-in-Spring Tour (early April to early June), general admission includes tours of the 18-room American Sampler Tour, plus 16 elegant rooms normally seen by reservation only, and the self-guided garden tours. The garden tram is offered for an additional fee.

From early June through mid-November, general admission includes the Sampler Tour, the garden tram tour and the self-guided garden tour.

From mid-November until early April, the Sampler Tour, the self-guided garden tour, and an audio-visual presentation are part of the general admission fee.

Two-hour reserved tours are offered from early January through early April, and from early June through mid-November. These tours offer an intimate, in-depth look at a selection of room settings. Small groups allow the guides to personalize each tour. Tour guests must be 12 or older.

Yuletide at Winterthur, 21 rooms decorated in holiday finery, is offered in late November through the end of the year by reservation only. Children of all ages are permitted on this tour, and those under 16 pay a reduced rate.

The museum and gardens are open Tuesday through Saturday from 10:00 A.M. to 4:00 P.M. Sunday and holidays the hours are NOON to 4:00 P.M. For information and reservations, contact the Reservation Office, Winterthur Mansion and Gardens, Winterthur, DE 19735 or call (302)654-1548.

Directions: From Philadelphia take I-95 south to Exit 7, Route 52 north. Winterthur is located on Route 52, six miles northwest of Wilmington.

Calendar of Events

January

Early:

Mummers Parade. Philadelphia. Contact: City Representative's Office, Room 1660, Municipal Services Building, Philadelphia 19107. (215)568-6599.

Flower Show. Fairgrounds, York. York County Visitors' Information Center, P.O. Box 1229, York 17405. (717)755-9638.

Mid:

Lee Birthday Celebration. Alexandria. Contact: Alexandria Tourist Council, 221 King Street, Alexandria, VA 22314. (703)549-0205.

Late:

Welcome Spring Display. Longwood Gardens. Contact: Longwood Gardens, U.S. 1, Kennett Square 19348. (215)388-6741.

February

Early:

Love Themes From Tudor England. London Brass Rubbing Centre in Washington. Contact: The London Brass Rubbing Centre, Washington Cathedral, Mount Saint-Alban, Washington, D.C. 20016. (202)364-9303.

Mid:

Chocolate Festival. Hershey. Contact: Hotel Hershey, Hershey 17033. (717)534-3098.

Mummers String Band Show of Shows. Civic Center, Philadelphia. Contact: Mummers Association, c/o Sure Music, P.O. Box 94, Broomall 19008. (215)356-2996.

Late:

Washington's Birthday Celebration. Valley Forge National Historical Park. Contact: Valley Forge National Historical Park, Valley Forge 19481. (215)783-7700.

George Washington Birthday Parade. Alexandria. Contact: Alexandria Tourist Council, 221 King Street, Alexandria, VA 22314. (703)549-0205.

Maple Sugar Festival. Tyler Arboretum. Contact: Tyler Arboretum, P.O. Box 216, Lima 19037. (215)566-9133.

March

Early:

Philadelphia Flower and Garden Show. Civic Center. Contact: Pennsylvania Horticultural Society, 325 Walnut Street, Philadelphia 19106. (215)625-8250.

Special Olympics. Shawnee Mountain Ski Area. Contact: Pocono Mountains Vacation Bureau, 1004 Main Street, Stroudsburg 18360. (717)421-5791.

Pennsylvania Charter Day. Conrad Weiser Homestead. Contact: Conrad Weiser Homestead, R.D. 1, Womelsdorf 19567. (215)589-2934.

Mid:

Tavern Days. London Town Publik House & Gardens. Contact: London Town Publik House, 839 Londontown Road, Edgewater, MD 21037. (301)956-4900.

April

Early:

Easter Conservatory Displays. Longwood Gardens. Contact: Longwood Gardens, U.S. 1, Kennett Square 19348. (215)388-6741.

Mid:

Daffodil Show. London Town Publik House & Gardens. Contact: London Town Publik House, 839 Londontown Road, Edgewater, MD 21037. (301)956-4900.

Late:

Sheep Shearing. Amish Farm & House. Contact: Amish Farm & House, 2395 Lincoln Highway East, Lancaster 17602. (717)397-3822.

Pennsylvania Crafts Fair. Brandywine River Museum. Contact: Brandywine River Museum, P.O. Box 141, Chadds Ford 19317. (215)388-7601.

French and Indian War Encampment. Conrad Weiser Homestead. Contact: Conrad Weiser Homestead, R.D. 1, Womelsdorf 19567. (215)589-2934.

May

Early:

Colonial Crafts Show. Colonial Pennsylvania Plantation. Contact: Colonial Pennsylvania Plantation, Ridley Creek State Park, Media 19063. (215)566-1725.

Philadelphia Open House. Contact: Friends of INHP, 313 Walnut Street, Philadelphia 19106. (215)597-7919.

May Day Garden Tour. Annapolis. Contact: Historic Annapolis, Inc., Old Treasury Building, State Circle, Annapolis, MD 21401. (301)267-8149.

Ellicott City May Day Arts Festival. Ellicott City. Contact: Howard County Dept. of Parks & Recreation, 3430 Court House Drive, Ellicott City, MD 21043. (301)992-2483.

Strawberry Festival. Peddler's Village. Contact: Peddler's Village, Lahaska 18931. (215)794-5306.

Mid:

Mercer Folk Festival. Mercer Museum. Contact: Bucks County Historical Society, Pine Street, Doylestown 18901. (215)345-0210.

Olde York Street Fair. Downtown York. Contact: York County Visitors' Information Center, P.O. Box 1229, York 17405. (717)755-9638.

Tulip Display. Hershey Gardens. Contact: Hershey Gardens, 621 Park Avenue, Hershey 17033. (717)534-3531

Mushroom Festival. Hewlitt Packard, Avondale. Contact: Chester County Tourist Promotion Bureau, 33 West Market Street, West Chester 19380. (215)932-8300, ext. 261.

Late:

Antique Show. Brandywine River Museum. Contact: Brandywine River Museum, P.O. Box 141, Chadds Ford 19317. (215)388-7601.

Laurel Blossom Time. Pocono Mountains. Contact: Pocono Mountains Vacation Bureau, 1004 Main Street, Stroudsburg 18360. (717)421-5791.

Memorial Day Parade and Ceremonies. Gettysburg and the National Cemetery. Contact: Gettysburg Travel Council, 35 Carlisle Street, Gettysburg 17325. (717)334-6274.

Chestertown Tea Party Festival. Chestertown. Contact: Kent County Chamber of Commerce, 400 High Street, Chestertown, MD 21620. (301)778-0416.

June

Early:

New Hope Flower Show. Throughout New Hope. Contact: New Hope Flower Show, Box 164, New Hope 18938. (215)862-2842.

Crafts Days. Pennsylvania Farm Museum of Landis Valley. Contact: Pennsylvania Farm Museum of Landis Valley, 2451 Kissel Hill Road, Lancaster 17601. (717)569-0401.

Elfreth's Alley Fete Days. Philadelphia. Contact: Elfreth's Alley Association, 126 Elfreth's Alley, Philadelphia 19106. (215)574-0560.

Patriot Days. Daniel Boone Homestead. Contact: Daniel Boone Homestead, Birdsboro 19508. (215)582-4900.

Mid:

Strawberry Festival. York. Contact: York County Visitors' Information Center, P.O. Box 1229, York 17405. (717)755-9638.

Steppingstone Arts & Crafts Day. Steppingstone Museum. Contact: Steppingstone Museum, 461 Quaker Bottom Road, Susquehanna State Park, Havre de Grace, MD 21078. (301)939-2299.

Strawberry Festival. 1758 Sun Inn. Contact: Restored 1758 Sun Inn, 564 Main Street, Bethlehem 18018. (215)866-1758.

Festival of Fountains (through August). Longwood Gardens. Contact: Longwood Gardens, U.S. 1, Kennett Square 19348. (215)388-6741.

Departure of the Continental Army. Valley Forge National Park. Contact: Valley Forge National Park, Valley Forge 19481. (215)783-7700.

Late:

Rose Festival. Hershey Gardens. Contact: Hershey Gardens, 621 Park Avenue, Hershey 17033. (717)534-3531.

Civil War Heritage Week (into July). Gettysburg. Contact: Gettysburg Travel Council, 35 Carlisle Street, Gettysburg 17325. (717)334-6274.

July

Early:

Vorspiel (through Labor Day weekend). Ephrata Cloister. Contact:
Ephrata Cloister Association, P.O. Box 155, Ephrata 17522.
(717)733-4811.

Freedom Festival. Independence Hall (and throughout Philadelphia).
Contact: City Representative's Office, Room 1660, Municipal Services
Building, Philadelphia 19107. (215)568-6599.

Civil War Relic & Collectors Show. Gettysburg. Contact: Gettysburg
Travel Council, 35 Carlisle Street, Gettysburg 17325. (717)334-6274.

4th of July Celebration. Hopewell Village. Contact: Hopewell Village
National Historic Site, R.D. 1, Box 345, Elverson 19520.
(215)582-8773.

Mid:

Benefit Dog Show. Friends of the Conrad Weiser Homestead. Contact:
Conrad Weiser Homestead, R.D. 1, Womelsdorf 19567. (215)589-2934.

Late:

Virginia Scottish Games. Alexandria. Contact: Virginia Scottish Games
Association, P.O. Box 1338, Alexandria, VA 22313. (703)549-0205.

August

Early:

Establishment Day. Hopewell Village. Contact: Hopewell Village
National Historic Site. R.D. 1, Box 345, Elverson 19520.
(215)582-8773.

Mid:

Civil War Reenactment. Ridley Creek State Park. Contact: Colonial
Pennsylvania Plantation, Ridley Creek State Park, Media 19063.
(215)566-1725.

Tavern Days. Alexandria. Contact: Gadsby's Tavern Museum, 134 North Royal Street, Alexandria, VA 22314. (703)838-4242.

Musikfest. Historic Bethlehem. Contact: Bethlehem Musikfest Association, 556 Main Street, Bethlehem 18018. (215)861-0678.

September

Early:

Fall Foliage Festival (through October). Pocono Mountains. Contact: Pocono Mountain Vacation Bureau, 1004 Main Street, Stroudsburg, 18360. (717)421-5791.

Pennsylvania Crafts Fair. Brandywine River Museum. Contact: Brandywine River Museum, P.O. Box 141, Chadds Ford 19317. (215)388-7601.

Red Rose Rent Day. Conrad-Pyle Rose Gardens. Contact: Red Rose Inn, West Grove 19390. (215)869-3003.

Celebration of the Arts. Delaware Water Gap. Contact: Pocono Mountains Vacation Bureau, 1004 Main Street, Stroudsburg, 18360. (717)588-6705.

Reenactment of the Battle of the Brandywine. Brandywine State Park. Contact: Brandywine State Park, Rt. 1, Chadds Ford 19317. (215)459-3342.

Mid:

Penn's Landing In-Water Boat Show. Philadelphia. Contact: National Marine Manufacturers Association, 353 Lexington Avenue, New York, NY 19106. (215)449-9910.

Fall Festival (through October). Fairmount Park. Contact: Fairmount Park Commission, Belmont Avenue and West River Drive, Philadelphia 19131. (215)568-6599.

Colonial Military Reenactment. Brandywine Battlefield State Park. Contact: Brandywine Battlefield State Park, P.O. Box 202, Chadds Ford 19317. (215)459-3342.

Chadds Ford Days Country Fair. Chadds Ford. Contact: Chadds Ford Historical Society, P.O. Box 27, Chadds Ford 19317. (215)388-2308.

Candlelight Walking Tour of Chestertown. Chestertown. Contact: Kent County Chamber of Commerce, 400 High Street, Chestertown, MD 21620. (301)778-0416.

Harvest Market (through October weekends). Brandywine River Museum. Contact: Brandywine River Museum, Rt. 1, Chadds Ford 19317. (215)388-7601.

Late:

Ephrata Fair. Fairgrounds. Contact: Ephrata Fair, P.O. Box 492, Ephrata 17522. (215)267-3744.

Chrysanthemum Display (through mid-October). Hershey Gardens. Contact: Hershey Gardens, 621 Park Avenue, Hershey 17033. (717)534-3531.

Fall Festival. Hopewell Village. Contact: Hopewell Village National Historic Site, R.D. 1, Box 345, Elverson 19520. (215)582-8773.

Steppingstone Museum Fall Harvest Festival. Susquehanna State Park. Contact: Steppingstone Museum, 461 Quaker Bottom Road, Havre de Grace, MD 21078. (301)939-2299.

October

Early:

Founders' Week Celebration. Germantown Historical Society Museum. Contact: Germantown Historical Society, 5214 Germantown Avenue, Germantown, Philadelphia 19144. (215)844-0514.

William Penn Heritage Day. Cornwall Iron Furnace. Contact: Cornwall Iron Furnace, P.O. Box V, Cornwall 17016. (717)272-9711.

Harvest Days. Pennsylvania Farm Museum of Landis Valley. Contact: Pennsylvania Farm Museum of Landis Valley, 2451 Kissel Hill Road, Lancaster 17601. (717)569-0401.

Apple Harvest Festival. South Mountain Fairgrounds. Contact: Gettysburg Travel Council, 35 Carlisle Street, Gettysburg 17325. (717)334-6274.

Mid:

Antique Auto Club of America Fall Meet. Hershey. Contact: Hersheypark Arena, 100 West Hersheypark Drive, Hershey 17033. (717)534-3900.

Historic Fallsington Day. Village of Fallsington. Contact: Historic Fallsington, Inc., 4 Yardley Avenue, Fallsington 19054. (215)295-6567.

Gemutlichkeit. York Fairgrounds. Contact: York County Visitors' Information Center, P.O. Box 1229, York 17405. (717)755-9638.

Harvest Festival. Quiet Valley Living Historical Farm. Contact: Quiet Valley Living Historical Farm, Stroudsburg 18360. (717)992-6161.

Harvest Feast. Colonial Pennsylvania Plantation. Contact: Colonial Pennsylvania Plantation, Ridley Creek State Park, Media 19063. (215)566-1725.

Late:

Heritage Day. Daniel Boone Homestead. Contact: Daniel Boone Homestead, Birdboro 19508. (215)582-4900.

Heritage Day. Conrad Weiser Homestead. Contact: Conrad Weiser Homestead, R.D. 1, Womelsdorf 19567. (215)589-2934.

"At the Sign of the Plough" Oyster Festival. Golden Plough Tavern, York. Contact: York County Visitors' Information Center, P.O. Box 1229, York 17405. (717)755-9638.

Historic Hike. Annapolis Heritage Week. Contact: Historic Annapolis, Inc., Old Treasury Building, State Circle, Annapolis, MD 21401. (301)267-8149.

Heritage Day. Pennsbury Manor. Contact: Pennsbury Manor, Morrisville 19067. (215)946-0400.

Pumpkin Day. Tyler Arboretum. Contact: The Tyler Arboretum, P.O. Box 216, Lima 19037. (215)566-9133.

Oktoberfest. Shawnee Mountain Ski Area. Contact: Shawnee Mountain Ski Area, Shawnee-on-Delaware 18356. (717)421-7231.

November

Early:

Apple Festival. Peddler's Village. Contact: Peddler's Village, Lahaska 18931. (215)794-5306.

Chrysanthemum Festival. Longwood Gardens. Contact: Longwood Gardens, U.S. Rt. 1, Kennett Square 19348. (215)388-6741.

Mid:

Anniversary of Lincoln's Gettysburg Address. Gettysburg National Cemetery. Contact: Gettysburg Travel Council, 35 Carlisle Street, Gettysburg 17325. (717)334-6274.

Late:

Gimbels Thanksgiving Parade. Philadelphia. Contact: Gimbels, Market Street East, Philadelphia 19107. (215)568-6599.

A Brandywine Christmas (through early January). Brandywine River Museum. Contact: Brandywine River Museum, P.O. Box 141, Chadds Ford 19317. (215)459-1900.

Holiday Candlelight Tour. Rock Ford Plantation. Contact: Rock Ford Plantation, 881 Rock Ford Road, Lancaster 17602. (717)392-7223.

Christmas in Hershey (through December). Hersheypark. Contact: Hersheypark, 100 West Hersheypark Drive, Hershey 17033. (717)534-3900.

Christmas Tree Celebration (through early December). Green Hills Farm. Contact: Green Hills Farm, Perkasie 18944. (215)249-0100.

December

Early:

Victorian Christmas at Wheatland. Lancaster. Contact: Wheatland Foundation, 1120 Marietta Avenue, Rt. 23, Lancaster 17603. (717)392-8721.

Christmas in Germantown. Germantown Historical Society Museum Complex. Contact: Germantown Historical Society, 5214 Germantown Avenue, Germantown, Philadelphia 19144. (215)844-0514.

Alexandria Scottish Christmas Walk. Alexandria. Contact: Alexandria Tourist Council, 221 King Street, Alexandria, VA 22314. (703)549-0205.

Dickens Christmas. The Ebenezer Maxwell Mansion. Contact: The Ebenezer Maxwell Mansion, 200 West Tulpehocken Street, Philadelphia 19144. (215)438-1816.

Christmas in Annapolis. Annapolis. Contact: Tourism Council of Annapolis & Anne Arundel Co., 171 Conduit Street, Annapolis, MD 21401. (301)268-TOUR.

Wassail Tour. Ridley Creek State Park. Contact: Ridley Creek State Park, Media 19063. (215)566-1725.

18th Century Christmas. Brandywine Battlefield State Park. Contact: Brandywine Battlefield State Park, P.O. Box 202, Chadds Ford 19317. (215)459-3342.

Holly Ramble. Tyler Arboretum. Contact: The Tyler Arboretum, P.O. Box 216, Lima 19037. (215)566-9133.

Winter Festival. Grange. Contact: The Grange Estate, P.O. Box 853, Havertown 19083. (215)446-4958.

Christmas City Night Light Tours. Bethlehem. Contact: Bethlehem Area Chamber of Commerce, 459 Old York Road, Bethlehem 18018. (215)868-1513.

Christmas Display & Christmas Tree Lane. Longwood Gardens. Contact: Longwood Gardens, U.S. Rt. 1, Kennett Square 19348. (215)388-6741.

Fairmount Park House Christmas Tours. Philadelphia. Contact: Museum of Art, P.O. Box 7646, Philadelphia 19101. (215)787-5449.

Moravian Christmas Putz, Bethlehem. Contact: Central Moravian Church, Main and West Church Streets, Bethlehem 18018. (215)866-5661.

Mid:

Festival of the Christmas Tree. Downtown York. Contact: York County Visitors' Information Center, P.O. Box 1229, York 17405. (717)755-9638.

Reenactment of Washington's March. Valley Forge National Historical Park. Contact: Valley Forge National Historical Park, Valley Forge 19481. (215)783-7700 ext. 73.

Late:

Live Bethlehem Christmas Pageant. Community Arts Pavilion. Contact: Chamber of Commerce, 459 Old York Road, Bethlehem 18018. (215)868-1513.

Reenactment of Washington Crossing the Delaware. Washington Crossing State Park. Contact: Washington Crossing State Park, Washington Crossing 18977. (215)493-4076.

Topical Cross Reference

Agriculture

Arts

Children (attractions with special interest for children)

Food and/or Wine

Gardens

History

Military

Nature

Religion

Transportation

Museums

Geographical Cross Reference

Baltimore

Berks County

Brandywine Valley

Bucks County

Chester Area

Delaware

Germantown

Lancaster County

Maryland

New Jersey

North of Philadelphia

Northwest of Philadelphia

Philadelphia

Pocono Area

Reading and Surrounding Area

Virginia

Washington, D.C.

West of Philadelphia

Western Suburbs of Philadelphia

West Virginia

About the Author

Jane Ockershausen Smith has covered the Middle Atlantic states as a travel writer for better than a decade. Her books, *The Washington One-Day Trip Book*, *One-Day Trips Through History* and *One-Day Trips to Beauty & Bounty* all include attractions in the Philadelphia area. The author's special interest in this part of Pennsylvania dates from her college years at Pennsylvania State University. She taught for part of her senior year in the suburbs of Philadelphia.

Jane Smith now teaches creative writing at a community college in Maryland and also offers a course on traveling through American history.

A member of the Society of American Travel Writers and the American Society of Journalists and Authors, she contributes regularly to the five *Journal* newspapers in the Washington metropolitan area and to *Country Magazine*. Her stories have appeared in *The Washington Post*, *The Washingtonian*, *The Washington Times*, *AAA World*, *The Chicago Tribune*, *Buffalo News*, and *The Oregonian*. Mrs. Smith lives with her husband and daughter in Bowie, Maryland.

TO HELP YOU PLAN AND ENJOY YOUR TRAVEL IN THE MID-ATLANTIC AREA

INNS OF THE SOUTHERN MOUNTAINS　　　$8.95
The first comprehensive guide to the 100 best hostelries of the Appalachians between the Shenandoah and the Great Smoky Mountains National Parks. Author Pat Hudson, a native of Tennessee, has personally visited each place. To meet her standards an inn must offer not only quality hospitality but also introduce guests to the heritage and/or natural beauty of its area. Excellent photos and maps covering VA, WV, KY, TN, NC and GA.

WASHINGTON ONE-DAY TRIP BOOK　　　$7.95
101 fascinating excursions within a day's drive of the capital beltway—out and back before bedtime. The trips are arranged by seasons and accompanied by calendars of special events, map and notes on facilities for the handicapped.

ONE-DAY TRIPS TO BEAUTY AND BOUNTY　　　$8.95
Would you believe there are more than 150 garden getaways in and around Washington, D.C.? Something beautiful and refreshing for every season and taste, including special longer trips to 10 of the most magnificent East Coast gardens.

ONE-DAY TRIPS THROUGH HISTORY　　　$9.95
Describes 200 historic sites within 150 miles of the nation's capital where our forebears lived, dramatic events occurred and America's roots took hold. Sites are arranged chronologically starting with pre-history.

THE BALTIMORE ONE-DAY TRIP BOOK　　　$8.95
This generously illustrated guide offers a unique combination of old and new sights in the historic port: the first commissioned ship of the U.S. Navy, for example, nearby the outstanding National Aquarium and World Trade Center. Plus the update of Baltimore's ethnic festivals and eateries, refurbished hotels, glittery shops, galleries, music, dance and theater.

(See next page for a convenient order blank)

Also:

Florida One-Day Trips (from Orlando). What to do after you've done Disney. **$4.95**

Call it Delmarvalous. How to talk, cook and "feel to hum" on the Delaware, Maryland and Virginia peninsula. **$7.95**

Old Alexandria. Copiously illustrated walking guide to George Washington's hometown. **$5.95**

Going Places With Children. More Than 400 things for kids to see and do in Washington, D.C. **$5.95**

Footnote Washington. Tracking the engaging, humorous and surprising bypaths of capital history by one of the city's most popular broadcasters. **$7.95**

Mr. Lincoln's City. An illustrated guide to the Civil War sites of Washington, as readable as it is informative. **$12.95**

Order Blank for all EPM books described here. Mail with check to:

EPM Publications, Inc.
Box 490, McLean, VA 22101

Title	Quantity	Price	Amount	Shipping
Philadelphia One-Day Trip Book	_____	$8.95	_____	$1.50 each book
_____	_____	_____	_____	_____
_____	_____	_____	_____	_____
_____	_____	_____	_____	_____
_____	_____	_____	_____	_____
		Subtotal	_____	
	Virginia residents, add 4% tax		_____	

Name _____   **Shipping** _____

Street _____

City _____ **State** _____ **Zip** _____

| | | **Total** | _____ |

Remember to enclose names, addresses and enclosure cards for gift purchases.
Please note that prices are subject to change. Thank you.